Managing Change in
a Unionized Workplace

Managing Change in a Unionized Workplace

Countervailing Collaboration

KIRK BLACKARD

QUORUM BOOKS
Westport, Connecticut • London

Library of Congress Cataloging-in-Publication Data

Blackard, Kirk, 1941–
    Managing change in a unionized workplace : countervailing
collaboration / Kirk Blackard.
      p. cm.
    Includes bibliographical references and index.
    ISBN 1–56720–348–5 (alk. paper)
      1. Trade-unions—Great Britain. 2. Industrial relations—Great
Britain. 3. Organizational change—Great Britain. I. Title.
HD6664.B527 2000
331'.0941—dc21   99–40352

British Library Cataloguing in Publication Data is available.

Library of Congress Catalog Card Number: 99–40352
ISBN: 1–56720–348–5

First published in 2000

Quorum Books, 88 Post Road West, Westport, CT 06881
An imprint of Greenwood Publishing Group, Inc.
www.quorumbooks.com

Printed in the United States of America

The paper used in this book complies with the
Permanent Paper Standard issued by the National
Information Standards Organization (Z39.48–1984).

10 9 8 7 6 5 4 3 2 1

To Marcia, Chris, and Drew

With all my love

Contents

Contents

Figures

Acknowledgments

It has been my intention in writing this book to discuss practical applications of important management principles. I am grateful to have worked for a company like Shell Oil, which encouraged such principles and provided room for experimentation and learning. I would like to especially acknowledge three people who more than any others helped fashion my beliefs about management and labor/management relations. The late Verle Whittington, formerly Vice-President of Employee Relations for Shell Oil Company, taught me the importance of the law as a framework for labor/management relations. Verle's bulldog tenacity also provided a model for that required to fashion a collaborative labor/management relationship. Jack Mahaffey, formerly President of Shell Mining Company, helped me understand the symbiotic relationship between work and people. He taught me the value of having the work drive the organization and of allowing people the freedom to learn for themselves how to best do the work. Bill Hopgood, currently Senior Vice-President, People, for United Airlines, helped me appreciate the value that a collaborative union can bring to an organization, as well as the necessity for a systems view of the labor/management relationship. I would also like to thank many friends from the then Oil, Chemical, and Atomic Workers International Union for their lessons on labor/management relations. Special thanks go to Bob Wages, formerly President of the International Union, Allen Barnes, and Ron Holloway. Many thanks to the colleagues and friends with whom I have commiserated over the years and who have willingly spent their time to read part or all of the manuscript and provide very helpful ideas and feedback: Sheila Blackstock, Fran Bulawa, Jim Gibson, Glen Gilchrist, James Hoose, Larry Hunter, Phil Jones, Mac MacIver, Christy McWilliams, Tom Ryan, and John Unger. Most of all I would like to thank my wife Marcia, and our sons Chris and Drew. Chris and Drew helped out on research and preparation of the manuscript when time permitted, and are a source of pride to us both. Thanks to Marcia for her support and love throughout my Shell career and this project.

Managing Change in a Unionized Workplace

Chapter 1

Introduction

A scene from *The Horse Whisperer*, a novel by Nicholas Evans, sets the stage for this book. Annie is a stereotypical New York businesswoman. Her daughter's horse has been involved in a terrible riding accident that left it explosively violent and almost impossible to deal with. Annie has contacted Tom Booker, a Montana cowboy with a reputation for helping resolve such situations. She says, "The reason I'm calling is that I understand you help people who've got horse problems." Booker responds, "No ma'am, I don't." Annie was silent for too long, and Booker could tell he had thrown her. He then explained, "It's kind of the other way around. I help horses who've got people problems."[1]

When management thinks it has union problems, it usually has management problems. While the union is rarely blameless in such a situation, management sets the tone for the relationship and initiates most of the actions that define it. More importantly, if there are problems, management is the party best positioned to fix them. But doing so isn't easy. Management must change itself, devote its best efforts to improvement, and do what it can to encourage a reciprocal response from the union. Improving a labor/management relationship is a journey through uncharted waters, where the parties must themselves figure out what to do and how to do it. The purpose of this book is to suggest a philosophy and provide ideas for leading such a journey. It is a management book, written from a management perspective, primarily to a management audience.

Given the book's one-sided perspective and the controversial history of the labor/management relationship, readers should understand at the outset where I've been and what I believe. I was an employee in the management ranks of Shell Oil Company for almost 30 years. I worked in both union and non-union locations, in line jobs managing operating organizations and in staff human resource jobs, in small field locations and Shell's international headquarters, in

Gillette and London. I identify with ''management'' and my beliefs are fashioned by this background. These beliefs are the foundation of *Managing Change in a Unionized Workplace*.

I believe people, and how they perform, are the key to any organization's viability and competitiveness. Further, people work for people, not companies, and the attitudes among them, and between groups of individuals, define the human equation that determines success or failure. Where a union is present, the reciprocal attitude between it and management is a key element of that equation.

I believe that historically unions have played an important and positive role. They have been necessary to counteract the short-term focus—and in some cases outright greed—of management, particularly during times when management was more closely associated with ownership. Unions are still necessary in many workplaces. Some managements still haven't gotten the message and are prone to exploit employees under the guise of competitiveness. If these managements do treat workers with dignity and respect, they do so only because they want to prevent them from electing a union.

But I have a different view with regard to other workplaces. Increased geographical mobility, higher education and skill requirements, and improved social safety nets have improved the relative power of individual employees. Social legislation of the last 30 years, most of which was adopted under union pressure, gives individual employees effective legal recourse against most inappropriate management actions. More importantly, however, many in management now realize that treating employees right and allowing them to contribute and grow in their jobs is necessary to further the interests of managers themselves and their stakeholders. Thus, I believe unions are not necessary in a workplace managed in the enlightened self-interest of its stakeholders.

I believe, however, that a management strategy to get rid of a union is folly. Such a strategy clearly violates the law and, notwithstanding the legal implications, makes no sense. Except for rare cases, when employees elect a union, they need it. While management may believe this need declines over time, employees are likely to disagree and continue to feel a need for their union. Therefore, efforts to escape from a union are likely to be self-defeating because they violate the law, have little probability of success, and negatively affect employee morale and commitment. In summary, once employees elect a union, it is a legitimate party in the employment relationship unless employees on their own initiative choose to make a change.

I believe that, for the most part, management has done a poor job of managing union relationships. While some enlightened employers have done better, many have jealously guarded their legal and contractual rights, imposed their authority when they have had the power to do so, taken reactive countermeasures that prolong negative cycles of conflict, and solved problems with compromises that ''split the pie'' and do nothing to acknowledge union needs or increase the benefit to all. Most efforts to improve relationships have focused on incremental improvement in current systems by seeking new answers to old questions, rather than broad transformation to completely new approaches and systems. Management has tended to believe that with more horses and men it can put Humpty Dumpty together again, when in fact it must ask entirely new questions if it hopes to get new answers that will insure success in the changing times ahead.

My experience convinces me that new answers do exist. My first job was handling labor issues in a large petrochemical complex that had experienced a difficult, very antagonistic eleven-month strike five years earlier. The environment was still acrimonious. Employees were told what to do, how to do it, and when to do it. Little communication occurred between management and union, and what did take place was through formal channels. Management insisted on all its rights, took unilateral action whenever legally permissible and it had the power to do so, and pushed the margins in administration of the labor contract. As a result, union legal challenges were common, grievance and arbitration activity was high, and productivity was poor. Another strike occurred during my first year of employment. Management and union were true adversaries. It was a world that emphasized winning the war with the union rather than beating the competition, making money, or advancing the purpose of the organization.

Over the years, men and women of good faith among management and union leadership improved the situation at this complex and at other unionized facilities within the company. The improvement was significant and helpful, but essentially incremental. It emphasized doing old things better with less acrimony and establishing a level of accommodation that minimized overt conflict. But it did little to elicit the potential synergy that a union can provide, recognize the interests of the union and its leadership, or implement systemic changes likely to become part of the organization's fabric over the long term.

During most of the 1980s I managed a series of Shell's non-union mining operations where we emphasized trusting, high involvement, team-based work environments. For the first time, I experienced the value that involved, committed employees can bring to an organization. In the early 1990s I was assigned responsibility for Shell Oil Company's labor relations. I brought to that assignment a conviction that continuing improvement in employee performance was required for the company's success and that collaboration with their union was the key to the major, systemic change so often required to improve employee commitment and productivity. This coincided with a period of company-wide transformation led by Phil Carroll, Shell Oil's CEO. Thus, the environment was perfect for transforming the relationship between Shell's management and the labor unions representing a large portion of Shell employees.

Leaders of the Oil, Chemical and Atomic Workers International Union and other unions representing Shell employees were willing to work to find a better way of handling our relationship, and we embarked together on a journey, with few directions or guideposts to show the way. We made mistakes, but learned as we went, succeeded in bringing about major changes, and created an entirely new relationship that, while not perfect, has served the best interest of all the parties.

My experiences, observations, and research have convinced me that there are better ways for management and unions to work together than are commonly practiced. No single approach fits all situations, however, and solutions cannot be designed with a cookie cutter. Instead, the parties must work together in good faith to figure out what to do and how to do it. Thus, the chapters that follow do not provide an answer. Rather, they present new questions and provide new ideas for management and union to consider together as they journey to a better and more productive working relationship.

Not all union leaders will be willing to take this journey. One must acknowledge the rather sordid history of certain elements within the labor movement and the fact that some union leaders continue to hold themselves and their own self-interest above their duty to the employees they represent. And they are willing to serve their self-interest with actions that are, at best, antithetical to the collaborative working relationship this book advocates. Managers who must deal with such individuals have my sympathy. I believe, however, that they are the exception, particularly among union leaders directly involved in workplace issues, and that a vast majority of union leaders make a good faith effort—for the most part successfully—to balance their own self-interest with the duties of their office. When this is the case, a journey to a better and more productive working relationship is possible.

This journey must proceed in the midst of uncertainty and excruciatingly difficult and fast-paced change. How management and union work together to adapt to and manage that change will be the test of whether the journey is a success, and how such change is managed will define their relationship.

The pace of change is perhaps the most striking feature of today's business environment. We continue to see change, unprecedented in both speed and magnitude, driven by factors such as increasing globalization of the market place, limited resources, faster communication, increasing competition and interdependence, increased government involvement, continuing technological improvements, difficulties in the world economy, and the changing home environment. A new business vocabulary has evolved, including terms such as process redesign, reengineering, restructuring, governance, empowerment, decentralization, transformation, learning organizations, strategic alliances, mergers, acquisitions, networks, and on and on! A Price Waterhouse study indicates that more than 800 books on the subject of change were published from 1989 through 1994.[2] There is no reason to believe the pace will decline, and every reason to believe it will accelerate.

The acceleration will be led by successful companies themselves, as the most effective way to cope with change is to help create it. Charles Handy notes in *The Age of Paradox* that, absent major intervention and fundamental change, all successful business enterprises have a clear and predictable life cycle.[3] They start slowly and with great difficulty, grow and gain momentum and strength, and then move into a period of decline. A business can be successful over the long term only if it fundamentally changes itself, preferably at the peak of its success and before decline begins. But change will happen, whether early in the cycle to prevent decline or later in the cycle when disaster is imminent and the necessity for change is obvious to everyone. The best companies will introduce changes such as new information technology; redesign of business processes for speed, efficiency, and flexibility; and new links with customers, suppliers, and even rivals. Most importantly, they will change their relationship with employees to continually give them more opportunities to contribute to the success of the enterprise and more input into their daily work lives.

This unprecedented change will lead to fewer jobs in many cases and more in others; different roles and responsibilities for existing jobs; new or revised work rules; changes in pay, benefits, and hours of work; and other changes affecting employees and their families. Employees will resist much of the change, both individually and through their elected union representatives. This will confirm their union as a legitimate player in the change process and require management to work not only with employees but also with the union that represents them.

Change must be managed at two levels in a unionized workplace. Management must make all the individual business changes, both large and small, that are necessary to remain competitive in the rapidly changing world. It may also need to change its relationship with its union. A union is in a position to delay, prevent, or make such changes more difficult, and what it elects to do will be largely determined by its relationship with management. If that relationship is less than positive, therefore, management must improve it before the company can effectively make the many business changes that are required.

Changing its relationship with a union requires management to address a key failing in most such efforts of the past: the inability of the parties to deal with the apparent dichotomy between the need for improved work systems and broader employee involvement in areas frequently not addressed in formal collective bargaining (the business changes), and matters subject to collective bargaining pursuant to the National Labor Relations Act (NLRA or the Act) or covered by the labor contract (the union issues). Many past labor/management change efforts have addressed one but not both of these areas, and the failure to effectively address both with a systemic approach has led to their downfall.

Addressing this dichotomy is the primary objective of the chapters that follow. Many books on labor law and bargaining strategy address the contractual and legal issues. Organization Development professionals and others have written extensively in the areas of strategic human resource management, change management, employee involvement, and other concepts and processes for improving organization performance. But the two rarely meet. Little literature has addressed the unique implications of such management concepts in a union setting, or attempted to integrate them with the requirements of labor contracts or the NLRA. My objective is to close this gap. I will describe relevant management concepts and then share thoughts on their application in a unionized workplace. I will not develop or articulate any new theory of organization change, advocate an easy fix, or attempt to provide ready-made techniques that solve all problems. The issues being addressed are not that simple. Rather, my hope is to challenge the reader with some new ideas and some different ways of thinking about the labor/management relationship.

This merger of ideas from the organization effectiveness and labor relations disciplines will, I believe, assist CEOs, general managers, and senior Human Resources (HR) executives in developing and implementing strategic human resource management strategies that will foster a high performing organization. It also will help Organization Effectiveness (OE), HR, and legal practitioners as well as first-line supervisors as they strive to make the changes necessary to implement those strategies. It will not provide easy answers. Rather, it will provide a common frame of reference to assist all levels of management in thinking more deeply about their own organization and the people in it, appraising every situation individually, identifying the problems involved and the decisions that must be taken, and analyzing options for proceeding. Management can then make its own judgments about how to more effectively implement change in the unionized workplace involved.

Part I provides a perspective for the remainder of the book. It briefly reviews the evolution of labor/management cooperation, describes various types of labor relationships, and examines the key differences between managing change in a non-union and a unionized workplace. This perspective should help readers think more deeply about a basic philosophy for dealing with a union and how to apply leading-edge management ideas and concepts to operationalize it. Key themes of Part I are:

1. Labor/management relationships have evolved over time and fall somewhere on a continuum between open warfare and efforts to create labor/management partnerships. Even those relationships near the partnership end of the continuum, however, usually leave much to be desired.

2. Management in a unionized workplace is governed by laws that do not apply in a non-union environment. These laws, particularly those relating to bargaining and labor contracts, are a major factor in the management of change.

3. Management must face more sources of resistance, more reasons for resistance, and a greater ability to resist in a unionized than a non-union workplace.

Part II presents the philosophical and conceptual context for the remainder of the book. Its purpose is to provide a framework for thinking about the labor/management relationship and a standard against which the ideas and practices outlined in Part III can be assessed. Key themes of Part II are:

1. ''Countervailing Collaboration,'' the fundamental operative philosophy of the book, is a pluralistic philosophy that acknowledges the inevitability of conflict but aims to capitalize on the synergy of the union's divergent interests, primarily through effective management of change.

2. Change management in a unionized workplace must integrate general change concepts with the unique aspects of a unionized workplace.

Part III introduces key practices for maintaining a positive labor/management relationship and managing change effectively. Each chapter briefly overviews the principles of a particular management concept and presents ideas for how those principles can be applied in a unionized workplace. The philosophy and concepts developed in Part II are the key themes that run through all of the chapters.

NOTES

1. Nicolas Evans, *The Horse Whisperer* (New York: Delacorte Press, 1995), p. 121.

2. Price Waterhouse Change Integration Team, *The Paradox Principles* (Chicago: Irwin, 1996), p. 16.

3. Charles Handy, *The Age of Paradox* (Boston: Harvard Business School Press, 1994), pp. 49–67.

Part I

Perspective

Chapter 2

Background

We have to understand where we are to decide where we want to go, and we can only understand where we are in the context of where we've been. Thus, although the history and current state of each labor/management relationship will be different from others, a brief review of their common heritage provides a starting point for assessing where we are and thinking about where to go. The purpose of this chapter is to present a brief overview of that common heritage and the state of labor relations to which it has evolved.

HISTORICAL OVERVIEW

Organized labor in the United States had its genesis half a century before the Civil War. Rapid population growth, the rise of a class of wage earners, and their concentration in urban communities provided an opportunity for a labor movement. Development of larger business units and the employment practices of their owners and managers created the need. Conditions such as long hours, low pay, dirty and unsafe working conditions, sweatshops, and the exploitation of women and children had to be changed. So employees formed unions.

The movement was largely local and on a relatively small scale until the 1850s. The Civil War and its aftermath, however, gave unions an impetus for growth, and the modern American labor movement got its start in the 1880s. This was a time of upswing in the business cycle and substantial immigration of skilled blue-collar workers into the U.S. labor force. The environment was conducive to change, and unions, driven by a consciousness of scarcity and limited opportunity, tried to cause change and improve the lot of workers. They fought with employers to increase wages to keep up with inflation and rising productivity, to improve labor conditions that most affected workers (particularly long hours of work), and to increase worker job security. The push for change still exists today as unions continue to work to insure that employees they represent are treated with dignity and respect, and that employers provide continually improving wages, hours, and conditions of work.

Unions also have caused political change. They have supported laws aimed at directly improving the life of workers, such as those creating minimum wages, fair labor standards, Social Security, unemployment compensation, Medicare, Medicaid, housing subsidies, government training, plant shutdown protections, and various anti-discrimination statutes. Importantly, their efforts led to passage of the Wagner Act of 1935. This legislation established labor's right to affect future change within a company by setting forth the principle of majority rule for the selection of employee bargaining representatives and requiring employers to bargain collectively with these representatives in respect to rates of pay, wages, hours, or other conditions of employment.

Unions have not only sought to cause change and get more for their constituents. They also have aimed to preserve earlier gains and prevent management-initiated changes they believe are not in the unions' or the employees' best interest. This role of protecting the status quo has become common in recent years as companies have attempted to respond to competitive pressure by reorganizing, retrenching, and downsizing. Companies frequently have attempted to reduce pay, benefits, and job security, while at the same time increasing employee contribution through expanding job roles and higher expectations of employees. In their drive for competitive advantage employers have frequently tried to get the best of both worlds—lower employee cost and greater employee contribution. They have resorted to various means of obtaining union acceptance of such change and frequently have used difficult ''concession bargaining,'' as has been the case in the steel, auto, transportation, meatpacking, electrical, textiles, aerospace, and other industries. Concession bargaining has led to settlements incorporating new and different wage systems, increased management flexibility in work assignments, increased management control over benefits costs, and many other changes thought necessary for businesses to remain competitive and viable. Unfortunately, these settlements usually have had a corresponding detrimental effect on employees, at least in the short term, and on the labor/management relationship.

Not surprisingly, change, whether initiated by employees and the union to improve their work life or by the company to improve competitiveness, has usually been problematic. Change is difficult under most circumstances, and the additional parties and interests involved where a union exists has made it uniquely complex and challenging. Instances of labor/management cooperation have occurred, and bargaining has in some cases been relatively smooth where the parties recognized employee needs, changes in the marketplace, and the need for management, unions, and employees to adjust with changes of their own. More frequently, however, change has involved a contest of wills that acknowledged little or no mutual interest. In some cases, needed changes have never been made or have been delayed until their usefulness has been reduced. In other cases, the change process has been so hard fought and bitter that the value of potential improvements has been substantially diminished by the cost of the fight, or the changes have been difficult or impossible to effectively implement because of lack of support or continuing resistance.

Given this history, some companies and unions have decided there must be a better way and that it involves attempting to work together. Such cooperative moves primarily have been initiated by management, and predictably have evolved over time. In *Creating Labor-Management Partnerships*, Warner Woodworth and Christopher Meek describe various phases in the evolution of approaches to labor/management cooperation since around the time of the enactment of the NLRA in 1935.[1] These phases, with exceptions from time to time, have evolved generally as follows:

- Focus on resolving impasses between unions and companies involved in contract negotiations.
- Attempts to reduce labor/management friction by improving two-way communication and opening management to concerns and complaints on most any subject, while retaining all management "rights" and viewing management as the unilateral problem solver.
- Management-oriented organization development in which management attempts to effectively go around the union and create a climate of cooperation and open communication directly with employees.
- Joint union/management support of organization development efforts to address specific, ad hoc issues of mutual concern on a project-by-project basis rather than as part of an ongoing process.
- Negotiating a union/management agreement to establish a cooperative partnership to address issues of mutual concern that are not part of the collective bargaining agreement or past practice.

Unfortunately, many efforts to establish greater cooperation have not met with resounding success. Some never got off the ground or failed early in the process, convincing both labor and management that cooperation is not feasible. Many that were initiated by management as a last-ditch effort to save a troubled or failing enterprise had initial success, only to fall into neglect when company performance improved to a viable level. Other efforts were successful in addressing easy issues of obvious mutual concern but went away in the face of difficult, seemingly intractable issues common in a mature collective bargaining relationship. Few have exhibited major success over the long term.

LABOR/MANAGEMENT RELATIONSHIPS

The quality of labor/management relationships has over the years ranged from the good, to the bad, to the ugly. This range has been variously described. In *A*

Behavioral Theory of Labor Negotiations the authors discuss conflict, containment-aggression, accommodation, cooperation, and collusion.[2] In *Collective Bargaining and Labor Relations* the authors describe conflict, power bargaining, accommodation bargaining, and cooperation.[3] The authors of *Mutual Gains* describe confrontation, armed truce, working harmony, and union/management cooperation.[4] Although essentially any grouping would work, open warfare, adversarial, accommodating, and partnership will be used to represent points on a continuum of management/union relationships that provides a context for discussion in the remainder of this book. The behavior described in these examples exists in the labor/management world, although a particular relationship is likely from time to time to include company and union behaviors depicted in several of the models. They are discussed as discrete models only to help in thinking about where on the range a situation is and where it could be.

Open Warfare

Labor/management relationships in the United States are based on a heritage of exploitation, resistance, and industrial warfare. This history began in the colonial days with the extensive use of indentured servants and convict labor, over whom the masters had almost complete authority, including the legal authority to administer corporal punishment. Isolated strike actions took place before the Revolution. With the first establishment of permanent labor unions shortly after the Revolution, the strike became a favorite weapon for attempting to increase wages and improve job security. Although the power of unions ebbed and flowed over the years, conflict was never far from the surface. Events such as the Haymarket bombing, the Molly Maguire Riots, and the Railway Strike in the late 1800s convinced much of the public that union elements were criminal in character, inclined to riot, assault, arson, or whatever tactics appeared necessary to accomplish their purpose. Employers responded with equally unsavory actions such as violent anti-union campaigns, strong-arming Pinkertons, lockouts, black lists, and yellow-dog contracts. Intense antagonism and violence continued in many areas after the turn of the century, with the coal mines of West Virginia and Colorado, and the copper mines of Michigan, being scenes of bloody fights. While the worst situations began to decline after passage of national legislation in the 1930s, severe conflicts continued, particularly as World War II was ending. In October after VJ Day nearly 9,000,000 workdays were lost due to strikes.

Such conflict hopefully is a thing of the past. Over the last several years, however, several situations have occurred that can only be described as industrial warfare. For example, in 1990 Pittston Company discontinued health care benefits for retirees and after bargaining for a year a coal miner's strike erupted. The strike was characterized by replacement workers, people laying their bodies in front of coal trucks, strikers dressed in camouflage clothes, pickets, arrests, injunctions, sympathy strikes, security guards, and millions of dollars in fines. When Frank Lorenzo bought Eastern Airlines in 1986, he sought $250 million in labor cost reductions. The International Association of Machinists responded with slowdowns, pickets, and boycotts. Personal and institutional animosities got out of hand. All this, plus other issues, led the previously troubled firm into bankruptcy and ultimately liquidation. Also in 1986, when the air traffic controllers union illegally struck to enforce its demands, President Reagan terminated the strikers and hired permanent replacements, resulting in decertification of the union. In 1991 Caterpillar and the United Auto Workers (UAW) engaged in a bitter battle that resulted in a 163-day work stoppage and acrimonious public campaigns against the company.[5] The 1998 UAW/GM strike, while absent the extensive public acrimony of earlier situations, can only be described as economic warfare.

In the early days open warfare typically involved management that did not accept the right of the union to exist and that often acted marginally if at all within the rule of law. Management actions were driven by anti-union animus and efforts to marginalize or get rid of the union whenever feasible. The union, perhaps in response to management behavior, saw management as having few if any redeeming virtues. Major and continuing hostility existed, with management frequently abusing the terms of the contract and flouting the law and the union engaging in antagonistic collective activities or violent and unlawful behavior.

As a general rule, more recent open warfare has involved less anti-union animus, violence, and unlawful activity. Most recent warfare has resulted from differing perceptions of threatening competitive pressures, disagreements as to how these should be addressed, and frequent insensitivity on the part of each side to the needs of the other. The warfare is primarily economic. But like earlier warfare, such activity is self-destructive and creates a state of disequilibrium that cannot exist over the long term. Either problems are addressed and the relationship improves, the union is marginalized or decertified, or the company suffers the economic consequences of both the cause and effect of the warfare.

Adversarial

The parties in adversarial relationships have much the same mindset as those involved in recent open warfare, but they have avoided its overtly destructive and public manifestations. They operate within the law and contract as they reasonably interpret them but are true adversaries in essentially every sense of the word. They behave as though they see their basic roles as to oppose or resist the other, whom they fundamentally view as the enemy. In standoff after standoff there is a declared winner and loser. Winning is important, even if the ultimate cost is greater than the gain. The parties typically look first to legal rights and coercive power to resolve issues, and consequently each strives to maximize its own legal position and power and minimize that of the other.

Management drives change by asserting its rights and power, and conceding as little as possible in required negotiations. The union, on the other hand, seeks to maximize resistance by enforcing the existing contract and its rights under the NLRA to the limit. Matters can easily get out of hand and escalate to open warfare.

The following are more specific examples of management behavior in an adversarial relationship:

- Recognizing the right of the union to exist but attempting to marginalize or discredit it whenever feasible, frequently by neglect rather than confrontation.
- Frequently going around the union with employee communication and other attempts to attain employee commitment.
- Providing the union only that information it requests and that management is required by law to provide.
- Making changes and taking actions unilaterally whenever legally permissible; discussing matters with the union only when and to the extent required by law.
- Pushing the edge to get its way; making contract administration interpretations favorable to it and where permissible implementing its decisions without union agreement after bargaining to impasse.
- Defending its actions by delaying or hardball tactics in arbitration, almost regardless of the merits of the case.
- Reserving most problems until the contract expires and then attempting to use its power to force union concessions.
- Managing the business to maximize its coercive power as compared to the union.

Union behavior in an adversarial relationship is likely to include the following:

- Acknowledging the legal right of the management to direct the work force, but seeking to thwart that right at almost every turn.
- Encouraging the work force to actively resist most company actions.
- Using the grievance procedure excessively to resist management actions.
- Filing repeated, burdensome requests for information that is of only marginal relevance or value.
- Reserving most problems until the contract expires and then attemping to use its coercive power to force company concessions.
- Taking frequent actions to promote union solidarity and enhance its power vis-à-vis the company.

Behavior of employees in an adversarial relationship usually mirrors that of the company and union. They comply with instructions of management because they believe they have to, insist on a literal interpretation of the labor contract, look for ways to challenge supervisor directions, resist discussing any issues

relating to their performance outside the presence of a union representative, and unfailingly support the union on essentially all issues, regardless of merit. As a result, their productivity is less than it could be.

The disadvantages of an adversarial relationship are obvious. Necessary or desirable change is impeded. Low morale and constant bickering hinder normal business by diverting time and energy of both management and employees from positive to counterproductive activities. The parties are walking a fine line, and more destructive open warfare can easily emerge. Overall, the ability of the company to compete is severely impaired.

Accommodating

An accommodating relationship exists where there is a genuine effort on the part of both the company and the union to reconcile their differences, keep the peace, and establish a working relationship in which issues are handled in ways both parties find acceptable. The parties act like friends, are willing to constructively try to solve most problems, and even work together on an ad hoc basis to anticipate issues and develop procedures to address them. Typical management behavior in an accommodating relationship includes the following:

- Publicly demonstrating signs of institutional respect for the union.
- Administering the labor contract in good faith, taking into account the views of the union.
- Providing more information, earlier, particularly as it relates to the company's position on a matter.
- Seeking involvement of the union on specific, narrowly defined issues or when management needs help to counteract a major threat.
- Advising the union of planned changes in advance and bargaining in good faith.
- Establishing joint advisory committees with closely circumscribed roles in areas of mutual interest such as health, safety, and training.
- Limiting use of coercive power.
- Senior managers developing personal relationships of trust with union leaders, and relying on this personal relationship to minimize resistance to company initiatives.

The typical union response would include behavior such as:

- Reacting constructively to company proposals and where there are disagreements, trying to work them out.
- Attempting to resolve problems before they reach the formal grievance procedure.
- Participating in cooperative processes proposed by management.

- Generally supporting company actions that do not negatively affect it or its membership.
- Limiting overt use of coercive power.

Relationships based on accommodation are quite common and typically are characterized as good ones. But they concentrate on minimizing the negative impact of the union rather than finding opportunities to make the best of the relationship. The parties don't have a joint vision of what success is. Management tables its solutions (rather than jointly developing solutions) and attempts to persuade the union to go along, frequently by trading concessions in return. It fosters active communication and other efforts to get along, but its real objective is to neutralize the union, take away its desire to resist, or co-opt it into supporting management activities. It does not try to benefit from the union as a representative of employee views and interests. Therefore, it does not get improved solutions derived from resolution of differing views or improved implementation derived from mutual ownership of the solution.

Employees working in an accommodating environment are also likely to be accommodating. They participate in programs established by management to enhance company performance, particularly in areas such as safety and training. They do their jobs with minimum supervision and generally have a friendly working relationship with their supervisors. On balance, they believe management will try to do the right thing.

Thus, an accommodating relationship minimizes the potential negatives associated with having a union and probably maintains the competitive status of the company in question because it is no worse that most competitors. But it fails to take advantage of opportunities for synergy that exist in a union workplace.

Partnership

Many knowledgeable people advocate partnerships as the preferred state in labor/management relations. One writer argues that a "corollary partnership with the union leadership must be formed" to create the most successful partnership with represented employees.[6] Others advocate transformation from an adversarial to a partnership relationship as a basis for labor/management cooperation on product quality.[7] And still others argue for creation of labor/management partnerships as a strategy for achieving national economic success.[8]

One can hardly disagree with the objectives of a good partnership. Among those commonly discussed are increased trust, attention to the self-interest of both parties, balanced rewards and risks, improved communication, consistent goals and values, recognition of the worth of individuals and their right to be treated with dignity and respect, fairness, openness, individual creativity, and individual growth. It has been suggested that partnerships lead to "improved working conditions, increased employee morale, greater job security, enhanced competitive advantage, fewer grievances, and a more positive organizational climate."[9] Certainly, accomplishing such objectives should lead to the employee commitment and involvement that tends to maximize organizational performance.

"Partnership" within the labor/management context, however, is defined differently by different people. Much partnership rhetoric appears to be all-inclusive, if rather ill-defined, covering essentially all efforts of the parties to improve the way they work together. For example, "Partnerships . . . are defined as relationships between companies and people who share common goals, strive to achieve them together, and do so in a spirit of cooperation, collaboration and fairness."[10] "*Partnership* is about creating the ideal work environment that will allow everyone to fully participate in helping to satisfy their customers."[11] Other definitions have a more limited scope. Woodworth and Meek describe a partnership as "*a formal, negotiated system of labor and managerial joint consultation and decision making,*"[12] which does not include, but rather is parallel to, the system of bargaining that addresses traditional collective bargaining issues such as work schedules, compensation, benefits, and basic shop-floor rules.

Thus, the meaning of a labor/management "partnership" is largely in the eyes of the beholder, but it will always fit somewhere on a continuum represented by the following:

- Comprehensive partnership—an association of partners with joint interests and accountability who share in risks and rewards.
- Parallel partnership—an agreed system of joint decision making limited to matters not covered by collective bargaining.
- Environmental partnership—a work environment that encourages an open, collaborative relationship.

This book endorses the objectives and most of the practices associated with labor/management partnerships of all descriptions. Its principles of countervailing collaboration, however, are based on the view that comprehensive partnerships are not feasible in the labor/management relationship, parallel partnerships miss opportunities, and referring to a collaborative relationship as a partnership causes unnecessary problems.

Comprehensive Partnerships. An association of true partners with joint interests who share in risks, rewards, and accountability is essentially impossible because of the differing fundamental characteristics of management and unions. They have different historical backgrounds, cultures, roles, and objectives. More importantly, management is ultimately accountable for decisions affecting the viability and economic success of the enterprise and the union is not. The parties to a comprehensive partnership, however, are generally thought to be mutually accountable for the consequences of their decisions, at least to the extent of their relative ownership in the partnership; and it follows that there is co-determination in decision making. While there is value in sharing power and decision making with employees and their union, where management is accountable for the performance of the enterprise and wishes to maintain a commensurate ability to make the ultimate economic decisions, co-determination and a true comprehensive partnership are not feasible.

The essentially involuntary nature of the union/management relationship also precludes a comprehensive partnership. In most cases, unions have represented employees at a particular location for a long period of time, and neither management nor union leadership has chosen the other as a partner. They are there by force of history. If the union is of a more recent vintage, it probably came in over the objection of the management, which is not an ideal way of selecting a business partner. So neither party has a choice as to who the other party in the relationship will be, and neither can get out of the relationship under reasonably acceptable terms. Thus, a key element of good partnerships—the ability to select a partner and to get out if it doesn't work—is missing in the company/union situation.

Finally, there is a significant imbalance of power between the parties. Some would disagree that an imbalance typically exists, given the substantial power certain unions have exhibited in various industries where companies have little economic ability to defend against strikes and other union initiatives. But in its broader context, companies are nearly always more powerful in the sense that management is in an advantaged position in the ongoing relationship. It has the information, resources, and incentive to take the actions that define the relationship. This gives companies a level of power relative to unions that makes a comprehensive partnership unlikely. As Mariotti says in *Power of Partnerships*, "When one of the partners has some form of power over the other, this power must be very carefully controlled or the partnership will turn into the cliché that makes *partnership* the most overused and abused word in business relationships."[13]

Charles Heckscher in *The New Unionism* provides supporting historical evidence. He observes that "the fact that the major examples of 'partnership' have appeared primarily in companies that are in severe trouble raises immediate questions about its value as a model for the future." He notes that partnerships have developed only where there has been a strong union and a weak company. The weak companies are usually 100 percent organized and have been damaged by a sudden increase in competition. Heckscher finds nothing mysterious about "partnerships" in this context, and concludes that "one should not look to these efforts for a general model for the future."[14]

Parallel Partnerships. Less comprehensive partnerships that are separate from and parallel to the collective bargaining process also are problematic. This limited or parallel approach typically is totally voluntary, and either party may withdraw at any time. The process is limited to items that are of mutual concern and not covered by the labor contract or by past practice. Such partnerships have an appeal and can work well in addressing certain issues, but in the broader context they have some compelling shortcomings.

The most significant disadvantage of parallel labor/management partnerships is that by definition they exclude areas of the business that are most likely to represent troublesome issues and substantial opportunities for improvement in the way the parties work with each other. Bargaining is required on most subjects of direct importance to employees, and in any mature collective bargaining relationship most such subjects are covered by the labor contract or past practice. If these are not included in the collaborative efforts of the parties, many opportunities for improvement will be lost. A company cannot maintain its competitive position if the focus of its efforts at management/union collaboration does not include issues of most importance to employees.

Excluding bargainable subjects from a partnership would be more feasible in an ideal world where good answers are always found, and agreements are reached without any trading or pressure. But the different interests and roles of unions and management mean such situations are rare if they exist at all. Parallel partnerships can provide the lubricant that makes solving certain issues possible standing alone, but in the end some give-and-take will be required in most situations. When this happens, excluding bargainable or contractual issues limits the ability of management to bargain and puts it at a significant disadvantage because what the union has to trade is generally contained in the contract, either directly or through practice. This means that if matters subject to bargaining or in the contract are off limits, and the union therefore has nothing to trade, management faces a situation where "what is yours is yours, and what is mine is negotiable."

Finally, a parallel partnership that does not include contractual or practice issues is not likely to address the systems aspects of change: those interrelationships among the various parts of the organization that mean a change in one part will affect, and be affected by, other parts. For example, work systems of the type that might be addressed in a parallel cooperative partnership are directly related to issues such as pay, seniority, or the grievance procedure—all of which are covered by contract. These relationships are not likely to be recognized or dealt with in a parallel partnership that excludes bargainable issues.

Environmental Partnerships. Use of the word "partnership" should be avoided in describing an open, collaborative working relationship. One can argue that "partnership" embodies the best that can be hoped for in the labor/management relationship and should be clearly articulated and held out to employees as a goal, with the view that it could drive improvement and at worst do no harm. Another view is that holding out a "partnership" as a goal may itself create problems. Many employee and union leaders believe unions must not abandon their adversarial posture as they seek to exploit opportunities to participate in decision making or make gains for themselves. Employees with this philosophy are likely to see participation by union leaders in a "partnership" as collusion with management rather than pursuing their best interest. Accordingly, even union leaders who see value in cooperation may for political or practical reasons be unable to agree to partner or to be seen as participating in a partnership with management, even though they would be willing to work with management in a rhetorically different or less formal arrangement.

Further, just using the language or claiming a partnership can be a negative. Doing so suggests a need for something that goes beyond existing processes and implies that the positive characteristics of partnerships cannot exist organically in all those routine labor relations processes that must be maintained to make the business work. Partnership rhetoric can create expectations among both represented employees and senior management that the parties will act as partners on all issues. When problems and setbacks in the relationship occur, as they inevitably will, they are seen as failures that thwart the expectation. This can kill trust and cause the partnership to fail, which exacerbates the initial setback and starts a downward spiral in the relationship.

THE CHALLENGE

This brief history and overview of labor/management relationships suggests that there are gaps to be filled and challenges to be met. Most relationships between labor and management leave room for improvement. Management's challenge is to think more broadly than making peace, and to go beyond incremental improvements in a system that remains fundamentally unchanged. It must do more than change its relationship from adversarial to accommodating, or from accommodating to a partnership that misses opportunities or has a high potential to fail or even backfire.

Management's challenge is to create a relationship with its union that not only minimizes the negatives management perceives are associated with unionization but also uses the union's presence to the extent possible for a competitive advantage. It can only do this through recognizing the differences that have contributed to the checkered past and present of labor/management relations and using those differences constructively to foster organizational excellence. An effective organization recognizes that labor/management relationships don't have to be a zero-sum game and brings differences together in a synergy that makes the combined contribution of all involved greater than the sum of their individual contributions. Properly managed, the conflict of differences in a unionized workplace can:

- Enhance creativity through constructive challenge and interchange of ideas.
- Improve decisions through thoughtful consideration of different information and different views.
- Facilitate implementation through involvement, mutual understanding, and buy-in.
- Foster personal and organizational learning through mutual problem solving.

Management's challenge is to foster a relationship that not only keeps the peace but also takes advantage of such opportunities. To do this, management in a unionized workplace must develop and implement a philosophy that aims to use the value of the union as an organic part of the company's human resource strategy. In many cases, this will require major change. Unfortunately, management can only require itself to change. Therefore, its challenge is to change itself and what it does, and expect that union leaders and employees will reciprocate. Parts II and III outline a philosophy and practices for doing this.

KEY POINTS

1. The labor movement was born out of the desire to create change, and how change has been managed over time has defined the labor/management relationship.

2. Cooperative efforts between management and labor have evolved over time, but have generally not met with resounding success.

3. Labor/management relationships can be categorized as either open warfare, adversarial, accommodating, or partnership.

4. Open warfare and adversarial relationships are counterproductive on their face.

5. Accommodating relationships aim to remove the negatives frequently associated with unions but fail to take advantage of potential opportunities.

6. Although there is much to be said for the aims of labor/management partnerships, they are inherently unstable and not likely to be viable over the long term.

7. Management's challenge is to lead change to a relationship that takes advantage of what unions have to offer as an organic part of the organization's human resource strategy.

NOTES

1. Warner P. Woodworth and Christopher B. Meek, *Creating Labor-Management Partnerships* (Reading, Mass.: Addison-Wesley, 1995), pp. 52–70.

2. Richard E. Walton and Robert B. McKersie, *A Behavioral Theory of Labor Negotiations*, 2nd ed. (Ithaca, N.Y.: ILR Press, 1965), pp. 186–188.

3. E. Edward Herman, Alfred Kuhn, and Ronald L. Seeber, *Collective Bargaining and Labor Relations*, 2nd ed. (Englewood Cliffs, N.J.: Prentice-Hall, 1987), pp. 74–76.

4 Edward Cohen-Rosenthal and Cynthia E. Burton, *Mutual Gains*, 2nd ed. (Ithaca, N.Y.: ILR Press, 1993), p. 12.

5. Woodworth and Meek, *Creating Labor-Management Partnerships,* pp. 4–8.

6. John L. Mariotti, *The Power of Partnerships* (Cambridge, Mass.: Blackwell, 1996), p. 123.

7. Edward Cohen-Rosenthal, ed., *Unions, Management, and Quality* (Chicago: Irwin, 1995), p. 137.

8. Woodworth and Meek, *Creating Labor-Management Partnerships*, p. 28.

9. Ibid., p. 29.

10. Mariotti, *The Power of Partnerships*, p. xvii.

11. Cohen-Rosenthal, *Unions, Management, and Quality*, p. 138.

12. Woodworth and Meek, *Creating Labor-Management Partnerships*, p. 28.

13. Mariotti, *The Power of Partnerships*, p. 22.

14. Charles C. Heckscher, *The New Unionism* (Ithaca, N.Y.: Cornell University Press, 1988), pp. 120–121.

Chapter 3

Legal Framework

Later chapters will advocate an approach to managing change that addresses both parties' interests through openness, collaboration, and mutual gain and minimizes reliance on the parties' legal or contractual rights. Since the interests of the parties cannot always be accommodated, however, situations will inevitably arise where they feel a need to use their rights under the law or their contract. Managers do not need to be lawyers or experts in labor law to handle most such situations, but they must have a basic understanding of the law of collective bargaining. This chapter is intended to provide that understanding.

The basic law covering management/union relationships in the United States, except for the airline and railroad industries, is the National Labor Relations Act (NLRA or "the Act"), passed in 1935 (Wagner Act) and amended in 1947 (Taft-Hartley Act) and again in 1959 (Labor-Management Reporting and Disclosure Act). Five provisions of the Act provide the legal framework for managing change.

- *Section 9 (a).* Representatives designated or selected for the purpose of collective bargaining by the majority of the employees in a unit appropriate for such purposes, shall be the exclusive representatives of all the employees in such unit for the purposes of collective bargaining in respect to rates of pay, wages, hours of employment, or other conditions of employment.
- *Section 8 (a) (5).* It shall be an unfair labor practice for an employer—to refuse to bargain collectively with the representatives of his employees.
- *Section 8 (b) (3).* It shall be an unfair labor practice for a labor organization or its agents—to refuse to bargain collectively with an employer, provided it is the representative of his employees.
- *Section 8 (d).* For the purposes of this section, to bargain collectively is the performance

of the mutual obligation of the employer and the representative of the employees to meet at reasonable times and confer in good faith with respect to wages, hours, and other terms and conditions of employment, or the negotiation of an agreement, or any question arising thereunder, and the execution of a written contract incorporating any agreement reached if requested by either party, but such obligation does not compel either party to agree to a proposal or require the making of a concession.

- *Section 301 (a).* Suits for violation of contracts between an employer and a labor organization . . . may be brought in any district court of the United States having jurisdiction of the parties.

The basic law has been interpreted by decisions of the National Labor Relations Board (NLRB or "the Board") and federal courts. These decisions establish minimum requirements for a company/union relationship and prescribe standards of behavior for both parties. From a management of change perspective, four issues are key:

- What is bargaining?
- When is bargaining required?
- What subjects require bargaining?
- What right does management have to implement a change if the union doesn't agree?

The first, second, and third questions should not be a concern in most cases, as discussion with and active involvement of unions in essentially all planned changes are effective business practices regardless of what the law requires. The fourth question is more problematic, however. Whether or not management can implement a change without union agreement affects the relative bargaining leverage of the parties and determines the dynamics of negotiations. If management can implement without agreement, it has the right to act. If it cannot, the union has the right to prevent action. Management's right to implement without agreement—if it exists at all—depends on its having met the bargaining requirements raised by the first, second, and third questions. Therefore, all are important, and each will be considered below.

WHAT BARGAINING IS

The requirement of both parties to "bargain" as described in Section 8 (d) of the Act is the threshold legal requirement for management of change in a unionized workplace. The board and courts have outlined several key aspects of this requirement.

With Union Representatives

Bargaining must be with appropriate union representatives rather than directly with employees. Management has a right to communicate directly with employees in many areas, but direct dealing is prohibited in others. Where it is attempting to develop a collaborative, high involvement relationship, management can easily cross the line and attempt to deal directly with employees where doing so is prohibited. This not only violates the law but also can create distrust on the part of union leaders who may see it as an effort to undercut them. Several cases demonstrate the difference between situations where management must deal with union leaders and where it may deal with employees.

In an early case a company extended an offer to one segment of a group of represented employees. The union challenged the action and the Board noted that this was an attempt by the employer to bypass the union, tantamount to dealing directly with employees on matters appropriate for bargaining. It held the company in violation of the Act, stating with respect to the bargaining requirement that "On the part of the employer, it requires at a minimum recognition that the statutory representative is the one with whom it must deal in conducting bargaining negotiations, and that it can no longer bargain directly or indirectly with the employees."[1]

In another case management polled employees as to their feelings concerning a contract clause being negotiated with the union. The union complained, and the NLRB concluded that although management may explain to employees the reasons for its actions and bargaining objectives, it must accept the union as their exclusive agent. This means it cannot determine for itself whether or not employees support its position but instead must rely on the union for such information.[2] In a similar case an employer solicited employee opinions as to desirability of a shift schedule being negotiated with the union. The Board found this unlawful because "by soliciting the sentiment of the employees on a subject to be discussed at the bargaining table, Respondent was usurping the Union's function and attempting to arm itself for upcoming negotiations."[3]

In another case management maintained a problem-solving procedure under which an employee complaint would be accepted and dealt with only if union representatives were not involved. The Board concluded that this was unlawful direct dealing and that the union had a right to be involved without regard to whether the grieving employees wanted it.[4] Similarly, where management established safety and fitness committees and resolved issues with them that were identical to those it was unable to resolve with the union, the Board found direct dealing in contravention of Section 8 (a) (5).[5]

Notwithstanding this line of cases, management can directly involve represented employees under many circumstances. It has the right to direct the work force and to discuss matters that are not subjects for required bargaining. It may solicit ideas and suggestions from employees as long as it does not deal with them on proposals or resolving issues. Such involvement is more clearly valid if there is a good-faith effort to separate out bargainable issues and assure the union it has the exclusive right to bargain them.

Legally permissible direct dealing is likely to be of little value if the union resists, and management cannot legally insist on the right to deal directly with employees on subjects where bargaining is required. Therefore, the preferred way to involve employees directly is to discuss the process with union leaders and arrive at a mutual understanding as to how management will work with employees. To get union agreement, management must avoid undercutting the organization or minimizing the influence of its leaders. Instead, the company must offer a union an opportunity for gain through its involvement in determining what the direct employee dealing will be, in managing it, and in monitoring the results.

Good-Faith Bargaining

The NLRA does not compel either party to agree to a proposal, to make a concession, or to engage in fruitless marathon discussions; nor does it allow the Board or courts to sit in judgment on the substantive terms of a negotiation. The Act does, however, require sincere, ''good-faith'' discussions with an intent to settle differences and arrive at an arrangement. While this concept may be difficult to define, the Board has given the following guidance: ''Good-faith bargaining thus involves both a procedure for meeting and negotiating, which may be called the externals of collective bargaining, and a bona fide intention, the presence or absence of which must be discerned from the record. It requires recognition by both parties, not merely formal but real, that 'collective bargaining' is a shared process in which each party, labor union and employer, has the right to play an active role.[6]

The NLRB and courts do not rely on isolated acts or statements to find violation of the bargaining requirement. Instead, they consider the totality of the circumstances and the employer's conduct. They require a willingness to meet at reasonable times and ''cooperation in the give-and-take of personal conferences with a willingness to let ultimate decision follow a fair opportunity for the presentation of pertinent facts and arguments.''[7] Management must negotiate with a view toward reaching agreement, if possible, rather than merely going through the motions. Accordingly, actions that obstruct or inhibit the actual process of discussion or that reflect a cast of mind against reaching agreement are prohibited. For example, imposing preconditions to negotiations, unreasonable delay, or outright refusal to meet would be evidence of an unfair labor practice.

While the Act emphasizes the process of bargaining rather than forcing a particular result, it nevertheless requires more than ''surface bargaining,'' or going through the motions without any serious intent of reaching agreement. Surface bargaining could include making proposals that do not attempt to reconcile differences, making regressive offers, refusing to take a definite position, and other dilatory tactics.[8] On the other hand, actions such as the following indicate good-faith bargaining: willingness to meet at mutually convenient times and places, offering of proposals, making concessions, timely response to union questions, fully explaining management positions, soliciting proposals and input from the union, and reaching agreement.

Although the Act does not require agreeing to proposals or making concessions, it does prohibit "take-it-or-leave-it" positions when they indicate an unwillingness to negotiate. For example, where management took a take-it-or-leave-it position, refused to explain its position to the union and employees, and implemented its decision after few discussions, the Board held that a violation had occurred.[9]

Supplying Information

Bargaining requires employers to supply the union, upon request, with sufficient information to enable it to understand and intelligently discuss the issues raised. This requirement extends to information that is relevant: directly related to the union's function as the bargaining representative and reasonably necessary for the performance of this function.

Relevance has been broadly defined. Courts have required an employer to disclose information relating directly to unit employees and their conditions of employment unless it plainly appears irrelevant.[10] A union may obtain even broader information with a showing of relevance. For example, in one case a hospital was required to provide an agreement concerning its affiliation with another hospital after a showing that the affiliation agreement was relevant to the union's duty to bargain.[11] In addition, the duty to provide information extends beyond the period of contract negotiations and applies to the policing of the administration of the contract during its term.

Providing information regarding a company's general financial situation is an exception to the presumption of relevance, as the burden generally is on the union to demonstrate the relevance of financial information, even where the company is raising general financial need as a basis for its position. However, where a company asserts inability to pay in response to a union demand, it must back up this demand by providing appropriate information requested by the union.

Where an employer refuses to provide information because of a claim of confidentiality the Board and courts weigh the competing interests of the employer and the union in the requested information, and the type and extent of disclosure required will depend on the circumstances of the particular case. In reaching this balance the Board places the burden of demonstrating a legitimate claim of confidentiality on the employer resisting production of the information. It generally does not consider the interests of individual employees as compelling, and they are subordinated to the collective interest of the unit.

WHEN BARGAINING IS REQUIRED

Absent a union, an employer has discretion over decisions and changes affecting the enterprise as long as existing laws are not violated, and such decisions and changes may be implemented lawfully without bargaining with or consulting employees. This right has been referred to as the management reserved rights doctrine. Where a union is present, however, this freedom is limited by the requirement to bargain and comply with any contract that results. Management must understand these limitations and learn to work within them to manage change effectively.

The legal requirement to bargain must be considered when initiating changes involving "bargainable" subjects: those subjects which under the law the parties either may or must bargain, excluding only matters that are illegal (such as a union shop that requires all employees to become a member of the union in order to retain their job) or that must be included in a contract upon request (such as a union recognition clause where the union has been certified as a union representative). Whether or not bargaining is required will depend primarily on the status of the labor contract and the type of subject being considered. Figure 3.1 demonstrates the primary decision points for addressing these issues.

No Contract in Force

After a union has successfully organized a facility and has been recognized as the collective bargaining representative of a group of employees, both it and the company have an obligation to bargain in good faith to reach an initial contract covering wages, hours, and conditions of work. No contract is in force, and all bargainable subjects are "open" for negotiation. All bargainable subjects are also open for negotiation after a contract has existed but is in the process of expiring. Either party may serve notice of termination or modification of the contract 60 days prior to its expiration date. When this is done, the contract stays in full force and effect for 60 days or until its expiration date, whichever occurs first. However, during this period, and until a new contract is executed, all bargainable subjects are open and bargaining is required on wages, hours, and conditions of employment.

Generally speaking (except for permissive subjects, discussed below), all economic weapons are available to the parties when a contract is not in force and issues are open for negotiations. The union may strike (assuming any contractual no strike provisions have expired) and the company may lock employees out (after any contractual no lockout provision has expired) or implement the terms of its last offer (subject to requirements to be discussed below).

Contract in Force

The process of collective bargaining generally results in a collective bargaining contract between the company and the union intended to stabilize the employment relationship for its term. "Collective bargaining is not an end in itself; it is a means to an end, and that end is the making of collective agreements stabilizing employment relations for a period of time, with results advantageous both to the worker and the employer."[12] Therefore, when a contract is in force,

Figure 3.1
Bargaining Decisions Flow Chart

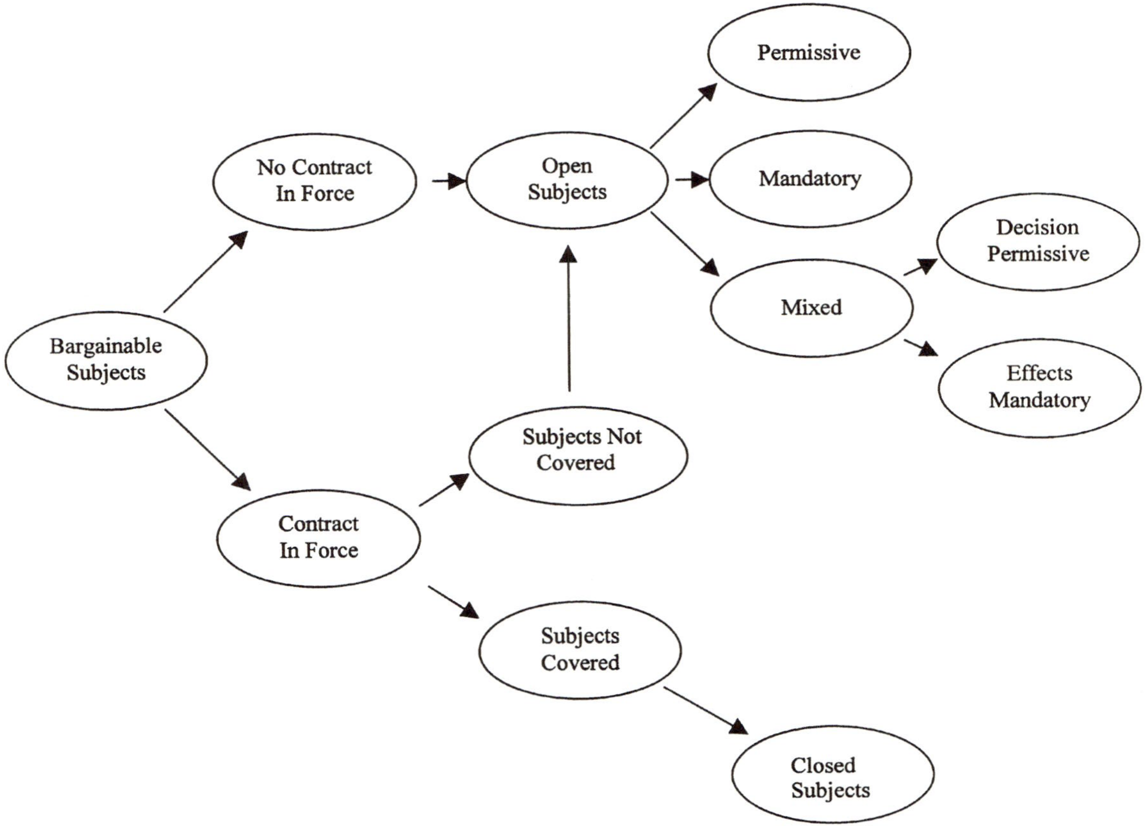

subjects covered by its terms are considered "closed" from bargaining and the Act does not require either party to discuss or agree to any modification of the terms and conditions contained in the contract.

Labor contracts, like other valid commercial contracts, are enforceable obligations of the parties, and where one is in force, neither party may terminate or modify it without mutual agreement. The contract may be enforced pursuant to Section 301 (a) of the Act, which provides that suits for violation of contracts between an employer and the union representing its employees may be brought in any U.S. district court having jurisdiction of the parties. The federal courts apply federal substantive law fashioned from the policy of our national labor laws to enforce such contracts.

More typically, however, the parties themselves have agreed to private arbitration as a means of enforcing their labor contract. Arbitration has been the centerpiece of collective bargaining agreements from the beginning. Courts presume that alleged violations of a labor contract are to be decided by an arbitrator and take a broad view of what matters are covered by the arbitration provision. The Supreme Court has noted that the grievance/arbitration procedure is a part of the continuous collective bargaining process and "Apart from matters that the parties specifically exclude, all of the questions on which the parties disagree must therefore come within the scope of the grievance and arbitration provisions of the collective agreement."[13] Thus, matters covered by the contract are subject to enforcement and are closed to bargaining, as demonstrated in Figure 3.1, unless both parties wish to discuss them.

Management may propose a change in a closed subject and attempt to convince the union to bargain and ultimately to agree. But the Act does not require the union to even discuss a modification of terms and conditions contained in a contract for a fixed period, and management is prohibited from implementing changes unless the union consents. For example, in one case an employer who had entered into an agreement covering wage rates attempted during the term of the contract to implement an incentive wage system. The union challenged and the Board noted that a bargain had been struck for the term of the contract and "neither party is required under the statute to bargain anew about the matters the contract has settled for its duration, and the employer is no longer free to modify the contract over the objection of the union." This was held to be true even though the contract did not specifically mention wage incentives because "such incentives are inseparably bound up with and are thus plainly an aspect of the payment of wages, a subject expressly covered by the contract."[14]

Subjects not covered by the contract, however, are open for bargaining even when a contract is in force, as indicated in Figure 3.1. In one case the employer maintained that except for subjects expressly reserved for further negotiations in a reopening clause, a contract created a static period in the relationship even as to issues that were not covered by the contract or discussed in the negotiations. The court disagreed and held that it was the company's statutory duty to bargain "as to subjects which were neither discussed nor embodied in any of the terms and conditions of the contract."[15] This concept has been applied even where such benefits have become a recognized term of employment. Of course, whether matters were discussed and whether they were in fact addressed in the contract can be the basis of disagreement.

Where a matter was discussed but not included in the contract, results have varied. Generally, however, courts have been reluctant to hold that a party loses a right to bargain by merely discussing a subject in previous bargaining. For example, in one case the parties during contract negotiations discussed inclusion of a provision covering Christmas bonuses, but the union withdrew its proposal and nothing on the subject was included in the contract. When the employer wanted to change the formula for computing bonuses, it was required by the Board to bargain with the union.[16] A matter will be closed to bargaining only if during contract bargaining it was fully discussed or consciously explored and the union consciously yielded or clearly and unmistakably waived its interest in the matter. In the absence of such a specific waiver of bargaining rights, the Board is reluctant to deprive employees of their right to bargain on a subject. When the contract is silent, it will not infer a bargaining waiver.

SUBJECTS OF BARGAINING

As indicated in Figure 3.1, open subjects may be mandatory, permissive, or mixed subjects for bargaining.

Mandatory Subjects

The Act requires the parties to bargain over ''wages, hours, and other terms and conditions of employment.'' The Board and courts have held that subjects contemplated by this language are ''mandatory'' subjects of bargaining, and unless a party has waived its rights by previous agreement, changes in them must be bargained upon request. Many decisions are clearly mandatory because they are an aspect of the relationship between employer and employee that obviously involves wages, hours, or conditions of employment. Examples are basic hourly rates, piece rates, shift differentials, incentive plans, layoffs, severance pay, holidays, vacations, recalls, production quotas, work rules, transfers, meal prices, seniority, work schedules, employee pensions, insurance, duration of the contract, and grievances under the contract. Other decisions involve managerial concern for economic viability that goes well beyond the employment relationship, and whether they are mandatory depends on the facts of the case. Some examples in this category are contracting out, supervisors doing certain work, and leasing arrangements. Management should seek legal counsel before refusing to bargain with its union concerning a change in such areas.

Permissive Subjects

Decisions that have only a very indirect and attenuated impact on the employment relationship are nonmandatory, or permissive. Bargaining is not required with respect to them but is permitted if both parties choose to do so. Such situations typically are at the core of the union's operation or the company's business.

An example of the first situation is where an employer insisted on a ballot clause calling for a pre-strike secret vote of employees as to the employer's last offer and a recognition clause that excluded as a party to the contract the International Union, which had been certified as the employee representative. The Supreme Court noted that a contract embodying both proposals would be legal and enforceable. The union, however, was not required to bargain, as the subjects were not a mandatory subject of bargaining because the ballot proposal dealt with relations between employees and their unions and the recognition clause was an attempt to evade the duty to bargain with the "certified" representative.[17] Other examples of permissive subjects involving relations between employees and their union include union fines and discipline, union organization structure, and union dues structure.

A change at the core of the company's business was presented where an employer sold a retail truck dealership in a franchising agreement without bargaining in advance with the union representing the workers. The union alleged the failure to bargain the decision was a violation of the Act. A majority of the Board dismissed the complaint, noting

decisions such as this, in which a significant investment or withdrawal of capital will affect the scope and ultimate direction of an enterprise, are matters essentially financial and managerial in nature. They thus lie at the very core of entrepreneurial control and are not the types of subjects which Congress intended to encompass within "rates of pay, wages, hours of employment, or other conditions of employment." Such managerial decisions ofttimes require secrecy as well as the freedom to act quickly and decisively. They also involve subject areas as to which the determinative financial and operational considerations are likely to be unfamiliar to the employees and their representatives.[18]

Other examples of permissive subjects involving managerial discretion are choice of advertising, product design and type, financing arrangements, benefits for already retired employees, corporate or other structure of the business, composition of the official or supervisor force, general business practices, plant locations, production schedules, and methods of manufacturing.

Mixed Subjects

A third type of management decision is one that has a direct impact on employment but has as its primary focus a fundamental entrepreneurial issue wholly apart from the employment relationship. In such cases, management is generally not required to bargain the issues necessary for the profitable running of the business. However, the NLRB and courts generally balance the interests of the union and employees by requiring bargaining over the effects of such decisions.

For example, where bargaining is not required on a decision to close part of a business, the employer nevertheless would be required to bargain on the procedures for lay-off and severance pay for affected employees unless that subject were already covered by the contract.

MANAGEMENT RIGHT TO IMPLEMENT

Whether, and under what circumstances, a company may implement a change without union agreement is a major factor in the power relationship between the parties and a key determinant of whether agreement is likely. If a union knows the company is prohibited from acting, it may have little incentive to agree. On the other hand, if it knows that after bargaining in good faith management has the right to act, it may have a greater incentive to compromise and reach the best agreement it can, particularly if it does not have the right to strike to stop the company.

Where closed subjects are concerned, management may not implement a change if the union objects. These matters are covered by contract, and the contract governs during its term. The union has an unfettered and enforceable right to insist that management abide by its agreement, although if the contract has a no-strike provision the union would be prohibited from striking to prevent management action.

Where permissive subjects are not covered by contract and therefore are open for bargaining, the party implementing a change is not required to bargain and may unilaterally implement the change at its discretion. The other party may not legally resist the change, insist on its position to the point of impasse, or bring economic pressure to bear in the dispute. Thus, management has an unfettered legal right to implement change of permissive subjects.

The right to implement changes in mandatory subjects open for bargaining is not so clear-cut. Bargaining does not require reaching an agreement, but for change to be implemented bargaining must be pursued until there is an agreement or until bargaining has reached an impasse. As early as 1937, the U.S. Supreme Court noted that the NLRA does not compel agreements between employers and employees or their representatives.[19] This view was confirmed in 1970 when the Supreme Court summarized the purpose of the Act as it relates to the bargaining requirement and whether agreement is required.

The object of this Act was not to allow governmental regulation of the terms and conditions of employment, but rather to ensure that employers and their employees could work together to establish mutually satisfactory conditions. The basic theme of the Act was that through collective bargaining the passions, arguments, and struggles of prior years would be channeled into constructive, open discussions leading, it was hoped, to mutual agreement. But it was recognized from the beginning that agreement might in some cases be impossible, and it was never intended that the Government would in such cases step in, become a party to the negotiations and impose its own views of a desirable settlement. This fundamental limitation was made abundantly clear in the legislative reports accompanying the 1935 Act. The Senate Committee on Education and Labor stated:

> The committee wishes to dispel any possible false impression that this bill is designed to compel the making of agreements or to permit governmental supervision of their terms. It must be stressed that the duty to bargain collectively does not carry with it the duty to reach an agreement, because the essence of collective bargaining is that either party shall be free to decide whether proposals made to it are satisfactory.[20]

Although neither party is obligated to yield its position or reach an agreement, either may insist on its position on an open and mandatory subject to the point of impasse. From management's perspective, this means that

An Employer violates his duty to bargain if, when negotiations are sought or are in progress, he unilaterally institutes changes in existing terms and conditions of employment. On the other hand, after bargaining to an impasse, that is, after good-faith negotiations have exhausted the prospects of concluding an agreement, an employer does not violate the Act by making unilateral changes that are reasonably comprehended within his pre-impasse proposals.[21]

Determining when an impasse exists is often difficult. Fruitless marathon bargaining sessions are not required, however, as an impasse exists where there are irreconcilable differences or after good-faith negotiations have exhausted the prospects of concluding an agreement. The Board has considered matters such as the following in determining whether negotiations have reached an impasse:

- The bargaining history.
- The good faith of the parties in negotiations.
- The length of the negotiations.
- The importance of the issue or issues as to which there is disagreement.
- The contemporaneous understanding of the parties as to the state of negotiations.

When a true stalemate or impasse occurs after good-faith bargaining on an open and mandatory subject, the employer is free to make unilateral changes consistent with the offer that the union has rejected. However, the employer cannot grant greater benefits than those proposed to the union or make changes to wages, hours, or working conditions that were not discussed during the bargaining. In response, a union generally may strike (without regard to the presence of an impasse) unless prohibited by a contractual no-strike provision.

KEY POINTS

1. The obligation to bargain requires employers to provide union representatives with relevant information and discuss matters with them in a sincere effort to settle differences and arrive at an agreement.

2. Bargaining is not required on closed (covered by contract) or permissive subjects (not contemplated by "wages, hours, and conditions of work").

3. Bargaining is required on subjects that are mandatory (contemplated by "wages, hours, and conditions of work") and open (not covered by contract).

4. After bargaining on an open and mandatory subject has reached an impasse, management may implement the terms of its last offer.

NOTES

1. *General Electric Company*, 150 NLRB 194 (1964).
2. *Obie Pacific, Inc.*, 196 NLRB 458 (1972).
3. *Harris-Teeter Super Markets, Inc.*, 310 NLRB 217 (1993).
4. *Circuit-Wise, Inc.*, 306 NLRB 766 (1992).
5. *E. I. DuPont De Nemours*, 311 NLRB 893 (1993).
6. *General Electric Company*, 194.
7. *NLRB v. Jacobs Mfg. Company*, 196 F. 2d 680 (2d Cir. 1952).
8. Charles S. Loughran, *Negotiating a Labor Contract*, 2nd ed. (Washington, D.C.: BNA, 1992), p. 133.
9. *American Meat Packing Corporation*, 301 NLRB 835 (1991).
10. *NLRB v. Item Company*, 220 F. 2d 956 (5th Cir. 1955).
11. *Mary Thompson Hospital v. NLRB*, 943 F. 2d 741 (7th Cir. 1991).
12. *NLRB v. Highland Park Mfg. Company*, 110 F. 2d 632 (4th Cir. 1940).
13. *Steelworkers v. Warrior Navigation Company*, 363 US 574 (1960).
14. *C & S Industries, Inc.*, 158 NLRB 454 (1966).
15. *NLRB v. Jacobs Mfg. Company*, 684.
16. *Beacon Journal Publishing Company*, 164 NLRB 734 (1967).
17. *NLRB v. Wooster Division of Borg-Warner Corp.*, 356 US 342 (1958).
18. *General Motors Corporation*, 191 NLRB 951 (1971).
19. *NLRB v. Jones & Laughlin Steel Corporation*, 301 US 1 (1937).
20. *Porter Company v. NLRB*, 397 US 99 (1970).
21. *Taft Broadcasting Company*, 163 NLRB 475 (1967).

Chapter 4

Resistance

Resistance is "any conduct that tries to maintain the *status quo* in the face of pressure to change it."[1] It is inherently neither good nor bad. While managers intent on a particular change see resistance as an unwelcome obstacle to be overcome, it is not always counterproductive. Resistance frequently presents another point of view in a perfectly rational reaction to a planned change. It can provide a check-and-balance that protects valuable systems or practices from change that is too fast. Resistance can also stimulate innovative problem solving and foster alternate options that may be better for employees and the organization.

Resistance can also slow or stop the pace of needed change, in which case it is a problem to be managed. Managing resistance can be difficult in any workplace, but where a union is present, management must face more sources of resistance, more reasons for resistance, and greater ability to resist than where one is not present. Understanding these aspects of resistance is a prerequisite to formulating a labor relations philosophy and change theory for a unionized workplace.

SOURCES OF RESISTANCE

Resistance to change in a unionized workplace can come from represented employees, the union, or non-represented employees. While individuals within each group may have much in common, they also are different in many ways. Each group has its own unique needs and interests that must be addressed to effectively deal with their resistance.

Represented Employees

Represented employees include all employees within the bargaining unit that elected the union and authorized it to deal with the company. Most change of the type being addressed in this book directly or indirectly affects them. They typically have much in common, as they are all represented by the same union, are (or will be) covered by the same contract, and do work of the classifications covered by the contract. Typically they are of the same or similar educational level and perhaps of similar socioeconomic groups. They may dress alike or wear identical uniforms. But they are far from homogeneous. Represented employees may or may not be members of the union or pay dues to it, depending on individual employee preference and union security provisions contained in the labor contract. They may be strident union activists, ambivalent about unions, or even anti-union. Their work situations may vary greatly, depending on factors such as age, relative seniority, job classification, shift schedule, level of competence, existing pay rate, marital or family status, or other individual factors. All have their own individual background, personality, needs, and aspirations. Small differences can have major consequences. For example, a management decision to lay off in seniority order could have no impact on one person but cause job loss to another similarly situated in every respect except for having been employed one day less.

Because of the many differences, management changes may have different effects on different individuals, and their level of resistance may vary accordingly. Management must anticipate and plan for this variation as it implements change. It must also remember, however, that the felt needs and attitudes of individual represented employees are frequently affected by the presence of a union. A union introduces a completely new set of cultural, social, organizational, and psychological considerations for the employees it represents, and union leaders can have a pervasive influence on them. Employees may subrogate their own interests to those of the union and identify more with the union than the company. If this happens within an adversarial management/union relationship, we/they attitudes can develop where individual employees resist first and ask questions later.

The Union

Reference to "the union" means different things under different circumstances. While it necessarily contemplates the collective voice of employees, the authority and scope of the individuals representing that voice, and potentially leading resistance, can vary greatly. For example, union resistance could be led by ad hoc individuals or groups of employees speaking with only notional authority, departmental stewards on the shop floor, local facility union leadership, union local leadership where the "local" covers more than one facility, ad hoc or standing union committees, union participants on joint committees, or national or international union leaders. Individuals in such roles could be self-selected, appointed by senior union leadership, elected by the represented employees at the facility, or elected by a broader group of union members. They might have no official responsibility or responsibility within a small portion of the facility, across the entire facility, across several facilities of a company, across several companies, or across several industries. Their authority to speak for the union may also vary greatly: they may have significant authority in a very autocratic union structure or little authority in a more democratic union where leaders are very responsive to the wishes of their membership. They might or might not be employees of the company concerned.

The union is rarely the direct target of management change, but it is the spokesman for, and alter ego of, the employees who often are the target. Consequently, the union becomes the leader in carrying out employee wishes and resisting management change. Its resistance hopefully is based on how leaders anticipate the change will affect employees they represent. Realistically, however, how the change is likely to affect the union as an institution and individual union leaders is an important consideration in determining whether and how the union will resist. It is an equally important issue for management to consider when implementing change.

Non-represented Employees

Non-represented employees such as administrative, technical, and supervisory staff are frequently overlooked in the change process in a unionized workplace. Policies and conditions of work applicable to some non-represented employees may be different from those for represented employees. They may have little or no association with the union or represented employees, be ambivalent about the union as an institution, and identify closely with management, where they see their future career. Those who are managers and supervisors may be expected to implement change that affects the represented work force. With so little in common with the change targets, such employees are not likely to resist.

Other non-represented employees, however, may have a strong mutuality of interest with represented employees or the union. They may have worked much of their career as a represented employee and may continue to socialize with bargaining unit employees, retain bargaining unit rights, and perhaps even continue to be union members. They may be subject to the same or similar policies and benefit programs as represented employees and therefore be affected by change in the same way as represented employees. At a minimum, their pay and benefits are likely to be affected by pay levels negotiated by the union. Non-represented employees in this situation may have essentially the same desire to resist a change as represented employees. Since they have no collective voice and are frequently part of management, formal resistance is unlikely. As a key player in the change process, however, they are positioned to have great influence on the ultimate result. Their actions or lack of action can cause change to succeed or fail.

REASONS FOR RESISTANCE

Represented employees, union leaders, and non-represented employees can all resist change. Whether they in fact do, and if so, the extent and method of resistance, varies greatly, depending on the issues involved and the expected impact of the change. This means a cookie cutter approach to dealing with resistance will not work, and that various groups and individuals within those groups must be dealt with differently. How they should be dealt with frequently depends on the reason they are resisting.

In *Managing Change and Making It Stick* Roger Plant describes two types of reasons for resistance. Systemic resistance is a cognitive reaction that arises from lack of appropriate knowledge, information, skills, and managerial capacity. Behavorial resistance is an emotional reaction based on perceptions and assumptions. He notes that management of resistance requires attention to both forms. Systemic resistance must be addressed by providing appropriate information and communication, while behavorial resistance demands attention to issues such as prejudice, perception, and assumptions that do not necessarily involve facts.[2]

In *Effective Change* Andrew Leigh takes the analysis a bit further and describes four types of reasons for resistance. Cultural resistance arises from a challenge to the values, traditions, practices, or customs of the organization. Social resistance results when relationships such as group solidarity or group norms are threatened. Organizational resistance occurs when changes are likely to affect formal arrangements such as organizational hierarchy, status differentials, or people's power or influence. Psychological resistance is based on selective perception of whether a change is positive or detrimental.[3]

The ideas of Plant and Leigh provide a basis for articulating three fundamental reasons for resistance in a unionized workplace: substantive, cultural, and process. Substantive reasons embody cognitive issues where the targets believe, rightly or wrongly, that their work life will become less desirable if the change is implemented. Cultural reasons include challenges to individual and organizational values, beliefs, customs, and biases that cut to the heart of employee and union identity. Process reasons arise when changes could affect the union as an organization, raise political issues, or affect the bargaining process between management and the union.

When management is devising a change strategy it must not only anticipate who will resist but also understand and empathize with the substantive, cultural, and process reasons that may cause them to resist. Such reasons may apply to represented employees, union leadership, or non-represented employees. More often than not, several causes work together in any particular case.

Substantive Resistance

Resistance is for substantive reasons if employees believe the substance of their work life—broadly speaking—will be affected. This substance includes wages, hours, and working conditions, as well as less tangible issues such as feelings of job security, ego and psychological needs, and expectations for the future. Represented employees, unions, and non-represented employees are all rational human beings who will resist if they believe a planned management change in these areas will do them more harm than good.

Some changes are so clearly to the disadvantage of employees that management fully understands the negative impact and why the union and employees resist. For example, where a competitive, profitable company sets out to reduce pay when there is no short- or long-term economic reason for doing so other than to create even higher profits, everyone would anticipate and understand the resistance. It occurs because the substance of employee work life will in fact be hurt by the change. The more usual case, however, is that management and the targets of the change have different views as to the impact of the change. For example, in many cases of concession bargaining management does not fully understand why employees object so intensely or how concessions it believes are so badly needed will actually hurt employees. The impact, however, is in the eyes of the beholder. Whatever the reason, it is quite common for employees and unions to perceive management actions as having negative impacts, even though management believes they are necessary. The parties see the potential impact differently for several reasons.

Different Information. Where the parties have different expectations of change they often are acting on different factual information. As the initiator of the change, management frequently fails to involve the union or share with it and employees all the information that has gone into the decision. Its reason for withholding information may range from trying to keep the union in the dark for perceived negotiating advantage, to negligence, to legitimate reasons of confidentiality. In other cases management shares information, but because of lack of trust, the union or employees do not believe what they hear. Whatever the reason, when the parties are operating on the basis of different information they are likely to disagree on what the impact of a change will be. When this happens, employees and union leaders are likely to assume the worst and resist the change.

Different Perspectives. Sometimes we see what we believe rather than believe what we see, or what we see is determined by what we need. This is particularly true in the workplace, where employees frequently look to their work and the employment relationship for their individual identity and self-esteem. Even where the parties are dealing with the same facts concerning a change, they see the likely impact differently because they have different perspectives and needs. Their different perspectives color what they see and cause employee expectations of change to be different from management's. For example, a management seeking to implement a change that relaxes work jurisdiction or seniority rules may honestly believe the change is in the best interest—certainly over the long term—of the company and the affected employees, as it improves efficiency but also makes jobs more challenging and meaningful. On the other hand, employees trained in a craft see it as their primary identity, and a change requiring them to do other things may dilute their sense of belonging. Or employees raised in the union tradition whose parents were laid off after work rule changes are likely to presume that increased efficiency reduces job security. When employees see change through such eyes they resist, and often management doesn't understand.

Different Time Perspective. Hopefully, management takes actions that insure the viability of the business and preserve jobs for as many employees as possible over the long term. If so, it may be required to balance these interests against the more immediate interests of current employees. For example, management could believe changes such as job consolidations, contracting out, or wage reductions are necessary to maintain competitiveness and ensure a viable enterprise several years down the road. Employees currently on the payroll, however, have more immediate concerns. In looking out for their own self-interest, they will not willingly make a sure sacrifice of their own job security or income for the possible benefit of future employees. Even if union leaders recognize the company's longer-term concern, political pressure may cause them to support a group of older employees who would be hurt now by the change and not be around to take advantage of the potential benefits. In such cases, the different time perspective can cause both employees and their union to resist an action that management believes is in their overall best interest.

Disagreement as to How Much Is Enough. The parties may agree that a substantive change is positive, yet disagree as to whether it goes far enough. For example, management may propose a small wage increase when the union and employees want and expect a larger one. Their differing views can result from different assessment of external guideposts, disagreements as to history, greed on the part of one or both parties, or other such issues. Regardless of the reason, even a positive change that is not enough can cause resistance.

Hidden Agendas. Management hopefully initiates most changes for reasons that are honest and transparent. If employees and the union resist, their reasons for doing so hopefully are equally honest and understandable in the context of the discussion above. Change can, however, also be initiated by management or resisted by a union for more covert reasons arising from personal beliefs of individuals, political needs, or bureaucratic pressures on those making the decisions. For example, management might make a particular proposal because of a bias of a senior manager or peer pressure on the CEO. Likewise, a union might resist because of the bias of a particular union leader or because a union leader believes resistance will enhance his chances of winning a union election. In such cases, the real motives of the parties may be hidden, causing misunderstanding as to why the parties are doing what they are doing.

Cultural Resistance

Values, beliefs, biases, and other deep-rooted influences derived from our history and experiences create the culture within which we live, and this culture fosters certain needs and expectations that value maintaining the status quo. This desire to maintain the status quo manifests itself in several ways in a unionized workplace.

Habit and Inertia. Changes that disrupt our expectations "produce a loss of the psychological equilibrium we unconsciously prize,"[4] creating a human inertia that causes people to cling to certainty and oppose interruption of the status quo. Change is an individual and personal matter, but with few exceptions, we are more comfortable with what we know or can predict with a reasonable degree of certainty than with what we don't know or can't predict. Since change nearly always involves uncertainty, we resist it.

The reaction of many people to the introduction of computers and to advances in computer technology is a good example. Many managers and professional employees with established records of success were slow to begin using computers notwithstanding persuasive evidence that they were easy to learn and would improve productivity. Likewise, many represented employees are comfortable with their current jobs, work assignment practices, seniority systems, or other procedures that make their lives stable and predictable. Union leaders like the stability of the status quo, particularly where it is part of a strong sense of history and institutional pride associated with the union. Resistance to change under these circumstances is not surprising.

Loss of Control. Conner also notes that "major change is loss of control."[5] He observes that the reaction of different people to a change frequently varies greatly, depending not only on the actual impact on the individual but also on the extent to which the individual believed he could affect the change. Mink et al., citing work by Gordon Lippitt and Alvin Zander, note that one of the reasons individuals and groups resist change is that they were not involved in the planning.[6] Stated differently, they lack control over the change.

The issue of control is important in any workplace. Individual employees, whether represented or not, are likely to resist change initiated by management because it reminds them of the extent to which management has control over their lives. The uncertainty that almost inevitably surrounds change exacerbates the real or perceived loss of control.

The existence of a union compounds the issue. Employees elect unions because they want more control over their work life. Unions represent themselves as providing this control, and the law provides them a structure for bargaining through which they can legitimately attempt to exercise it. The contractual right of a union to share control of change with a company may have been gained by past struggles and hard-fought negotiations. Not surprisingly, unions are reluctant to allow any change that suggests to the employees they represent that they do not have the expected level of control.

Unions also are reluctant to allow change that could be seen to set a precedent that minimizes control in future cases. Therefore, employees and the union must consider not only whether the substance of a particular change is positive or negative but, perhaps more importantly, whether the process used by the management to implement it will tend to jeopardize any rights they have to control similar changes in the future. For example, an employer's attempt to unilaterally impose an obvious benefit such as an increase in pay or a bonus might meet strong resistance. Employees, and particularly the union, might uniformly view such change as positive from a substantive viewpoint but resist its unilateral implementation because of fear of loosing a degree of future control in matters relating to pay.

Indictment of the Past. Tichy and Devanna in *The Transformational Leader* argue that ''Perhaps the most significant resistance to change comes from the fact that leaders have to indict their own past decisions and behaviors to bring about change.''[7] This resistance often is a result of how they view change. Marilyn Ferguson notes in *The Aquarian Conspiracy* that there are four kinds of change: ''*Change by exception* says, 'I'm right, except for _____.' *Incremental change* says, 'I was almost right, but now I'm right.' *Pendulum change* says, 'I was wrong before, but now I'm right.' *Paradigm change* says, 'I was partially right before, and now I'm a bit more partially right.' ''[8]

Unfortunately, it is easy to view all change as pendulum change and an indictment of the past. Management, employees, and union leaders tend to forget that circumstances change, the information base grows, and over time people learn better ways of doing things than were possible at an earlier time. When they forget these things they conclude that by initiating or acceding to change, they are implicitly condemning the past—frequently their own past. This leads to resistance.

Managers no doubt often fail to initiate needed changes because they don't want to indict themselves, and the concern also causes union leaders to resist. Typically union leaders are in a political position where they serve at the will of the membership, and as with any politician, acknowledging a mistake, whether implicitly or explicitly, can have dire consequences. Whether particular leaders were involved in initiating a contractual provision or practice to be changed, actively supported it, or merely tolerated it during earlier periods of their administration, their acceding to a change initiated by management is likely to be interpreted by the membership as proof that they were not doing their job properly. This will be remembered when election time arrives. The easier course for union leaders may be to refuse to acknowledge need for the change and resist it, regardless of its substantive merits.

Process Resistance

To serve their constituency effectively, union leaders must first get elected and stay in office and then bargain agreements with management that employees believe are appropriate. Management changes that appear to detract from the ability of leaders to accomplish either process will be resisted, regardless of their substantive merit.

Political Processes. Unions, to a greater or lesser extent, are fundamentally democratic institutions where leaders are elected through a political process. The internal governance procedures of national unions are spelled out in their constitutions. While detailed procedures vary from union to union, typically a periodic convention is the supreme authority and delegates to the convention are selected by secret ballot. Principal officers may be elected by the convention or by a direct referendum of all members of the union, but in either case members have the opportunity to elect national officers at least every five years. The officers are generally responsible to executive boards, the members of which are also selected by the membership. Local union leaders, whether key officers or departmental stewards, are selected in similar, but frequently more political and democratic, processes. Local members, in accordance with local union by-laws, elect their leaders using procedures that almost invariably allow direct participation of all union members. Thus, most union leaders, particularly at the local level, are responsive to the political pressure inherent in democratic institutions.

Individuals serve in union office for various reasons. They may serve for pay, prestige, status in the community, or because of devotion and dedication to the union cause. Regardless of the reason, those who serve as union leaders must continually be responsive to the wants and needs of their constituencies.

When management initiates a change that affects represented employees, union leaders must seriously consider the political impact of their response before deciding on a course of action. Taking an unpopular position could prevent their being reelected and cost them their job, individual self-respect, or both. This often means they must lead employee resistance to management changes, even when they are indifferent to the substance. As with other politicians, their first and greatest need is to get reelected, whether their motive is continued employment or continued ability to maintain the influence that union office provides. Management should not underestimate the influence of such considerations on the decisions of union leaders as to whether or not to lead resistance to a change.

Bargaining Processes. The collective bargaining process that governs most management-initiated change is an integrated process where no action stands alone, and what the parties do in one case can affect the handling of future cases. The parties must be concerned about the impact of current actions on situations or individuals in the future. This means that in order to enhance its bargaining position a union may logically choose to resist a change that, if viewed in isolation, would not be seen negatively. This can happen in two situations.

In much bargaining each party develops and presents its position on an issue or issues, and resolution ultimately occurs when one party persuades the other to change positions, or they trade one position for another until all are resolved. Where the parties have such bargaining practices, each is reluctant to agree with the other unless it gets something in return. If a quid quo pro is not obtained there is incentive to delay agreement until other, perhaps unrelated, opportunities develop to get something in exchange. Under these circumstances, some managements might defer making changes employees would like until they need to buy a concession from the union. On the other hand, when an employer proposes a change under these circumstances, a union's likely reaction is that management wants the change and is willing to up the ante, even on an otherwise positive change, in order to gain acceptance. This expectation of more, either then or later, causes union resistance.

In pattern bargaining a union attempts to negotiate identical wages, hours, or conditions of work across various work locations or in all or many companies of an industry. Examples are seen within many companies and in industries such as automotive, steel, and oil. Patterns may be attained by exerting economic force on a weaker employer to get certain concessions and then using those concessions as leverage against successively stronger companies. When a pattern exists, the union jealously guards it because a break in the pattern, even if otherwise justified in one company, could easily move to others where the change might be less appropriate from the union's point of view. Further, the existence of a pattern in an industry is a source of power for the national union because only it, as opposed to its locals, has the information and infrastructure to deal across an entire industry. This provides the national union with an incentive to resist any change that could break a pattern. Such factors lead a union to resist change at one location or employer, largely or solely because of the potential future impact on another location or employer.

TYPES OF RESISTANCE

Some level of resistance to change exists in all workplaces, whether union or non-union, and in a union workplace resistance can exist among employees who are not represented (e.g., supervisors, technical employees, and administrative staff) as well as among represented employees. Resistance may be passive, where employees do not actively resist but are demotivated or demoralized and unwilling to support the change effort. It may also be active, where employees take the initiative and actively engage in behavior to resist change.

Key differences exist, however, between resistance in a union and non-union workplace. Represented employees have most of the individual rights to resist change that are available for non-represented employees. In addition, a union can affect employee morale and their consequent passive behavior and also lead employees in a broader array of activities to actively resist management changes than are available to non-represented employees. Discussed below are some of the more frequently used actions, whether individual or collective, for resisting management change in a unionized workplace.

Failure to Support

Failure to actively support management initiatives is a major, insidious resistance mechanism in both union and non-union workplaces. In a typical difficult business environment, with scarce resources and pressure for growth, reduced cost, and increasing profits, a company's performance is judged in both absolute terms and relative to what its competitors are doing. To beat the competition, a company must be able to implement change that encompasses all its employees, integrates the best thinking and expertise available, and is faster and more efficient than changes competitors are instituting. This only happens when employees are broadly skilled, knowledgeable, and motivated to care about their jobs and to contribute more.

Under these circumstances, work force compliance is not enough. The very best efforts of all employees are required, and failure of all employees to provide their best effort can lead to an inadequate change effort, the competition winning, and resulting business failure just as surely as if employees actively resisted the change.

Individual Resistance

When employees elect a union to represent them they forgo the right to take certain actions individually with respect to management. For example, they cannot as individuals legally agree to changed wages, hours, or conditions of work; negotiate with management; or resist changes their union has agreed to or is negotiating. But they can individually resist management change in several ways.

Individually represented employees may resist change by speaking against it. Management in many companies encourages employees to speak out and express their views, including those that are contrary to management. Where speaking out is not encouraged, free speech protections and union contracts nevertheless typically accord individual employees the right to express their views and speak against a planned change. Such speech may lower morale or create a critical mass of opinion against a change, either of which could cause management to discontinue or defer a planned change or lead to collective employee action. This type of resistance can be positive if a better solution results, or negative if the change needs to be made and management defers to employee threats.

Individual employees also can take specific actions that slow or stop implementation of change. As a general rule, when management implements a legal policy or rule, employees are bound to comply with it. In fact, however, employees who want to resist a new policy or rule usually can; not openly and in strict defiance, but more subtly and perhaps only partially. Their actions can be just one small step beyond failing to support the change, or substantially more egregious. Behavior such as doing the minimum work required, refusing to work overtime, frequently confronting supervisors with objections and questionable concerns, and ridiculing management are all examples of individual resistance tactics. They are the same types of actions that, when endorsed and pursued on a continuing basis by groups of employees, would be considered an "inside game," discussed below. Whatever form it takes, such behavior can substantially reduce the positive impact of a planned change.

Process Hostage

The management/union relationship involves both substantive and process issues. As previously discussed, substantive issues are objective business matters such as wages, hours, and conditions of work, and process issues relate to the practices and procedures through which the parties decide and manage the substantive ones. Substantive changes directly affect employees and are the changes most likely to be resisted. One way unions resist substantive change, however, is by holding processes hostage, hoping that management will change its position on the substantive matter to preserve the process.

At the most elementary level, a union may simply refuse to discuss a company proposal that is not an open and mandatory subject of bargaining. The most common situation of this type is where management tries to change wages, hours, or conditions of work that are covered by a labor contract. In such case, the matter is closed to bargaining and the union could exercise its right to have a deal be a deal, refuse to talk about it, and effectively prevent a change.

Other types of situations are more complex, and may involve attempts by the union to resist change where it does not have the contractual or legal right to prevent it. Most union/company relationships include some cooperative processes such as joint committees or joint problem-solving task forces. Under normal circumstances, these presumably are mutually advantageous, as neither party is legally required to participate and either may withdraw or refuse to participate at any time. Because of their voluntary nature, the union may refuse to participate in them in an attempt to pressure management to change its position or to punish it for its actions. For example, a union might use a threat to withdraw from a joint training committee to pressure the company to discontinue plans to begin testing participants or to make other changes to which the union objects. If the union actually does withdraw from a cooperative process, its action creates an unfortunate circumstance where the best process for resolving a disagreement, or preventing future ones, is given up in an effort to prevent substantive change.

Grievance Procedure

Essentially all labor contracts contain agreements covering wages, hours, and conditions of work for a set time period and a grievance/arbitration procedure for enforcing these agreements. The company administers the contract and the union may use the grievance/arbitration procedure to formally contest a management action as an alleged violation, discuss it formally with management representatives, and have the issue decided by a neutral arbitrator if necessary. Thus, while the contract is in force, a union may prohibit implementation of a planned change that it can convince an arbitrator is contrary to the labor agreement. When the contract expires, however, the company may, after appropriate bargaining, implement planned changes at the peril of other union and employee resistance tactics.

Using an agreed grievance procedure to prevent management from making changes the union in good faith believes violate a labor agreement is a perfectly legitimate method of resisting change. Occasionally, however, the grievance process is used in less straightforward ways to resist management actions. These tactics, which may be part of an "inside game," involve filing of mass or harassing grievances, perhaps on issues previously decided in arbitration, in an effort to intimidate supervisors, strain management resources, or otherwise pressure management to back off a planned change. Such actions are typically orchestrated by union leaders, involve large numbers of employees, and are highly visible and confrontational. The grievances are processed within the grievance procedure and usually rejected by management. They are rarely arbitrated, however, because the union doesn't want to risk an adverse decision and the company has no need for a decision because confirmation of what it is already doing would be of little value. Such use of the grievance procedure may intimidate management into changing its position or build a reservoir of discontent and anti-company feelings that give the union additional bargaining leverage to prevail in its position when the contract is being renegotiated.

Inside Games

Inside games include a broad array of activities that workers can use within their workplaces to resist management actions or gain concessions from management. They may include any or all of the actions previously discussed but generally are more broad based, consistent, collectively supported, and threatening than the individual activities. The underlying strategy is to utilize a combination of activities, frequently with escalating levels of severity, to gain power by damaging production, reducing efficiency, and/or destroying employee/management relationships. Inside game tactics may including the following:[9]

- Symbolic demonstrations such as dressing alike, or wearing of buttons, arm bands, or T-shirts.
- Loading the grievance procedure.
- Confronting supervisors through behavior that is just short of insubordination but with similar effect, or at the other extreme, ending all relationships with supervisors except those that are absolutely required.

- Creating and maintaining a warlike atmosphere in which the union/management relationship is characterized as a continuing battle and warlike rhetoric is used to embarrass, pressure, and cajole company leaders to accept the union's position.
- Use of ridicule to denigrate management and turn employees against them.
- Work-to-rule, where employees are encouraged to do the minimum required to avoid discipline for insubordination through activities such as doing nothing unless directed by supervisors, following supervisors' direction to the letter even if obviously a mistake, taking no initiative to handle problems, or never making suggestions.
- Ending union/management cooperation by activities such as refusing to hold problem-solving discussions, serve on joint committees, or support community activities.
- Filing questionable charges against the management with government agencies such as OSHA, EPA, NLRB, and others.

Inside games typically represent the maximum pressure or resistance a union and/or employees can exert while remaining at work and not involving external parties. They can, however, also include some withholding of services through actions such as sick-outs or refusal to work overtime at a level that is costly to the company but not subject to charges of insubordination or interpreted as a partial strike. Unions such as those representing airline pilots can use sick-outs to great effect, as members are highly trained, difficult to replace, and under federal regulations can decide for themselves whether or not they are sick.

The cost to the union of a sick-out is less than a strike because many members continue working and those who are ''sick'' receive no strike benefits. Such actions can come at any time, giving management little time to prepare. They may, however, be considered as strikes in violation of contractual no-strike agreements and therefore subject to injunctions or fines against the union.

Strikes

Section 501 of the Act defines strikes to include ''any strike or concerted stoppage of work by employees (including a stoppage by reason of the expiration of a collective bargaining agreement) and any concerted slow-down or other concerted interruption of operations by employees.'' Strikers retain their employee status. After an unfair labor practice strike, initiated in response to unfair labor practices committed by the company, employees generally are entitled to their jobs back even if they have been permanently replaced. After an economic strike for the purpose of enforcing economic and other negotiating demands, an employer may not discharge employees but may hire permanent replacements and refuse striker requests for reinstatement unless a vacancy exists.

Economic strikes are more common in bargaining situations. In an early decision the NLRB, no doubt influenced by the circumstances surrounding most strikes at that time, said ''a strike exists when a group of employees ceases work in order to secure compliance with a demand for higher wages, shorter hours, or other conditions of employment, the refusal of which by the employer has given rise to a labor dispute.''[10] Economic strikes are also used in concession bargaining, where employees strike to resist changes proposed by management, such as proposals for reduction in wages or expansion of work flexibility. Such strike activity historically has been the primary weapon of unions against managements with whom they had major disagreements. It is legally permissible and employers generally are prohibited from taking punitive or discriminatory actions against employees who engage in it.

The NLRA does, however, specifically prohibit strikes for certain purposes, and certain types of strikes and related activities are not ''protected'' activity, allowing an employer to lawfully discharge or discipline an employee for participating in them. The following types of strikes or strike activities fall within these categories, allowing management to take action to prevent their use:

- Forcing a person to cease doing business with another person (a secondary boycott).
- Forcing an employer to transfer work from one group of employees to employees of the striking union, or for purposes of ''featherbedding.''
- Sit-down or sit-in strikes where employees remain on the employer's premises but take possession of the property, prevent access, or are involved in sabotage.
- Partial or intermittent strikes where employees remain at work but refuse to perform certain assigned work.
- Strike misconduct where employees resort to aggravated violence such as assaults upon non-strikers, destruction of property, or egregious use of profane and insulting language to humiliate or intimidate non-strikers.
- Strikes in breach of contract, where the labor contract between the parties contains an express or implied no-strike clause.
- Strikes where the union is insisting to impasse on a permissive bargaining subject.

Strikes generally are used only in the most serious disputes and as a last resort after other processes for resolving issues have broken down. Decisions are made on the basis of which party has the most power. Relative power is determined by the ability of the union and employees to withhold their services and forgo their pay for whatever period of time is necessary, as compared to the company's ability to sustain the business without the services of the striking employees. Thus, strikes involve mutual hurt, and except in the rarest of cases, everyone loses.

In many situations the threat of a strike is a more powerful action for forcing the union's position than a strike itself. Management typically recognizes the cost of a strike—both in immediate economic terms and in long-term impact on employee performance—and will make significant concessions to avoid these costs. But once a strike begins, many of the costs are behind it, positions harden, and each party seeks to recover its costs by insuring concessions from the other.

If a party has the power to do so, it may insist on positions that go beyond what it would have settled for before the strike began.

Picketing

Picketing is the patrolling of an employer's premises by one or more persons. It typically is used in connection with a strike to encourage workers to stay on strike, prevent replacements from taking over striker jobs, and gain public sympathy for the strike. Where no strike exists, pickets may be used to publicly protest various actions of management or employment standards that are considered sub-par.

Picketing includes a range of activities. At one end of the range, it is limited to one or two persons and conducted in a non-threatening way to communicate the union's position to represented employees, non-represented employees, management, contractors, customers, and the public at large. At the other end of the range, picketing is a device to threaten and intimidate management, employees, or those desiring to do business with the company. In these cases, larger numbers of pickets typically are involved and they use whatever techniques of intimidation are necessary to increase the power of the union.

As a general rule, picketing has a clear ingredient of communication and therefore is a protected, legal activity. However, mass picketing or picketing accompanied by threats, intimidation, or violence will in most cases be held to be illegal. In addition, picketing to force or require an employer to recognize or bargain with a union or in connection with secondary activity is likely to be an unfair labor practice and therefore not protected by the Act.

Boycotts

Boycotts can include many different types of behavior but in their simplest form are merely refusals to deal with a particular business. In a consumer boycott, a union tries to bring economic leverage on a company by persuading employees and the public not to purchase its products. Tactics could include activities such as picketing, handbilling, and publication of an ''unfair'' or ''we-do-not-patronize'' list.

Boycotts may be used in connection with a strike as an additional tool to create economic hurt and force the company to agree with the union's bargaining position. They require significant time to implement and make effective, however, as it is necessary for the union to communicate its views and cause the public to change its buying habits. Further, they cannot be turned off immediately and can cause long-term damage to a company that is not in the union's or the employees' best interest. Therefore, they typically are used only in connection with strikes that are bitter and long lasting. In addition, boycotts may be used to address issues of concern to a union when it is unwilling to strike (perhaps when it feels it does not have the member discipline or economic substance to prevail over the company) or legally prevented from doing so (perhaps to protest a social position taken by the company).

As a general rule, boycotts are legal, as unions may use publicity to truthfully advise union members, customers, and the public that goods are produced by a company with whom it has a dispute and to discourage purchase of those goods. However, the boycott area is a legally complex one and several types of boycott activity are illegal or unprotected (e.g., secondary product boycotts and certain boycotts relating to union recognition).

Corporate Campaigns

A corporate campaign "means [exploiting] vulnerabilities in all of the company's political and economic relationships—with other unions, shareholders, customers, creditors, and government agencies—to achieve union goals."[11] Corporate campaigns are essentially public relations campaigns designed by unions to generate external pressure on an employer to change its policies. They are intended to put indirect pressure on a company by pressuring individuals or other firms that do business with or have interlocking directorate ties with it.

In corporate campaigns unions attempt to exploit companies' vulnerabilities, destabilize their operations, and bring economic hurt to force agreement with union objectives. Tactics have included use of the various in-plant devices discussed above, plus external efforts such as bringing pressure on board members or executives as individuals, soliciting political figures or other community thought leaders to bring pressure on a company, attempting to reduce stock prices by spreading unfavorable publicity, pressuring customers and vendors to cease doing business, inducing federal or state agencies to intervene to the detriment of the company, and communicating directly to groups such as shareholders, investors, creditors or customers.[12] The campaign itself can include a wide array of confrontational tactics from which unions are free to choose in varying combinations and to various extents.

From a union perspective, corporate campaigns have several advantages. Elements can be used in connection with strikes or other forms of resistance to further increase the leverage against a company. They are of special value to a union, however, where the union is reluctant to call a strike because the employer can operate its business without striking employees or where employee commitment to a strike is weak. Further, elements of a corporate campaign may be one of the union's few weapons in those cases involving broad managerial discretion (e.g., the decision to shut down a plant or handling of social issues) where management is not required by law to bargain and a strike would not be protected.

KEY POINTS

1. Where a union is present, management must face more sources of resistance, more reasons for resistance, and greater ability to resist than where one is not present.

2. Bargaining unit employees, the union, and non-union employees are all potential sources of resistance to management-initiated change.

3. They may resist change for substantive, cultural, or process reasons.

4. Resistance to change may be both passive and active, and may include:

- Failure to actively support
- Individual employee resistance
- Holding cooperative processes hostage
- Use of grievance procedure
- Inside games
- Strikes
- Picketing
- Boycotts
- Corporate campaigns

NOTES

1. Andrew Leigh, *Effective Change* (London: IPM, 1988), p. 69.

2. Roger Plant, *Managing Change and Making It Stick* (London: HarperCollins, 1987), p. 19.

3. Leigh, *Effective Change*, p. 70.

4. Daryl R. Conner, *Managing at the Speed of Change* (New York: Villard, 1993), p. 126.

5. Ibid., p. 74.

6. Oscar G. Mink, Pieter W. Esterhuysen, Barbara P. Mink, and Keith Q. Owen, *Change at Work* (San Francisco: Jossey-Bass, 1993), p. 82.

7. Noel M. Tichy and Mary Anne Devanna, *The Transformational Leader* (New York: Wiley, 1986), p. 77.

8. Marilyn Ferguson, *The Aquarian Conspiracy* (Boston: Houghton Mifflin, 1980), p. 72.

9. Herbert Northrup, "Union Corporate Campaigns and Inside Games as a Strike Form," *Employee Relations Law Journal*, vol. 19, no. 4 (Spring 1994), p. 507.

10. *American Mfg. Concern*, 7 NLRB 753 (1938).

11. Industrial Union Department, AFL-CIO, "Developing New Tactics: Winning with Corporate Campaigns," 1985, p. 1.

12. Northrup, "Union Corporate Campaigns and Inside Games as a Strike Form," p. 507.

Part II

Philosophy

Chapter 5

Countervailing Collaboration

The picture presented in Part I is not, on balance, a pretty one. It shows a world of conflict between labor and management, littered with failed or only marginally successful attempts to work together. Open warfare and adversarial relationships are common and clearly counterproductive. Accommodating relationships and partnerships do exist and are more positive, but each has its deficiencies. Accommodation keeps the peace but misses opportunities to use what unions have to offer, while partnerships typically are either too narrow or too unstable to provide maximum benefit over the long term. These relationships exist in a legal environment that limits management flexibility, and employees and their union have substantial opportunity and power to resist management changes. In this environment, most companies would benefit from a new type of relationship with the union representing their employees: a stable, long-term relationship that minimizes counterproductive conflict, takes advantage of what the union has to offer, and benefits employees and the union as well as the company.

This chapter presents "countervailing collaboration" as a philosophy for moving in this direction. This philosophy acknowledges the countervailing interests between companies and unions, as well as the likelihood that some level of conflict will be a continuing characteristic of their relationship. It also posits that a labor/management relationship that recognizes the many interests companies and unions have in common and fosters collaboration among them is feasible and imperative for a high-performing workplace. The philosophy is summarized in the following concepts:

1. The labor/management relationship should be based on a pluralistic philosophy that acknowledges the inevitability of conflict and benefits from the synergy of the union's divergent interests.

2. How change is managed defines the labor/management relationship, and the unique aspects of that relationship require a special change model that specifically addresses union issues.

3. An effective labor/management relationship should avoid programs that address union issues independent of the whole organization. Instead, labor relations should be a fully integrated part of a systemic approach to human resource management.

4. Use of force as a last resort is appropriate in combination with efforts to foster a more effective working relationship.

5. Management must set the tone for the relationship and lead efforts to improve it.

The remainder of this chapter discusses these concepts and briefly outlines how other parts of the book relate to the countervailing collaboration philosophy.

THE COUNTERVAILING INTERESTS

Obvious differences exist between companies and unions. Each has a different history and cultural background, serves different customers, has different roles and responsibilities, and measures its success by different criteria. The most important difference is that each entity is accountable to a different constituency for employee behavior and well-being. This differing accountability for the same thing is the key wedge that forces difficulties between the two.

Peter Drucker has noted that "The first job of the executive is to make his organization perform."[1] Management is responsible for those fundamental business decisions of a financial and managerial nature that directly affect the scope and direction of the enterprise. These include issues such as products to be made and sold, location of facilities, production processes, customer relationships, and the many day-to-day decisions necessary for maintaining a viable business. Management is accountable to its shareholders for a secure investment with high returns; to governmental agencies for compliance with laws and regulations; to the public generally for operating within the law and maintaining high levels of commitment to health, safety, and the environment; to customers for providing products and services that offer value; and to other stakeholders that the company does business with or affects. Most important for our discussion, management is responsible to its employees for fair treatment that includes a safe and healthful workplace, reasonable compensation, and an opportunity for personal satisfaction and growth.

Unions, on the other hand, have entirely different responsibilities. They were born of the need to maintain the fundamental dignity of employees through organized resistance to practices of management. From the inception of the modern American labor movement in the 1880s, unions have presented a collective voice to counter management practices they felt were unfair to employees. Title I, Section 1 of the NLRA, Findings and Policies, notes that "The inequality of bargaining power between employees who do not possess full freedom of association or actual liberty of contract" and employers substantially burdens commerce, and commerce should be safeguarded by "restoring equality of bargaining power between employers and employees."[2] Passage of the Act gave protection to employees' ability to resist unfair management practices and attain favorable terms and conditions of employment through collective action.

In the early days, unions' primary efforts were to improve employee wages and working conditions. While unions continue to seek improvements in these areas, their recent, higher profile activities often have included protecting what employees have (concession bargaining), as employers facing serious competition have attempted to control costs by reducing wages and benefits or changing work rules. Unions have also been active in improving the quality of employee life. For example, many have provided counseling services, insurance, referrals, or other services of value to employees and their families. More recently, some unions have taken the initiative in fostering cooperation with management or have engaged in "partnerships" with management to mutually address issues of common concern.

Thus, both the company and union are accountable in certain respects for insuring proper management of the work force, and employees look to both for fair and equitable treatment. From a broader perspective, however, their accountability is very different. Union leaders head political entities and derive their authority from those they govern and to whom they are accountable. They are accountable to employees for attaining the best treatment and highest level of wages and benefits that can be sustained by the company without driving it out of business. The employees they represent determine whether they have been successful and the consequences of their performance. Management, on the other hand, is in a different situation. As indicated by Section 2 (11) of the NLRA, supervisors have the authority "in the interest of the employer, to hire, transfer, suspend, lay off, recall, promote, discharge, assign, reward or discipline other employees, or responsibly to direct them."[3] While the rights associated with this responsibility may be limited in individual cases by the labor contract, management nevertheless has the initial responsibility and is accountable over the long term, even for actions that were coerced by union pressure. It also is more broadly accountable. Managers are appointed to positions of power and are accountable to a chain of command for winning in the marketplace. They have a constituency and diverse accountability that is much broader than that of union leaders and requires managers to balance employee needs with many other stakeholder demands. Differences over how this balance is decided lead to labor/management conflict and challenge both parties to work together.

In summary, whether seeking to get more, preserve what they have, or improve employee life, unions have not assumed management's broad accountability. Only management is ultimately accountable for the actions resulting from the investment of the shareholders. When bad things happen—whether injury or death on the job, poor quality, falling profits, declining stock prices, bad publicity, investigations, or lawsuits—management must answer and be accountable to all its stakeholders. This responsibility must not be abrogated by the relationship with the union.

THE COLLABORATIVE CHALLENGE

Although management is accountable for everything that happens within the organization, the union also has a right to a say and important input on many issues. Management's challenge is to work with the union to insure that its presence creates, rather than destroys, value by helping to improve organizational excellence.

One must acknowledge from the outset that some managements have attempted to address these conflicting interests by severing their relationship with the union representing the company's employees. The authors of *Strategic Negotiations* describe three approaches management has used for dealing with labor unions, one of which is escaping the relationship.[4] They discuss escape strategies such as relocating operations, outsourcing work, creating conditions in which employees elect to decertify their union, or hiring replacements during a strike (who technically are still represented by the union but de facto may have little relationship with it). This book, however, is based on the premise that escape is not an appropriate management strategy, and management must respect the right of employees to organize and bargain collectively if they wish, regardless of its feelings about the value of unions. As a general rule, taking actions for the purpose of escape violates the National Labor Relations Act. From a more pragmatic viewpoint, such a strategy is also usually a bad decision when the disruption caused by a decertification election or legal challenge, the chance of failure, and the likelihood of continuing controversy are considered. This does not, of course, assume that actions such as outsourcing or plant moves are inappropriate when taken for legitimate business reasons. Such actions raise many of the difficult change issues that this book should help address.

The NLRA generally keeps management and unions together, absent an escape strategy, for as long as employees wish to have a union represent them. It also prescribes the legal parameters within which the parties must function, although the parameters leave great latitude for the parties to determine how they will work together. Over the years this latitude and the different accountabilities, roles, and objectives of the parties frequently have led to union/management relationships characterized by major conflict. Better relationships can be achieved, however, where the parties accept the inevitability of the relationship and the value of working together. The challenge is to do the best with what is available. Barry and Irving Bluestone note in *Negotiating the Future: A Labor Perspective on American Business* that

Regardless of the mechanism of managerial control, there is bound to be some level of conflict between labor and management since the objectives of workers and owners are never perfectly congruent. This is simply in the natural scheme of things. The problem is to figure out how to distribute power between labor and corporate management in such a way that all the stakeholders in the enterprise—workers, owners, and managers themselves—forge the best collective outcome possible within an economic and social environment riddled with constraints.[5]

The best possible collective outcome can be attained through a relationship that not only recognizes the inherent conflict between the parties but also notes their many common interests and integrates them into a collaborative relationship. Management's challenge is to develop that type of relationship.

The Relationship

Relationships in a unionized workplace are multifaceted. One aspect is the relationship among individuals: employees, supervisors, managers, and union representatives. The actions of each of these persons are critical to business performance, both as individual acts and as they contribute in the aggregate to the overall work environment. It is not the purpose of this book, however, to address those individual actions as such. To the extent that it addresses issues such as their beliefs, biases, talents, motivations, actions, and the personal relationships among them, it does so in the aggregate for their respective institutions or groups as a whole. The book's purpose is to deal with collective actions of management, the union, and the group of represented employees.

In this collective context the labor relationship is comprised of groups or institutions with their own interests, some of which overlap with others and some of which differ. The relationship is a function of the attitudes these groups—management, represented employees as a group, and the union—have toward each other.

The relationship starts with the attitude between

- the employer or "management," which is the aggregate of the top decision maker(s) and those company employees who are charged with controlling and directing the affairs of the enterprise, taken as a whole and ranging in a hierarchical sense from the board of directors through the first-line supervisors; and
- employees who are "controlled" by management.

The company and its employees are held together by overlapping areas of interest. The company's need for labor and the employees' need for work bring them together. The company cannot operate without employees; without the company, employees have no job. Many common interests exist within the relationship, such as what work is done, how it is done, what it costs, and how much employees receive for doing it. The work of employees determines whether the company will succeed or fail, and their behavior, performance, and treatment are central to the company's human resource policies. Where a union is not present, differing views and needs within the common area of interest are

Figure 5.1
Management/Employee Relationship without a Union

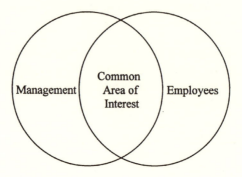

reconciled directly between the management and individual employees. This relationship is represented in Figure 5.1.

When employees organize, the relationship is expanded to include a union, composed of members and their elected leaders who in the aggregate are charged with representing the collective interest of the company's employees. The desire of the employees for a collective voice and their legal right to organize introduce the union. (Several unions may exist in many workplaces, with each representing a different group of employees. Where this situation exists, the relationship described below must be replicated for each union and employee group.) The union depends on both management and employees for its existence, and its presence introduces additional overlapping areas of interest. This creates a situation where certain areas of interest are held in common by all three parties, others are held in common only for employees and the company, others only for employees and the union, and yet others only for the union and company. These overlapping interests are demonstrated in Figure 5.2.

Thus, the relationship is one based on the reciprocal attitudes among three parties who have many different interests but are held together by their common interests.

The Interests

The key interest management, unions, and represented employees have in common is their interest in optimizing the results of their combined contributions to the relationship. Each party contributes different things. Management brings the capital and the ultimate accountability to the investor, the customer, and other stakeholders, along with the management and technical expertise necessary to fulfill its role. Employees bring their labor. More importantly, they must also bring the hearts and minds that really understand what's going on and, if given the opportunity and incentive, the commitment and ability to improve and innovate in ways that really make a difference. The union brings a single voice

Figure 5.2
Management/Employee/Union Relationship

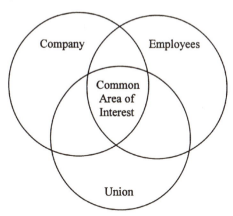

reflecting the collective environmental needs employees require to optimize their contribution. It also brings the ability to influence the hearts and minds of employees, either positively or negatively, as they decide whether to support or resist the company. This influence can be by virtue of the union's legal right to bargain for employees concerning conditions of work or by its more informal ability to lead employees it represents to support or not support management initiatives.

Each party's contribution to the relationship is essentially without value standing alone; it is of value only in combination with the contribution of one or both of the other parties. Thus, each has an interest in the others contributing as much as possible to an effective combination that maximizes the value of the whole. Management's interest is best served by a relationship that encourages employees and the union to contribute as much as they can to the combination.

One assumes the relationship with employees is the most critical to management because they, and not the union, are part of the company, and it is their work and the commitment of their hearts and minds that translate into the company's success or failure. For example, whether employees exhibit initiative and creativity in their jobs rather than just do what they are told is the type of issue that determines whether the company succeeds or fails. Since such employee behavior is affected by the relationship between employee and company, one easily assumes the union is of little, or even negative, value.

From a broader perspective, however, the relationship with the union is equally critical because it also has interests in the areas of overlap and has substantial influence over employee behavior in those areas. Management's relationship with the union may in fact be its first concern because the union can leverage the actions of the entire employee group. Its relationship with management will largely determine whether the union will use its leverage to prevent or support employee commitment to the company or to encourage the type of employee behavior management is looking for. In the example above, the attitude of the union may well be the largest factor in determining whether employees demonstrate initiative and creativity. Thus, management must view the union as a primary vehicle for influencing employee behavior in the overlapping area, and it must accept that in a unionized workplace it is unlikely to get the kind of employee commitment it needs without union support. As the authors note in *Strategic Negotiations*, "a growing body of research evidence confirms a high failure rate among employee commitment programs undertaken in a setting in which the union-management relationship remains arm's-length."[6]

Thus, management must acknowledge the countervailing interests of unions while simultaneously exploiting areas of common interests. Peter Drucker has noted that

Every single area of union activity is inevitably a management area, whether it be working hours or working conditions, job definitions, job assignments, hiring and firing policies, supervisory authority or seniority provisions . . . Hence the union is always a part of the governmental structure of the enterprise . . . It is shortsighted to the point of folly for any management to deny that the union necessarily concerns itself with problems which are "properly management's prerogatives."[7]

COUNTERVAILING COLLABORATION

"Countervailing collaboration" is a philosophy that acknowledges both the countervailing and common interests within the labor/management relationship and presents a framework for managing them to the parties' mutual advantage. The language describes the philosophy. A countervailing force is one that is different but that compensates for, counterbalances, or makes up for that which is missing. Collaboration means working with another. Thus, the language contemplates complementary forces working together to make up for what is lacking. The essence of countervailing collaboration is that labor/management relationships do not have to be zero-sum games and that the parties can work together to complement each other through a synergy that allows the combination to be greater than the sum of its parts. The language connotes a philosophy that acknowledges both the conflicting world in which companies and unions operate and the vision of what can be if they work together. It contemplates two parties with different roles, values, objectives, and accountability recognizing their differences and working together to develop a complementary relationship that is to the advantage of the company, its employees, and the union. The key elements of this philosophy are outlined in the sections below.

Philosophical Perspective

One's philosophy of labor relations is affected by how the world in general and labor unions in particular are seen. In *Labour Relations* Frank Burchill discusses three perspectives that are helpful in understanding the basis of a countervailing collaboration philosophy.[8] The first is a unitary perspective that

places emphasis on common objectives and the possibility of harmony. Where conflict arises, it is variously seen as the result of the activities of deviants and troublemakers or as arising from ignorance. In this model the productive enterprise has objectives which are in the interests of all associated with it. Managerial style often emphasises team spirit, working together and notions of leadership rather than of power. Sanctions are needed to deal with troublemakers and deviants and there is an emphasis on discipline at the place of work, and stronger laws to deal with such people.

In the unitary model, unions are seen as needing to be curbed and controlled, or alternately as an extension of management to assist with communication, unity, and control.

Burchill's second perspective is pluralism, which

acknowledges divergent interests within society and the organisation and accepts that there will inevitably be some conflict. The productive enterprise is a coalition and not all parties are committed to all of its formal objectives. Conflict is built into organisations, and society, because individuals, and groups, have interests which clash. In the employment relationship employees and managers often have objectives which differ; hours of work impinge on social life; change can necessitate redundancy; higher pay may compete with investment demands and so on.

In the pluralism model, unions are seen either as a nuisance or as necessary channels for discontent, and conflict can play a positive role in promoting change and efficiency.

The final perspective is conflict, which is rooted in Marxist analysis and holds

that society is essentially divided into two classes—those who own the means of production and those who do not. Those who own are concerned with maximising their profits by whatever means are available, and, regard labour as simply one factor of production to be exploited in a similar fashion to any other factor in pursuit of this objective. The owners of capital deal with labour only to the extent that they need it. Manipulation of labour might require concession and compromise, but these represent temporary devices used in the pursuit of absolute control.

The countervailing collaboration philosophy is based on the pluralistic perspective. It recognizes that fundamental differences between the parties make differences of opinion and some level of conflict inevitable. It also acknowledges, however, that the parties share many common interests, and where a union is present it is a necessary channel for employee discontent and involvement. It treats the fates of the parties as so intertwined that it is in management's best interest to foster a reasonable balance of its interests with those of the union. Therefore, the philosophy contemplates collaboration which allows and encour-

ages employees both individually and through their union to contribute all they
are able and willing to contribute, while protecting their own long-term best
interest.

Countervailing collaboration represents a natural evolution of management's
relationship with employees and their union, as follows:

- Management control—autocratic, bureaucratic, directive management of employees and
  similar rule, legal, power-based relationship with their union
- Organization development programs—participative, involving, team-based management of employees and a relationship with the union based on power or cooperation
  limited to certain well defined areas
- Countervailing collaboration—participative, involving, team-based management of employees supported by involvement of the union as an integrated part of the human
  resource system.

Countervailing collaboration envisions a real, substantial sharing of management processes, including the decision process, with union leaders. This puts
them in the room where most management decisions are made and gives them
an opportunity to provide input, influence decisions, and understand the results.
But it does not advocate joint decision making, economic democracy, co-
management, or any forum where the union has a vote on matters that are the
prerogative of management. Management is accountable for results, and giving
away its right to make the final decision is an abrogation of its responsibility to
its stakeholders.

Management of Change

Change is a process of moving from the current status to a new, desired state
in which a series of events—expected or not—unfold. Management of this process is the central focus of the labor relationship and a key element in the countervailing collaboration philosophy.

The relationship between management and union is largely irrelevant as long
as both are willing to live with the status quo. Life proceeds on its normal
course. The same jobs are assigned the same way, pay and benefits remain the
same, and working conditions remain unchanged. As a general rule, all parties
deliver on their promises and have their expectations met. When either party
fails to deliver, a predictable process that contains no surprises is used to address
the failure. How the union and management feel about each other doesn't matter
because the business is on autopilot and there is nothing to disturb the status
quo. A "no harm–no foul" situation exists.

In today's world, however, both external and internal forces continually create
dissatisfaction with the status quo and drive one party or the other to attempt
to change various aspects of the work environment. When this happens, the
union/management relationship becomes critical, for it affects what the parties

do and how they act in the change process; and it can drive issues such as what changes are made, when they are made, how much they cost, and how they are implemented. For example, management's relationship with the union would be a major factor in determining what happens in connection with a management plan to introduce new technology. If the relationship was based on fear, misunderstanding, or mistrust the union would strongly resist the change, go to great lengths to limit its application in order to reduce adverse consequences to employees, and push for extensive contractual language to guarantee protection. This could cause problems ranging from delay in implementation to restrictive associated work rules to actual termination of the plans. On the other hand, if a relationship is based on trust and understanding, the union is more likely to accept, or even support, the change and not as likely to require the same guarantees and protections. Thus, the state of the relationship largely determines what the parties do and how they act in the change process.

In a case of circular reasoning, however, what the parties do and how they act in the change process are the key determinates of the state of the relationship. The relationship is likely to deteriorate if management proposes changes in wages, hours, or conditions of work that are unfair or misunderstood or makes investment decisions that have significant adverse effect on employees. How management proposes the change and attempts to get it implemented may be even more important. For example, attempts to implement change unilaterally or inappropriate use of force are likely to hurt the relationship regardless of the merits of the substantive change itself. On the other hand, positive changes with fair impacts, or even unpopular changes implemented with full involvement and understanding, can improve the relationship.

In summary, the labor/management relationship is defined both by its effect on the management of change and by the effect management of change has on it. Understanding this self-reinforcing feedback loop and, where feasible, managing change to foster positive cycles is a key to the countervailing collaboration philosophy.

Integration

Stand-alone labor relations programs have a predictably short life cycle. Management sees a need to address a particular problem or improve the labor/management relationship. A plan based on plausible sounding theory and alleged successes elsewhere is proposed. Senior management and perhaps union leaders concur with proceeding. New training, procedures, and practices are implemented. There is initial success, possibly because the parties decide to address easy issues first. Over time, however, disappointments occur. The parties are unable to solve certain intractable problems, a company manager or union steward behaves badly, or senior managers or union leaders conclude they are not getting what they expected. Disappointment leads to cynicism and mistrust. The program is dumped, and in some cases a downward spiral in the relationship begins.

Management of a unionized work force is too complex to be addressed this way. More is required than a program, a relationship, a negotiation process, a way to resolve conflict, or rules to follow. Instead, all these and more must be integrated parts of the human resource management system of the enterprise. Everything that affects management, employees, and the union, and the relationships between these effects, must be managed as integral parts of the whole.

Countervailing collaboration is an integrated philosophy. It does not exclude—but rather includes and integrates—appropriate labor/management programs such as quality circles, quality improvement processes, total quality, team concept, team management, team development, or production quality teams. Programs such as these may be helpful or necessary in attaining the type of synergy and effectiveness desired. But they work over the long term only if they are effectively integrated with ongoing, fundamental processes such as those relating to wages, benefits, bargaining, contract administration, and dispute resolution. The countervailing collaboration philosophy suggests approaches for integrating all such processes to foster long-lasting results.

Forcing

Countervailing interests will not always be reconciled on the basis of collaboration and synergy alone. The world is not so simple. Where parties have different interests in an environment of scarcity, and abandoning the relationship is not an option, some situations inevitably develop where available resources do not fulfil the needs or desires of all the parties. When this happens, "distributive" bargaining, where each party attempts to force its will on the other, typically follows. Countervailing collaboration accepts this situation as inevitable and acknowledges that some issues will be determined by the parties' relative power.

Several research studies support combining forcing and collaboration to improve problem-solving effectiveness. The authors of *Strategic Negotiations* studied four bargaining scenarios among thirteen case histories and concluded that a combination of "forcing" followed by "fostering" provides the best opportunity for successful change, employee commitment, and union/management cooperation.[9] Several additional studies combining forcing and fostering are discussed in *Using Conflict in Organizations*. These also concentrate on forcing followed by fostering, but the authors suggest the two probably are not isolated modes but rather are components of a complex, cyclical behavior in which sequentiality is not a critical factor.[10] Countervailing collaboration adopts this view and holds that use of, or clear willingness to use, force provides the necessary discipline and balance required to solve some of the more difficult problems arising in the labor/management relationship. Further, how force is used, rather than the fact of its use, frequently is the major factor affecting the relationship.

Leadership

Although both parties have responsibilities in the labor/management relationship, management must lead efforts to improve it. Management represents the owners of capital and, combined with the owners, is responsible for the investment decisions that determine the opportunity for a relationship to exist in the first instance. It holds and is broadly accountable for the resources and information of most consequence to the relationship. In most cases management acts, and the union reacts. Therefore, management must determine the type of relationship it wants with the union representing its employees and manage its business to attain that relationship.

To change its relationship with a union, management must start "from where it is" and pursue improvement regardless of the union's reaction. The existing relationship with union leaders may be so bad that collaboration seems out of the question, and union leaders, for personal or other reasons, may have strong desires to perpetuate this situation. Or the relationship may be more positive, but political pressures nevertheless prevent union leaders from being seen as working with management. Union leaders are elected, and regardless of how they may feel personally, their constituency may want an aggressive approach with management. For such reasons, the union's willingness to collaborate may vary across a range in which union leaders are:

- Antagonistic and unwilling to even consider collaborative concepts.
- Cordial but unwilling to engage in collaborative efforts.
- Willing to collaborate informally on a case-by-case basis.
- Willing to agree to pursue systemic collaborative processes.

The more a union is willing to collaborate, the better. But countervailing collaboration does not require any particular starting point, union buy-in, or agreement to proceed. Rather, as a philosophy that considers unions and represented employees as an organic part of the whole human resource system, it helps management decide what behavior and actions are appropriate for a particular situation at a point in time. Management can, and should, take the initiative regardless of the existing relationship with the union or the union's attitude toward changing it. The state of the relationship may affect what management does, but it should not affect whether it takes actions to foster improvement. Most such actions involve improved management processes that have their own inherent value and also will, over time, lead to reciprocal action by the union.

Management can create the environment it wants by setting the tone and taking the actions that mirror its desired relationship with employees and their union. Joseph Jaworski notes in *Synchronicity* that "people in fact do create the future through our declarations, our actions, our way of being." Further, "the only world we can have is the one we also create together through our language and interactions," and this compels us "to see that our world, our communities, our organizations will change only if *we* change."[11]

If we—management—will change and exert leadership through who we are, what we value, what we do, and how we conduct our relationships, a work environment with completely new properties will emerge: an environment that mirrors who we are and how we act. That is the essence of countervailing collaboration.

IMPLEMENTING THE PHILOSOPHY

How-to books that describe programs or specific solutions lend themselves to an orderly point-by-point implementation procedure. A sequential discussion of what to do and how to do it accomplishes their purpose. This book is not that straightforward. Its purpose is to present a philosophy and ideas to challenge and help practitioners, in collaboration with union representatives, think through their own unique problems and opportunities and create their own future. This chapter has presented the underlying philosophy. The following chapter develops a change model for a unionized workplace that provides a working theory for dealing with change management, the central focus of the philosophy.

Part III discusses ideas and practices for building a labor/management relationship that is consistent with the countervailing collaboration philosophy and the parameters and constraints described in Part I. The ideas presented are not point-by-point explanations of how to implement each element, which is impossible for an integrated, systemic philosophy requiring a holistic approach. Rather, each chapter discusses certain management concepts and how they can be applied in a unionized workplace. The ideas in each chapter apply to the labor relations philosophy as a whole rather than just to its specific elements. Accordingly, readers who accept the principles of countervailing collaboration must read Part III with a view toward deciding for themselves which ideas will best support the philosophy within their organization and how to apply them for greatest effect.

KEY POINTS

1. The labor/management relationship should be based on a pluralistic philosophy that acknowledges the inevitability of conflict and benefits from the synergy of the union's divergent interests.

2. How change is managed defines the labor/management relationship, and the unique aspects of that relationship require a special change model that optimizes union involvement.

3. An effective labor/management relationship should avoid programs that address union issues independent of the whole organization. Instead, labor relations should be a fully integrated part of a systemic approach to human resource management.

4. Use of force as a last resort is appropriate in combination with efforts to foster a more effective working relationship.

5. Management must set the tone for the relationship and lead efforts to improve it.

NOTES

1. Peter F. Drucker, *The Changing World of the Executive* (New York: Truman Talley, 1982), p. xi.

2. 49 Stat. 449 (1935), as amended.

3. Ibid.

4. Richard E. Walton, Joel E. Cutcher-Gershenfeld, and Robert B. McKersie, *Strategic Negotiations* (Boston: Harvard Business School Press, 1994), p. 24.

5. Barry Bluestone and Irving Bluestone, *Negotiating the Future: A Labor Perspective on American Business* (New York: Basic Books, 1992), p. 133.

6. Walton, Cutcher-Gershenfeld, and McKersie, *Strategic Negotiations*, p. 12.

7. Peter F. Drucker, *The New Society: The Anatomy of Industrial Order* (New York: Harper and Row, 1949), p. 107.

8. Frank Burchill, *Labour Relations*, 2nd ed. (London: Macmillan, 1997), pp. 2–6.

9. Walton, Cutcher-Gershenfeld, and McKersie, *Strategic Negotiations*, p. 231.

10. Carsten De Dreu and Evert Van De Vliert, eds., *Using Conflict in Organizations* (London: Sage, 1997), p. 51.

11. Joseph Jaworski, *Synchronicity* (San Francisco: Berrett-Koehler, 1996), pp. 173, 175.

Chapter 6

Change Model

A key element of the countervailing collaboration philosophy is that how change is managed defines the labor/management relationship, and the unique aspects of that relationship require a special model that specifically addresses union issues. A special model is necessary because of the pervasive effect of the NLRA and the increased opportunities represented employees and their unions have to resist management-initiated changes. Thus, change must be grounded in a theory that recognizes the role of the law and the impact of the union on employee behavior. This chapter presents such a theory. It outlines some generally applicable change principles and presents a labor relations change model based on them. It then discusses how that model typically works in various types of management/union relationships and addresses its longer-term implications.

PRINCIPLES

Change means different things under various circumstances. It contemplates a difference but standing alone does not imply either quality or quantity. It does not distinguish between partial and complete change, successful and unsuccessful change, short- or long-term change, or change that makes a difference and change that doesn't. But certain general principles apply to all change.

Types of Change

This book is based on a broad definition of change that contemplates the end result being sought. It includes all the differences that are necessary to accomplish a current or future organization objective. The objective could be very narrow, requiring only a small change, or broad and long-term, requiring major organizational restructuring. It could be operational change or transformational change.

- Operational change is the long- or short-term change that is intended to cause contin- uous improvement in efficiency or effectiveness. Its primary aim is to do things right.
- Transformational change is broad based, usually longer term, strategic recasting of the form or nature of the organization and its people. It addresses broad areas of the organization, such as the technical, political, and cultural systems, and involves en- dorsing different beliefs, doing different things, and fundamentally changing relation- ships. It synthesizes new ideas to redefine and integrate the entire organization. Transformational change is primarily about doing the right things.

Most change that benefits the organization occurs in two phases:

- Direct change is immediate, specific change, such as a move to new machines, policies, or rules. It typically is not an end in itself, but rather is a means to accomplish an objective. Direct change frequently can be imposed on a target population of employees by requiring them to comply, but it has little value if the ultimate objective is not attained.
- Secondary change is the result of the direct change. For example, it is the change in the behavior of people (what they do and/or how they do it) and in the results they achieve from a direct change such as a new procedure, policy, or machine. Needed secondary change usually comes only when the right direct change is made and effec- tively implemented. Secondary change also can be the unintended consequences of a direct change that is poorly conceived or implemented.

Direct changes standing alone rarely accomplish meaningful improvement. Installing a new machine, publishing a new rule, negotiating a new contract, or implementing a new training program is of little value if the ultimate objective is not attained: if production does not improve, employee behavior does not change, or a redirection of the organization does not occur. Sandra E. Black and Lisa M. Lynch report in *Proceedings of the Fiftieth Annual Meeting, Volume 1* of the Industrial Relations Research Association that actual workplace practices are what really matter and that what is important

is not necessarily whether or not an employer adopts a particular workplace practice but how that workplace practice is actually implemented in the establishment. For example, whether or not a workplace has a total quality management (TQM) system has no (or even a negative) relationship to productivity, but the percentage of workers that get together to discuss workplace issues, a key component of TQM, does have a positive relationship to productivity. This suggests that what matters is how well you implement a workplace practice and not just whether or not you say you have it.[1]

The direct/secondary distinction is particularly important in a unionized set- ting. Managers and labor relations practitioners too frequently declare success when the union is forced to concede, a new contract is signed, or an arbitration case is won. The problem is that these direct changes frequently are worthless, either because positive secondary change does not follow or because unintended consequences do more harm than good.

Characteristics of Change

Three themes emerge from the literature to provide the theoretical underpinnings for organizational change. They are process, roles, and resistance.

Process. Change is a process and not an event. It is a process of moving the organization from the current flawed state, through a transition, to a more desirable state. Change is moving from "the status quo—an established equilibrium that continues indefinitely until a force disrupts it"; through transition, or "the phase during which we disengage from the status quo" and "develop new attitudes or behaviors"; to the desired state or "what we want."[2] "Because change is a process, events—often unexpected events—unfold over time."[3]

Roles. The change process requires different roles, and participants must fill several discrete, although related, roles for it to be effective. In *The Challenge of Organizational Change*,[4] the authors argue that the entire organization must participate if a change effort is to be successful and that the participants can be divided into three categories, as follows:

- "Strategists lay the foundation for change and craft the vision." They "are responsible for identifying the need for change, creating a vision of the desired outcome, deciding what change is feasible, and choosing who would sponsor and defend it." Strategists typically are seen as those at the top level of the organization.

- "Implementers develop and enact the steps necessary to enact the vision." They make it happen by managing the day-to-day process of change. Implementers generally are seen as those at the middle level of the organization.

- "Recipients, finally, adopt—or fail to adopt—the change plan." "These are the institutionalizers; their behavior determines whether a change will stick." They are typically seen as at the bottom of the organization, where it is believed resistance is most likely to occur.

Daryl Conner similarly outlines four distinct roles of participants in the change process: "A sponsor is the individual or group who has the power to sanction or legitimize change. . . . An agent is the individual or group who is responsible for actually making the change. . . . The individual or group who must actually change is the target. . . . An advocate is the individual or group who wants to achieve a change but lacks the power to sanction it."[5]

In *The Paradox Principles* the Price Waterhouse Change Integration Team identified four types of employees, or roles. Their "visionary," "catalyst," and "co-operator" are similar to the roles discussed above. But in addition, they identified the "stabilizer," which adds a new dimension:

Stabilizers are not stragglers blocking change. On the contrary, they facilitate change by continually creating and communicating models to interpret the changing environment and promote understanding. They act as beacons, shedding light on clarity and structure and articulating what can be counted on. Basing their opinions on logic and information, they create successive versions of order that are persuasive and stabilizing as the process moves forward.[6]

In these times of great change, it is easy to jump to the view that anything that gets in the way of change is negative and problematic. But that frequently is not the case. Change that is too great or too fast can become chaos and have unintended or bad results. Balance is required. The Price Waterhouse Change Integration Team has noted that "Rampant change in the absence of key elements of stability is chaos. Uncontrolled change fathers turmoil, not solid performance. Managers need stakes in the ground to guide change. Where such guideposts are missing or wobbly, change can be nothing more than a free-for-all—plenty of activity, too little real performance improvement."[7]

The sponsor and agent in a change initiative typically come from the ranks of management. The target can be any group or groups of employees. Anyone could be an advocate or a stabilizer, but both are important roles of the union. Regardless of where they exist, however, effective change requires all these roles working in concert.

Resistance. The third theme is that change requires overcoming resistance. Kurt Lewin is generally credited with creating the basic outline of the dynamics of the change process—the force field analysis.[8] This theory holds that an organization is not a static structure, but rather a dynamic one where equilibrium, or the status quo, is created by countervailing forces, typically called "restraining" forces and "driving" forces. Restraining forces tend to resist change, while driving forces tend to cause it. Such forces may exist inside or outside an organization. For example, factors such as traditions, laws, policies, values, beliefs, and biases can be significant restraining forces that tend to maintain the status quo. On the other hand, external events, changing laws, aggressive management, opportunities for benefit, and other similar factors can be driving forces for change. When an organization is in equilibrium, change can only occur if the drive or incentive to change exceeds the resistance and creates a disequilibrium that unfreezes the status quo. Disequilibrium can be introduced by changing the size or direction of a driving or restraining force, or by adding additional forces of either type. To maintain the new status over time the organization must be refrozen in a new state of equilibrium. When this happens the changed situation becomes the new status quo, and changing it requires a new cycle initiated by the introduction of a new force for disequilibrium.

General Change Model

Thus, organizational change is a process of moving from the current state to a preferred one. Different parties play different roles in the process and for change to happen, driving forces must overcome restraining forces to upset the equilibrium of the status quo. These characteristics have been reduced to formulas and described in various ways. In *Real Time Strategic Change*[9] Robert Jacobs notes that change happens when the product of dissatisfaction with the current state, a vision of what can be, and achievable first steps exceeds the resistance to the change, as follows:

Dissatisfaction × Vision × First Steps > Resistance to Change

Similarly, in *Change at Work*[10] the authors argue that change happens when the product of the level of dissatisfaction with the current state, the desirability of the proposed change, and the practicality of the change exceeds the cost of the change, as follows:

Dissatisfaction × Desirability of Change × Practicality > Cost

In *Large Group Interventions*, the authors endorse a similar formula.[11] In addition, they emphasize that all elements must be in place for such a process to be effective. For example, people in the organization may be highly dissatisfied, but change will not occur unless they have a vision of where they want to go or an understanding of the desirability of their change objective.

LABOR RELATIONS CHANGE MODEL

The formulas outlined above apply in a general sense regardless of whether or not a union is present, so a synthesis of them will be a starting point for a unionized model. A union represents an additional participant whose role does not fit any of the descriptions in the general model and whose presence can greatly increase resistance to change. Even though many employees wear two hats (as an employee and as a union member or officer), a union is an institution separate from the employees it represents. Therefore, to effectively manage change in a unionized workplace management must explicitly recognize the presence of the union and the unique considerations it requires. The general model will be adjusted accordingly to build the labor relations change model.

General Model

The following synthesis of the formulas presented above will serve as a starting point for development of a change model for a unionized workplace:

Change happens if:
Management Drive × Quality of the Change > Employee Resistance
to Change   Decision

In this model, management drive to change combines dissatisfaction and vision into a more comprehensive element that includes both the incentive and ability to make a change. It refers to management (even though others can drive change) because management-initiated change is the principle focus of this book, and the management role typically includes being the strategist and/or sponsor of whatever change is necessary for accomplishing organizational objectives. Managers are expected to take the lead in developing a vision of what can be and to function as the implementors and agents who accomplish that vision.

Quality of the change decision refers to making the best decision about what change to initiate and how to initiate it. The primary considerations are insuring that direct change can reasonably be expected to cause the desired secondary results and understanding the impact on employees and how desirable or undesirable the change is from their perspective.

Employee resistance is the action of the recipients or targets (and occasionally of agents as well) to maintain the status quo. Their level of resistance will be affected by how desirable or undesirable they perceive the change to be. If they perceive the change as desirable, they can become advocates.

In summary, in this model change happens if the management drive is strong enough and the quality of the change is good enough to overcome employee resistance. This formula will be the starting point for developing a labor relations change model.

Union Considerations

The presence of a union affects the labor relations change model in three areas not specifically addressed in the general model. First, where a union is present, legal requirements introduce a different, mandatory, change process that does not exist in a non-union setting and that tends to enhance organizational equilibrium. The NLRA requires bargaining, which can be a significant restraining force even though it rarely absolutely prevents management-initiated change. More importantly, the labor contract frequently absolutely limits a company's right to make certain changes during its term and provides substantial psychological resistance even after it has expired.

Second, the union can help improve the quality of change decisions if management will collaborate with it to exploit the value of the synergy that is potentially available. Union leaders can contribute their own experience and knowledge to decisions and increase the likelihood that the primary change can reasonably lead to the secondary change objective being sought. Considering their views on how employees will perceive the change can increase the likelihood of ultimate successful results. They also can be a stabilizer that helps prevent management from proceeding with ill-conceived changes that have little chance of success.

The third consideration is that the union is a substantial force for additional resistance. It may lead resistance as a representative of employee interests or to protect the union's institutional interests from the effects of change. It can do so by organizing and leading employees to actively and effectively resist through concerted action. When this happens, the "union" is seen as resisting. It also can be a subtle, or not so subtle, force for encouraging or preventing individual employee resistance through job actions. Either type of resistance can largely determine whether a change will be effectively implemented and the intended secondary results achieved.

In summary, a labor relations change model must address three key issues that are not present in non-union model:

- Legal and contractual constraints that limit management rights.
- Union ability to help improve the ultimate decision and/or provide an effective stabilizing force.
- Union collective resistance and its ability to influence individual employee behavior.

The Unionized Model

These differences suggest a unionized change model with different and additional elements, as follows:

General Model	Unionized Model
Management Drive to Change	Management Drive to Change
Quality of the Change Decision	Management Rights
Employee Resistance	Quality of the Change Decision
	Individual Resistance
	Union Resistance

These elements are combined into the following formula:

Change happens if:
Management Drive × Management × Quality of the > Individual + Union
to Change   Rights   Decision   Resistance   Resistance

Management Drive to Change. Management drive to change is similar to the same element in the general model. It is a function of management's dissatisfaction with the current state compared to its vision of what can be and its commitment to go forward with the change. Unless management, as the strategist and implementor of change, has the drive and commitment to pay the price necessary to attain the goals of change, the initiative will fail in the end. Such commitment arises out of a thorough understanding of the problem being addressed and the need for change. It is strengthened by a clear vision of the desired future and its advantage as compared to the status quo. Management drive to change typically increases as the problem or opportunity becomes larger, the need for change becomes better understood, and the vision of what can be becomes clearer. It is supported by the expertise, competence, resources, and bargaining power available to be used to deal with resistance and unfreeze the status quo.

Management Rights. Management rights is a new element in the unionized model. In a non-union workplace, management generally has an unfettered right to implement changes except where their substance is proscribed by law or regulation. This is not the case where a union is present. Consideration of management rights builds into the change model the issue of when and whether management has the right to implement a change. The NLRA requirement to bargain necessitates specific processes that can affect the timing and risks associated with implementation, and the labor contract absolutely prevents changes during its term that are contrary to its provisions, unless the union agrees. Thus, the law and contract impose obligations, rights, and powers on the parties that prevent management from unilaterally implementing many types of changes and that can materially affect the timing of others. These considerations are a significant factor in the union change model.

Quality of the Change Decision. Quality of the change decision addresses whether the best decision is being made from two perspectives. The first perspective concerns whether the planned direct change can reasonably be expected to cause the desired secondary result. All too often management isn't clear about what secondary objective it desires. Even when it is, its decision is often impaired by the influence of conventional wisdom or by lack of information as to whether the direct change has a realistic chance of attaining the secondary result. When either is the case, direct changes are likely to have unintended negative results. For example, a management implemented a broad job rotation procedure (direct change) in order to get increased job flexibility (secondary change). However, it did so without recognizing that improved effectiveness, not increased flexibility, should have been the desired secondary change and without any evidence that job rotation would add to effectiveness. As it turned out, the jobs were too complex to rotate as often as scheduled, so accidents increased and quality and productivity declined. In retrospect, the idea of job rotation arose because it was a fad. Management didn't really understand the complexity of the jobs being rotated and whether the frequent rotation was likely to create unintended consequences. So a bad change decision was made.

The second perspective to the quality of the change decision relates to its desirability to employees and the union. A change can have a positive or negative effect on employees and therefore either foster support or create resistance. Changes that are necessary and appropriate for all considered will not always be viewed as desirable by employees, and a hallmark of good management is a willingness to take unpopular stands that are necessary for the business and in the long term best interest of employees. To manage change effectively, however, management must predict how actions will be received and fashion its decisions to make their effect as desirable to employees as is feasible, thereby reducing their resistance to them.

Union Resistance. Union resistance is the collective and coordinated resistance of the group of represented employees, exercised pursuant to a union constitution and through elected leaders. Ideally, it represents an aggregation of the individual views of the members and is responsive to the interests of the employees in the bargaining unit. Unions may, however, also resist change to meet their own institutional needs. Such resistance may be led by employee union leaders who are personally affected and also have broader union objectives in mind, or by non-employee leaders who are not personally affected by the outcome of a change within the company. Union resistance is the primary force for formal resistance to proposed direct changes. For example, a union might prevent a direct change in the seniority system by refusing to agree during a closed contract or by striking when the contract is open.

Individual Resistance. Individual resistance is seen in the behavior of individual employees acting on their own initiative, although perhaps with encouragement from others. Individual actions may be for specific, rational reasons, as when employees resist staff cuts or pay reductions, or for more subtle reasons having to do with the fact that people generally don't like change. Human inertia is a compelling force that often causes employees to cling to what they know and oppose any significant change in their status quo.

When employees elect union representation they give up much of their right to individually resist management actions as a trade-off for substantially strengthening their right to resist through collective action. The NLRA prevents individual bargaining, and under various circumstances either the employer or the union may legally discipline an employee for resisting change in the face of the collective will. For example, an individual employee represented by a union has essentially no individual right to resist adoption of new work rules or contract language covering conditions of work. This must be done collectively. But direct change is of little value unless it is effectively implemented, and individual employees can in numerous ways, big and small, appropriate or not, informally resist implementation even though it is collectively agreed. This resistance must be overcome for positive secondary change to occur.

Every union workplace also has employees who are not represented by a union, such as supervisors, technical staff, and others who are thought leaders in positions to affect the views and actions of represented employees. Nominally, they are likely to be change agents who are unlikely to actively resist direct management change. By their actions or inactions, however, they can have a substantial impact on whether secondary change occurs, so they must be considered part of the individual resistance contemplated by the labor relations change model.

APPLYING THE LABOR RELATIONS CHANGE MODEL

The question now is how to apply the elements of the model to support effective change in a unionized workplace. As with the general model, management must use a process in which driving forces overcome restraining forces and create disequilibrium. However, it must also specifically consider the legal framework, the ability of the union to affect the quality of the decision, and the right of the union as well as employees to resist. Three cases will be used to demonstrate a range of change management processes in a unionized workplace. The cases are conceptual in nature and will not specifically fit any particular circumstance, but they do show how various elements of the change model are applied in different types of labor/management relationships and demonstrate the importance of considering all elements of the model.

Adversarial Relationships

Direct change is the objective and secondary change gets little attention in adversarial relationships. When management is sufficiently dissatisfied and has the power and legal right to make a change, it does so with little regard to views of the union and without any particular consideration of individual resistance or whether a desired secondary objective will be attained. The formula for change is seen as:

> Change happens if:
> Management Drive to Change $\times$ Management Rights $>$ Union Resistance

This is an expedient way of forcing direct change where management has the right and power and the costs are justified, but it gives no consideration to the need for secondary change. Resistance to the secondary objective is likely even after the primary change is implemented, as hard feelings and animosity created by forcing compliance through exercise of coercive power increase resistance and make positive results almost impossible to attain. Management gets half a loaf at best because there is no employee commitment or union support.

Accommodating Relationships

An accommodating relationship addresses some of these deficiencies. In this case management considers both primary and secondary change by dealing with both individual and union resistance. Management tries to accommodate both employees and union in order to reduce their resistance and further its agenda. The formula, which adds individual resistance, demonstrates this.

> Change happens if:
> Management Drive $\times$ Management $>$ Individual $+$ Union
> to Change   Rights   Resistance   Resistance

This case is a significant improvement over the adversarial one. The role of both employees and the union are acknowledged, and management tries to minimize reliance on coercive power by reducing their resistance to proposed changes. In its decision process management considers the secondary effect of its direct changes and the importance of union and employee support of its decisions. On the negative side, however, it does these things to minimize resistance and make the union more malleable rather than to take advantage of the synergy of countervailing views. The company's unilaterally decided agenda is the one being pursued, and the best that can be hoped for is that employees and the union will not resist and will go along with management's initiative.

Countervailing Collaboration

The countervailing collaboration case aims for more by aggregating all the elements into one system.

Change happens if:
Management Drive $\times$ Management $\times$ Quality of the $>$ Individual $+$ Union
to Change   Rights   Decision   Resistance   Resistance

Management Drive to Change. As in other cases, management drive to change requires commitment to filling the gap between dissatisfaction and vision. It also envisions use of power, but in a different way. Whereas coercive power is management's primary tool in the adversarial case, it is a tool of last resort when collaboration is the objective. In the collaborative case management attempts to reduce the need for coercive power by improving the quality of its decisions in ways that reduce employee and union resistance.

Management Rights. Management rights are a less significant issue in a collaborative environment. Management does not have to be required to bargain because it sees value in union input on almost all issues. Its right to implement change over union objections is used less frequently because more issues are resolved satisfactorily and management understands that reliance on forcing direct change is not likely to achieve its ultimate objective. Management rights continue as an element of the equation, however, because they are sources of management power and their use may be necessary in some situations.

Quality of the Change Decision. Quality of the change decision is the important addition to the change model in a collaborative workplace. Its addition suggests that management does more in its change effort than use force or attempt to minimize employee and union resistance. In this case, management tries to improve its decisions in order to minimize the ill-conceived actions that lead to unintended consequences and maximize those actions that add value by increasing the size of the pie. It also considers both employee and union needs and attempts to structure change so it is as desirable as possible from their perspective. When management decisions adequately consider such needs, direct change can be made more easily and with less use of coercive power. More important, however, effective secondary change is possible because employees and the union understand the change and have an opportunity to help make it as desirable as possible. As the authors note in *Change at Work*, "No matter how good the basic plan, if the leaders who advocate a change fail to work with the individuals that change will involve, they will not fully accept the change or let it affect their performance. Nothing will happen except more of the same."[12]

Change initiated by management can have two types of impact that affect whether employees and the union will accept and support it. Change has substantive impact when it either adds to or takes away from employee rights, benefits, or working conditions, thereby directly affecting employee work life. Increasing pay, reducing insurance coverage, or requiring more or different types of work are examples of changes that have substantive impact on employees. Negative substantive impact encourages resistance, while positive substantive impact encourages acceptance and support.

Change can also have process impact that may reinforce or be different from the substantive impact. The process impact relates to control and whether the union and employees believe they are maintaining or losing it. Control is important regardless of whether the substantive impact of the actual change is positive or negative. Conner states that "Major change occurs when people believe they have lost control over some important aspects of their lives or their environment."[13] This is particularly true in a unionized workplace. A major reason most employees vote for unions is a belief that a union will increase their control over their work lives, and unions intend to exercise control over wages, hours, and conditions of work. Therefore, even a management change initiative that is positive in substance will be actively resisted if it threatens the control that employees believe they have over their work lives through their union. For example, unions commonly reject offers of pay increases or bonuses where the employer retains the right to determine how much is paid or to whom. Unions frequently are concerned about discriminatory administration in such cases, but they also are simply unwilling to have employers exercise that level of unilateral control. This unwillingness is strengthened by their desire to avoid establishing a practice of employer control that could detract from the union's ability to resist in future similar situations.

In summary, the quality of the decision must be considered from many different perspectives. In addition to economic and other such considerations, management must consider whether the direct change is likely to get the intended secondary change, whether it is desirable from both an employee and union perspective, and whether both the substantive and process impacts have been addressed. Involving the union deeply in the change decision is the only way to address these issues.

Union Resistance. As in other cases, union resistance recognizes the union's legal right to delay or prevent direct change in many cases through its right to bargain or to insist on continuing application of the labor contract. It also recognizes the ability of union leaders to influence the behavior of individual employees and effectively determine whether desired results are achieved from a direct change. In a collaborative setting management's emphasis is on actions to minimize resistance rather than to overcome it.

Individual Resistance. Individual resistance recognizes the many ways individual employees can prevent change, primarily by action or inaction on the job that prevents effective implementation of direct change. In a collaborative environment, management emphasizes actions to minimize employee resistance rather than to force their compliance.

Integrating the Elements. The various elements of the change model work together in a system where each element affects and is affected by the others. All represent levers that can be used to foster both direct and secondary change. Different situations require emphasizing different elements, and which levers management should turn and how it should turn them varies from case to case. As a general rule, however, the countervailing collaboration philosophy suggests management should strive to increase its drive to change by developing a vision of what can be and sustaining the commitment to achieve it; maintaining but downplaying its management rights; improving the quality of its decisions in order to enhance the secondary results; and taking actions to reduce both individual and union resistance rather than use coercion to overcome them. Ideas for accomplishing such actions are discussed in the remaining chapters.

TRANSFORMATIVE IMPLICATIONS OF THE CHANGE PROCESS

Both operational and transformational changes are necessary for an enterprise to be viable and effective over time. The principles outlined in the labor relations change model apply to both because the two types of change work together in a close systemic relationship. Each affects and is affected by the other: how operational change is handled will have a long-term, transformational effect on the labor/management relationship, and the labor/management relationship will in turn affect how operational changes must be handled. This system is the basis of the emphasis on change in the countervailing collaboration philosophy.

Rosebeth Moss Kanter notes in *The Change Masters* that breakthrough changes "are likely to reflect the interplay of a number of smaller changes that together provide the building blocks for the new construction."[14] She calls this step-by-step, iterative process "logical incrementalism," and it is the way labor relationships are built. Positive operational change handled well leads to improved relationships and employee confidence that makes future change easier, but negative changes handled badly have the opposite effect. Correspondingly, a good management/union relationship makes change easier to handle well, while a bad relationship makes it much more difficult. This process becomes a cycle. As indicated in Figure 6.1, each direct operational change in actuality has two impacts: the secondary change that was its explicit objective and the subsequent impact on the labor relations climate. For example, if a management forces a change in how jobs are assigned (direct change), that change could

Figure 6.1
Transformational Change Cycle

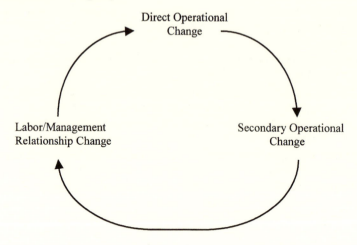

create a secondary short-term change of improved productivity but also degrade the labor relations climate because of the way the direct change was unilaterally imposed. When this happens, the worsened labor relations climate makes future changes more difficult, reduces the likelihood of their achieving the desired results, and increases the likelihood of further deterioration in the labor relations climate. And the cycle can continue. On the other hand, a primary change implemented in collaboration with the union is more likely to be effectively implemented with a positive secondary result and to be a factor in improving the longer-term labor relationship. The aggregation of the impact of many operational changes over time defines the labor/management relationship, for better or worse.

This analysis suggests that when implementing change in a unionized workplace management must implement appropriate direct change in ways that both attain the desired secondary change and foster a continuing positive transformation of the relationship.

KEY POINTS

1. Management must attain both direct and secondary change to achieve desired results.

2. To attain both direct and secondary change management must engage in a process that creates disequilibrium and unfreezes the organization. To do this, it must:

   • Be dissatisfied with the current state and have a vision of what can be, supported by resources and power as appropriate.

   • Minimize reliance on management rights.

   • Foster improved change decisions that can reasonably attain secondary results and are as desirable as feasible to employees and the union.

- Seek to minimize or remove union and employee resistance rather that to overcome it with power.
3. Labor/management relationships are transformed by the effect of many operational change processes over time.

NOTES

1. Sandra E. Black and Lisa M. Lynch, "The New Workplace: What Does It Mean for Productivity?" *Proceedings of the Fiftieth Annual Meeting, Volume I* (Chicago: Industrial Relations Research Association, 1998), p. 60.

2. Daryl R. Conner, *Managing at the Speed of Change* (New York: Villard, 1993), p. 88.

3. Murray`M. Dalziel and Stephen C. Schoonover, *Changing Ways* (New York: AMACOM, 1988), p. 11.

4. Rosabeth Moss Kanter, Barry Stein, and Todd Jick, *The Challenge of Organizational Change* (New York: Free Press, 1992), p. 379.

5. Conner, *Managing at the Speed of Change*, p. 106.

6. Price Waterhouse Change Integration Team, *The Paradox Principles* (Chicago: Irwin, 1996), pp. 43–44.

7. Ibid., p. 19.

8. Oscar G. Mink, Pieter W. Esterhuysen, Barbara P. Mink, and Keith Q. Owen, *Change at Work* (San Francisco: Jossey-Bass, 1993), p. 59.

9. Robert W. Jacobs, *Real Time Strategic Change* (San Francisco: Berrett-Koehler, 1994), p. 122.

10. Mink et al., *Change at Work*, p. 94.

11. Barbara Benedict Bunker and Billie T. Alban, *Large Group Interventions* (San Francisco: Jossey-Bass, 1997), p. 71.

12. Mink et al., *Change at Work*, p. 14.

13. Conner, *Managing at the Speed of Change*, p. 74.

14. Rosabeth Moss Kanter, *The Change Masters* (New York: Simon and Schuster, 1983), p. 289.

Part III

Practice

Chapter 7

Business Driver

To say that business need should be the driver of management-initiated change seems to state the obvious. Why would management initiate a change for any other reason? Implementing change in an organization is hard work. It takes effort, time, and usually money. There is risk of failure and of making matters worse. Nonetheless, management frequently initiates change for other than business reasons, and when it does, it typically gains nothing or adversely affects the business.

This chapter briefly discusses some principles of organizational ideology and the role of profits as a driver of change. It then addresses two situations where management often initiates change for other than legitimate business reasons and concludes with ideas for insuring that change in a unionized workplace is driven by the needs of the business.

PRINCIPLES

Reasonable people disagree about what is a legitimate organizational purpose and an appropriate driver of business decisions. Some say (or at least behave as though they believe) business purpose is purely financial: profit, earnings per share, return to stockholders on invested capital, a specified rate of return, or added value. Everything is for the stockholder. Some argue that the purpose of business is to produce things people need, when they need them, at a price they can afford and profit is only a means to accomplish this end. Others believe the purpose of business includes fixing society's ills.

In *Built to Last* Collins and Porras conclude that visionary companies are generally driven more by ideology than by profits. They describe ideology to include core values ("The organization's essential and enduring tenets—a small set of guiding principles'') and purpose (''The organization's fundamental reason for existence beyond just making money'').[1] This ideology is a vital, shaping force that drives management's behavior and decisions.

This book endorses the Collins/Porras conclusion that businesses should have a much broader purpose than just making a profit. But it also recognizes that profit is the objective that must drive the actions of most employees, most of the time, and that ''profitability is a necessary condition for existence and a means to more important ends. . . . Profit is like oxygen, food, water, and blood for the body; they are not the *point* of life, but without them, there is no life.''[2]

Or as Charles Handy notes in *The Age of Paradox*, ''A company will only be allowed to survive as long as it is doing something useful, at a cost that people can afford, and that generates enough funds for its continued growth and development.''[3]

Unless a company can make a profit over the long term it cannot sustain itself and attain its purpose. Profits must not be mediocre, but rather must beat the competition and allow for health, growth, and some level of financial flexibility if the company is to have any chance of delivering on any laudable social intentions it may have. Therefore, long-term profit enhancement should drive most management change decisions, particularly the operational decisions where a union is most likely to be involved.

This emphasis on profits presents another of the many paradoxes in the business world: most actions taken to enhance profit are advantageous to all stakeholders; not only stockholders, but also others such as customers, vendors, partners, society, and employees. All are important and must have their needs met, but employees inevitably are among the most critical, if not *the* most critical. Recognizing their contribution and treating them fairly and with respect is essential for organizational success. Where employees have elected a union to represent them, the union becomes an alter ego and a stakeholder entitled to respect and fair treatment as well. Fortunately, making a profit that allows the business to accomplish its purpose is also consistent with values that respect employees and their union.

The key to the paradox is that the basic needs of the business, employees, and union leaders are so closely aligned that what works for one usually works for all over the long term. What is good for the business is good for its employees and their union. Profit is necessary for survival and growth, which are necessary for a company to continue offering jobs to employees, whom the union can then represent. There can be no security for any employee in any business that doesn't make a competitive profit year in and year out, and individuals cannot achieve their personal ambitions unless their company makes money.

Emphasis on profit, however, can cause some difficult and unpopular decisions that may cause hurt or ask employees for more. Management, as the party responsible for making a profit and insuring the long-term viability of the business, must make them. Failure to do so is irresponsible toward all stakeholders, but particularly toward those employees and union leaders whose livelihoods depend on these difficult decisions.

Management must provide a context for such decisions by maintaining a socially acceptable level of pay and benefits, and providing fair and equitable treatment to all employees. Furthermore, management must make every effort to insure that changes to reduce cost, improve employee productivity, or otherwise enhance profitability do not create unnecessary pain or loss to employees or go beyond what is reasonably anticipated by the employment contract. Except in the most extreme cases relating to survival of the enterprise, management must insure that actions to further the business purpose do not require employees to receive less. Rather, they should ask employees to contribute more, as in today's competitive world every person must deliver more tomorrow than they did yesterday in order for the business to keep pace with the competition. Within this context, management must make the case to itself, employees, and unions that change for the purpose of improving profitability can be mutually beneficial.

Even seemingly innocuous demands to contribute more are likely to elicit resistance from employees and unions, as they usually involve extra work or doing things differently, both of which can conflict with strongly held union beliefs relating to work jurisdiction and job preservation. Such resistance is at the heart of the conflict frequently seen in concession bargaining and at some level is probably inevitable in the labor/management relationship. Thus, even changes intended to improve profitability that management feels have a minor impact on employees require a mutual understanding of the real impact and collaboration to insure that negative impacts on employees are minimized.

To reach this mutuality, management must value its employees and the contribution their union can make and share a purpose that justifies their increased contribution. This shared purpose must lead to management sharing with employees and the union: sharing power, information, involvement, and the results achieved from the improved employee contribution. The sharing is not owed or morally obligatory but occurs because management wants and expects it to lead to greater contribution from employees.

With common purpose and sharing, mutual gain can result. The opportunity to contribute more should mean that employees have more variety and autonomy in their work and are doing things that are highly significant for which they feel responsible. This hopefully causes them to see their work as more meaningful and gives them personal purpose in their lives and satisfaction from coming to work each day. Sharing means employees are not engaging in self-destructive behavior by working themselves out of a job and in fact see opportunity for personal gain in organizational improvement. In this situation an emphasis on profits benefits employees as well as the business; conversely, change that doesn't advance the purpose of the organization is not likely to help employees over the long term and is a pyrrhic victory at best for management.

PYRRHIC CHANGE

A pyrrhic victory is one that is gained at too great a cost. Unfortunately, many management changes are of little value and are attained at too great a cost to be justified because management has the wrong objectives. Trying to make someone feel good and trying to deceive employees or the union are objectives that lead to pyrrhic victories.

Feel-Good Change

If one assumes management intends the logical consequences of its actions, change frequently appears to be driven by motives other than business need. Such change intentionally or unintentionally makes someone feel good but is of little or no value because it does not improve the business. This can be the case for both operational and transformational change.

Feel-Good Operational Change. All managers would probably deny implementing change to make themselves feel good. We all believe we have higher motives. But there are three situations where management-initiated operational change has no other beneficial effect.

The warm feeling of personal popularity gained from changes that do not benefit the business becomes an end in itself for some supervisors and managers. It is frequently easier for them to give in to requests of employees or union leaders than to take an unpopular stand that is in the long-term best interest of all concerned. Managers may also initiate change to curry personal liking even though broader benefits are not likely to occur. While personal rapport is important for the collaboration that can provide significant advantage to the business, it is of marginal utility unless it can be leveraged well beyond the individual manager involved and attributed to the entire organization. Without such leverage, the cost of such changes are likely to exceed the benefit. Unfortunately, bought popularity does not provide the leverage, and it may become a negative cycle, as the chain of command frequently rewards it informally or through misuse of 360 degree assessments that emphasize feedback from subordinates. This can compound the good feelings, but it does no good to, and may even harm, the organization.

Feel-good operational change occurs more frequently, however, when direct change does not lead to secondary change that contributes value to the organization. Work rules are changed, but employees continue to behave in the same old way. Wages are cut, but costs go up. Contract language is changed, but there is no gain to the business. In such situations, management works hard, gains concessions, and negotiates contract changes allowing different overtime procedures, increased work assignment flexibility, wage savings, or other similar alterations in language or practice. Obvious and presumably positive direct changes are made. Management feels great, and the labor relations manager is promoted. But what has been gained? Has the change really achieved the sought-after improvement in the business operation? Are the results even measured? Frequently not!

Management often fails to attain desired secondary change because there is no cause/effect relationship between the direct change and a desired secondary objective. Conventional wisdom, habit, inertia, or failure to thoughtfully analyze likely results can drive management to initiate changes that have little chance of adding value. For example, management may be concerned about worker productivity. It notes that unrestricted job bidding on a seniority basis is creating turnover and views the turnover as causing costly, unwarranted training even though there is no data to confirm its actual impact on productivity. Management negotiates contract language that restricts job bidding, but the restrictions do not have the expected impact on productivity. The change limiting employee rights to bid and choose their jobs insures more experienced employees are on jobs and reduces training costs, having a positive result. On the other hand, it constrains employees in the management of their own work life and results in narrowly trained, inflexible, antagonistic employees who are less productive than before. Thus, where management doesn't thoroughly consider the likely result of its direct change and unintended consequences occur, early, brief good feelings among managers who conceived and negotiated the change may be the only positive result.

Finally, when direct changes initiated by management, and perhaps agreed to by the union, are never implemented, temporary good feeling is the only benefit. Changes initiated by labor relations staff or senior management may be for the right reasons. However, failure to establish or maintain administrative systems to manage the implementation, lack of understanding or support of first-line supervisors, or ambivalence or outright resistance by those directly affected may prevent the direct change from being implemented to achieve desired results. This is particularly true where a change is made without considering its systemic nature, as a change in only one part of an integrated system will be effective only for as long as management forces it to be. When management attention declines, the system springs back like a rubber band to its original position. For example, management may negotiate contractual work flexibility or change work rules, only to have nothing happen because affected employees resist and other parts of the system (e.g., role of supervisors or training programs for employees) are not changed to provide incentives or capability. Or management may negotiate a broad management rights clause requiring work teams but get no result because pay incentives and job security were not addressed and employees resist attempts to force teamwork. Whatever the cause, when direct changes are not implemented the only benefit is initial good feeling on the part of certain managers.

Feel-Good Transformational Change. Much of this book is devoted to convincing readers of the merit of a collaborative, mutually beneficial relationship between management and the union that represents its employees. Attaining this type of relationship where it does not already exist will necessitate difficult, sometimes costly change in how business is done with union leaders. It will require management to recognize and address the needs of union leaders, give them more time and attention, provide them a bigger role in day-to-day activities, and perhaps vest them with more power. These types of actions are costly to management in money spent, time utilized, or risks assumed. Management would not logically incur such costs without expecting a reward in the form of improved business performance.

But this is not always the case. Business logic notwithstanding, management may seek an improved union relationship without a clear vision of any expected return because it values the relationship in its own right. As the authors note in *A Behavioral Theory of Labor Negotiations*,

a company or a union may attempt to strengthen or to weaken the opponent out of personal preference and ideological conviction. Thus a conflict or cooperative relationship might be considered as an end in itself. An organization may have a general preference for a given type of relationship because it is congruent with its dominant social philosophy; and the persons who represent the organizations may prefer a certain kind of relationship because of their own personal outlook. Some people take pride in a positive relationship; they prefer friendly relations, also marked by mutual trust and concern.[4]

Thus, the personal beliefs or preferences of certain individual managers, whether driven by altruism or other considerations, may drive a change in the relationship with a union. People generally prefer amicable, supportive relationships to those that are adversarial. A good relationship makes management's life simpler, as arguments and disagreements are fewer. Managers and supervisors may believe (perhaps correctly) that their relationship with union leaders is a factor in their performance evaluations, and they get kudos from on high when the quality of their relationship with the union is good. Whatever the reason, when the relationship improves, one or several managers feel better.

But therein lies a paradox. Implementing change to improve the working relationship without an overriding motive of improving business performance is likely to backfire over the long run and lead to a worse relationship. There are several reasons for this paradox.

Effective change requires a systems approach that integrates the effect of the change across all parts of the organization. This means that when a change is made in one part of the organization, other parts must often be altered in unison. Change to improve the relationship with union leadership as an end in itself addresses only one part of the organization and is not likely to be effective over the long term because other related parts of the system are unlikely to be addressed. For example, involving union leaders more or giving them more power can be seen to disempower supervisors of represented employees unless supervisors are given appropriate training or a revised role. The organization's communication procedures may be affected and require change if union leadership is given earlier notice of pending issues. Or the management decision process will need to change if the union is given an enhanced role in that process. Since change solely for the purpose of improving the union relationship is not likely to address such issues relating to supervisors, communication, decision processes, and other related parts of the system, the value of any improvement in the relationship will be offset by problems created elsewhere.

Effectively changing a union relationship also requires continuity: continuing focus, dialogue, training, and support sufficient to create new institutions and a new culture that will weather the passing of time. Continuing efforts such as these are difficult to sustain and will not be sustained unless the incentive is broad and strong. They cannot be tied to one individual because individuals change beliefs, change jobs, or simply get frustrated or tired and fail to maintain the needed effort. More importantly, a relationship generally will not be viewed by a critical mass of the organization's decision makers as valuable enough to withstand tough business times unless there is broad consensus that it helps in dealing with difficult business issues. Without strong support, the effort required to maintain the relationship will be the first to go when management changes, the business gets more difficult, or costs must be cut.

Finally, pursuing a relationship for its own sake can lead to management granting substantive concessions to ''buy'' an improvement, which is likely to do more harm than good in the long run. If the relationship is the ultimate goal of greatest value, it becomes the substance being sought, and it seems natural for management to trade other, less valuable, things of substance. For example, a union might insist on a no-layoff agreement as a precondition for engaging in a collaborative effort, and management might be tempted to agree. But the no-layoff proposal is substance and the relationship is a process. Trading substance to improve or maintain the process can be a string with no end. The union can forever threaten to break the relationship or create a need for an improved one in order to gain a bargaining chip in a negotiation for substantive concessions. No company can afford to buy resolution of potentially never-ending process issues with substantive concessions that are otherwise unwarranted. In the example cited above, layoff protection may well be appropriate in connection with substantive changes in, for example, work rules. But it should not be traded for something as potentially ephemeral as a relationship.

More importantly, management trying to buy a relationship is likely to cause it to concede on matters of principle. Doing this will destroy its credibility, and credibility must be a hallmark of a good labor/management relationship. This can lead to a cycle where management buys a relationship that it then destroys by giving up a principle to buy its continuation. As Fisher and Brown note in *Getting Together*,

Don't try to buy a better relationship. While many people believe that they can demand (and achieve) substantive concessions as a prize for a ''good'' relationship, others believe that they can ''buy'' a good relationship by making substantive concessions. But again, giving in on a current problem will not help build a process for solving future problems. A good working relationship is not for sale. And to make a substantive concession for that purpose is likely to be counterproductive.[5]

The bottom line is that we cannot buy good relationships. They must be earned. Buying them may make the purchaser feel good for a time, but it will not help the business over the long run.

Deceptive Change

Deceptive change is change initiated by management under false pretext. Those who initiate deceptive change probably see it as accomplishing a business purpose, and it may in the short term. But in the long term, they only deceive themselves. The dishonesty at its core is so fundamental that deceptive change does not have a legitimate business purpose.

Deceptive Operational Change. Operational change is deceptive when the true management intent is hidden and employees or union leaders are misled. For example, in an attempt to negotiate contract concessions management might imply that continuous viability of the enterprise is at stake when the real issue is larger profits. Or management might claim it is contracting out work to get a specialized expertise when its real purpose is to get increased flexibility, lower cost, or prepare to operate during a strike.

The moral/ethical problems with such dishonesty are so obvious that they will not be discussed here. Instead, our issue is with the longer-term negative impact on the business, which cannot be overstated. This type of behavior is frequently transparent from the beginning, and if not, it will ultimately be exposed. When it does become obvious, it is likely to antagonize union leaders and cause them to use any available power to thwart management's future initiatives and insure they aren't misled again. It will destroy trust and probably lead to a reciprocal cycle of dishonesty between union leaders and management where ever-decreasing standards of conduct are justified as appropriate responses to the other party's conduct. For these reasons, management is unlikely to gain by its deception. If it does, the gain is almost sure to be short term and offset by losses when the truth is known, so that the end result is to impair, rather than enhance, business performance.

Deceptive Transformational Change. Transformational change is deceptive when management attempts under false pretext to improve its relationship with a union. While the deception may be for business reasons, the effort's fundamental dishonesty and possible illegality prevent it from being a legitimate business endeavor. Deceptive attempts to improve the management/union relationship fall into three categories.

Opportunistic change happens when management takes unfair advantage of unique circumstances. Management may seek cooperation from its union to address current economic distress or other short-term difficulties where both union and management can identify a common enemy. For example, the company may seek union help to beat foreign competition or to deal with domestic legislation that could substantially hurt the business. When management is genuinely seeking creative solutions and a combined effort leading to mutual gain, such initiatives are the essence of the collaboration advocated in this book. On the other hand, if management is "using the developments as a club to exact concessions from their workers while the rhetoric of cooperation muffles the blow,"[6] then the initiative is an opportunistic deception. When the problems are overcome and business health returns, the deception will be obvious and the union is likely to seek recompense that causes the company even greater difficulties than the original one.

Co-optation is management's objective if its real purpose in a collaborative initiative is to reduce the union's power or render it impotent or unwilling to resist changes management sees as in the company's best interest. Evidence that co-optation is the real motive exists, for example, where management talks co-operation but is interested only in its own agenda, limits collaboration to narrow areas selected by it, or publicly gives union leaders credit while privately excluding them from matters in which they have an interest. These types of activities are intended to get union leaders in management's tent where it is better able to control them. At best it misses out on the potential synergy of true collaboration, and at worst it creates a backlash of negativism that is detrimental to the business.

Management's motive is circumvention when it develops a relationship with the union in order to make it complacent so managers can make unilateral changes or deal directly with employees. Evidence of circumvention can exist at all levels of the organization: from the first-line supervisor who inappropriately resolves a contract complaint directly with the employee involved rather than through the union steward to the CEO who communicates initiatives directly with the work force without advanced discussion with union leadership. As with co-optation, circumvention misses out on the potential synergy of union collaboration and is likely to lead to union distrust, antagonism, and perhaps legal action to stop direct dealing.

In each of these categories the line between legitimate and inappropriate purpose is frequently subtle. When does an honest effort to address an economic problem become opportunistic deception? Or an effort to develop a smooth, congenial work atmosphere become co-optation? Or normal employer/employee communication become circumvention? In many senses the answer is in the eyes of the beholder. But it is critical for management to carefully examine its own motives and insure it is honest in what it does and how it does it. Only then can it build the continuity, trust, and credibility necessary for a countervailing collaboration relationship.

BUSINESS-DRIVEN CHANGE

What is business-driven change? It is not change implemented to make someone feel good or for deceptive reasons. This is inappropriate, and is not likely to help a company's business performance in the long run. Broadly stated, business-driven change is change that is intended to accomplish the purpose of the enterprise. In a ''for profit'' business this most often means it is intended to improve profitability. The remainder of this chapter suggests ideas for insuring that both operational and transformational change are business driven.

Business-Driven Operational Change

Operational change embodies those long- or short-term efforts for continuous improvement that enhance profit and further the business purpose. To insure it is driven by business need, management first must understand the key financial or other factors that contribute to profitability and organizational purpose: those factors that are measured and tracked over time, continuously improved, and used to dominate the competition, such as production per hour, defect rate, or on-time delivery rate. Improvement in such factors is the critical secondary change that is management's objective. Management must also understand what direct changes are available as levers to improve the various performance factors and how to pull those levers. For example, introducing new equipment or increasing work flexibility might be direct changes intended to cause a secondary change such as improvement in production per hour. Thus, business-driven operational change occurs when management pulls the right levers to cause improvement in identified performance factors.

Several performance factors are typically available to improve profitability. A key factor in all organizations, and the one most affected by labor/management relations, is the productivity of its people. Management's challenge is to identify those elements of employee performance that have a direct link to productivity and change them to cause improvement. Two elements of employee performance can be changed to improve productivity. They are:

- Employee effectiveness, or the capability of employees to produce the desired result. Employee effectiveness relates directly to their working on things that create value and their capacity to produce high quality results. Success is primarily a function of employees doing the right things.

- Employee efficiency, or the overall cost of employee effort as it relates to the results attained. In this context, employee efficiency is determined by how many units of work an employee can do within a set time, and at what cost. Success is primarily a function of doing things right.

Effectiveness and efficiency can be addressed in many different ways. Management may initiate broad organizational change that improves the structure or climate within which employees work: for example, redefining what employees work on, changing what is expected from them, providing enhanced training and development, or encouraging more worker participation. Or management can implement narrower operational change in areas such as work rules and practices, tools and equipment, and financial incentives. The objective is to implement direct change that leads to secondary improvement in effectiveness or efficiency.

The key to insuring that such change is business driven is effectively measuring the results. The measure of success should not be focused on the direct change; not on whether the rules were changed, the contract was revised, job duties were made more flexible, or more training was provided. Success on such issues may make responsible managers feel good, but standing alone it does nothing for organizational success. Rather, the secondary impact—the enhanced effectiveness or efficiency of the affected employees and the resulting improved profitability—is the test. Unfortunately, while measuring direct change frequently is fairly easy, measuring its secondary impact on effectiveness and efficiency is difficult because so many variables affect employee performance, and these variables can be impossible to isolate. Just doing the measurement at the right place—at the secondary and not the direct point—goes a long way. In addition, the following may be used to insure, at least in general terms, that the change will meet or has met business needs:

- Logic check relating to the need for the intervention, asking questions relating to the real needs of the business, why the primary change was undertaken, and the cause/effect relationship between the two.
- Study of literature/professional knowledge indicating whether the primary change will add value.
- Assessment of the quality of the implementation, considering whether "best practices" were used and whether the cost of implementing the change was reasonable.
- Employee and union feedback concerning effect of the change.
- Management feedback about changes in employee behavior and impact on the business.
- Financial improvement in the business unit of which the employees are a part, comparing performance before and after implementation of the change.
- Comparing performance with otherwise comparable groups where such changes are not implemented.
- Cost of the initiative in staff time and out-of-pocket expense.
- Study of trends and benchmark data such as number of employees, wage/salary cost, benefits cost, and legal compliance results/cost.

If most or all such considerations indicate a positive response, the change is accomplishing its business purpose.

Business-Driven Transformation of the Labor/Management Relationship

Trying to improve a labor/management relationship as an end in itself is ill advised. Management should not try to change the relationship unless it sees a business need: unless it believes the change in the relationship will further the purpose of the organization, typically by improving profitability.

The relationship itself—good, bad, or indifferent—has no inherent value. What is important is how the relationship influences employees and their union to support the goals of the business and to resist or support management change initiatives that affect the business. Thus, the business need for transforming the relationship is based on the fact that management cannot do it alone. Management cannot effectively implement the type of operational changes discussed in the previous section to improve effectiveness and efficiency without the support of employees and the union that represents them. Management can rarely, if ever, force improved efficiency. In fact, attempts to force improvements in efficiency are more likely to strengthen forces such as conflict, tension, and unhappiness that decrease efficiency. This raises the specter of management implementing direct change that makes managers feel good when the actual secondary result is negative. A different approach, however, can have positive business results. Argyris notes that:

The necessity for constantly increasing efficiency is a basic fact of business life. Yet increasing efficiency generates forces that in the long run decrease efficiency, and the problem is still unsolved; it may be worse than ever. So perhaps more can be gained by concentrating on weakening those forces that tend to decrease efficiency, rather than strengthening the forces which tend to increase efficiency. Basically, the only way out is to obtain the participation of the employees themselves in alleviating the factors that they have created to help keep production down.[7]

Employees are not likely to participate in alleviating factors they have helped create if their union has an adversarial, or even accommodating, relationship with their management. They will resist operational change intended to improve productivity, essentially without regard to its merits, if their participation is inconsistent with the labor/management relationship or if their union does not support the change. Thus, the business need for transforming the relationship is the need to have employees and their union participate in and support operational change that improves productivity, largely by removing factors that impair productivity. This participation must use synergy among management and union to improve the quality of decisions, insure mutual gain, and foster union and employee support for effective implementation. Employee participation is of most importance in this relationship because they are the ones who do the work. But critical dealings and negotiations are with union leaders, and they largely determine how employees act. Thus, there is a strong business need for a good relationship between management and unions.

Several studies support the view that an improved relationship with union leaders can lead to improved organizational performance. In *Unions in Transition*, the authors studied a number of plants and concluded that in most of them a cooperative union/management program raised productivity. They concluded,

in sum, a plausible reading of the productivity findings is that what matters is not unionism per se but how management and labor interact at the workplace. Higher productivity in union settings runs hand in hand with "good industrial relations" and tends to
be spurred by competition in the product market while poor labor reactions and protected
environments can produce the opposite.[8]

In *Labor-Management Cooperation* William N. Cooke cites survey results
from 194 unionized manufacturing companies reporting perceived changes in
product quality, worker productivity, and supervisor/employee relations. He recognizes the problems associated with statistical analysis of human behavior and
perceptions, but nevertheless notes that "the success of cooperative efforts are
dependent on union leader endorsement and participation," and "where union
leaders appear to be more actively involved in joint activities and where union
representation is more secure or stronger, joint efforts realize greater improvements."[9]

This cause/effect relationship can be explained by the notion that management's relationship with a union is only one part of a broader organizational
system, and a change in that part has repercussions throughout. It can best be
analyzed in the context of hierarchy theory in complex systems. Ahl and Allen
note in *Hierarchy Theory* that two types of systems exist: simple and complex.
A simple system is one that may have many parts, but in which details in one
part have no effect on other parts. A complex system, however, is one with
multiple parts or levels "in which fine details are linked to large outcomes,"
"the details of lower-level behavior have a profound effect on the upper level,"
and "low-level details . . . can exert an influence over high levels and affect the
behavior of the whole system."[10] Level is defined relative to the observer and
not to the external world, so both management and union leadership are lower
level relative to each other and to organizational performance. Each is positioned
to influence the other and organizational performance through the details of what
it does and how it behaves. This influence is amplified through positive feedback
and plays out in a chain reaction among various levels of the complex system.

The organizations in which we work are complex systems. Management behavior is "lower level" as compared to behavior of union leaders, so management must recognize that its actions affect union leadership. Union leadership
behavior is "lower level" with regard to employee behavior, so minor changes
in the fine details of how union leaders behave affect behavior of represented
employees, which can then affect organizational performance.

A key example of union leadership affecting employee behavior arises from
the fact that unions are a filter in communication between management and
employees. The filter affects employee perceptions of their needs and how those
needs are being met. When employees are inadequately informed or involved,
or do not view management information concerning efforts to meet their needs
as credible, they are likely to be demotivated or antagonistic and contribute less

than they can. On the other hand, if they perceive their needs are being met and they are being provided with opportunities to contribute, motivation is generally high. Union leaders are uniquely situated to affect this perception, for better or for worse. Management is prohibited by law from direct communication with employees in certain situations, in which case union leaders are the first, and perhaps only, avenue of communication. Even in situations where direct communication is appropriate, union leaders are in an excellent position to influence employee thinking for or against the company. Perception of needs and opportunities is a highly subjective process, greatly affected by the eyes through which they are viewed. In a union workplace, employees frequently view such factors through the eyes of the union leadership. If union leaders present a positive picture, represented employees are likely to be motivated to support the purpose of the organization; but if union leaders are negative, employees will be also.

A final thought: Management must acknowledge that in a unionized workplace employee commitment to the business will not be exclusive. However, employees can be loyal and maximize their contribution to the business even when they have strong loyalty to their union or to other entities. For this to happen, management must acknowledge the appropriateness of "twin citizenship" for employees: citizenship in their company and also in their union. Twin citizenship encourages employees to be loyal to both entities, and recognizes that neither entity has sovereignty over them, but rather they have loyalty to both. Under these circumstances there is no concept of we/they, and employees can willingly maximize their contribution without a feeling that their loyalty to their union is diminished. From the employee perspective, both the company and the union are "us," and the employee sees benefits from membership in each and from each accomplishing its purpose.

KEY POINTS

1. Profitability is not inconsistent with valuing people and is necessary for a business to accomplish its purpose.
2. Change should not be undertaken if the only reasonably foreseeable result is to make someone feel good or if it is for deceptive reasons.
3. Change should be driven by the purpose of the business. When this is the case:
   - Profit enhancement drives most decisions.
   - Operational change increases employee effectiveness and efficiency.
   - The management/union relationship fosters employee and union support of appropriate operational change.

NOTES

1. James C. Collins and Jerry I. Porras, *Built to Last* (New York: HarperCollins, 1994), p. 73.
2. Ibid., p. 55.

3. Charles Handy, *The Age of Paradox* (Boston: Harvard Business School Press, 1994), p. 168.

4. Richard E. Walton and Robert B. McKersie, *A Behavioral Theory of Labor Negotiations*, 2nd ed. (Ithaca, N.Y.: ILR Press, 1965), p. 201.

5. Roger Fisher and Scott Brown, *Getting Together* (Boston: Houghton Mifflin, 1988), p. 20.

6. Charles C. Heckscher, *The New Unionism* (Ithaca, N.Y.: Cornell University Press, 1988), p. 116.

7. Chris Argyris, *On Organizational Learning* (Cambridge, Mass.: Blackwell, 1992), p. 182.

8. Seymour Martin Lipset, ed., *Unions in Transition* (San Francisco: ICS Press, 1986), p. 323.

9. William N. Cooke, *Labor-Management Cooperation* (Kalamozoo, Mich.: W.E. Upjohn Institute for Employment Research, 1990), pp. 102–104.

10. Valerie Ahl and T.F.H. Allen, *Hierarchy Theory* (New York: Columbia University Press, 1996), pp. 29–33.

Chapter 8

Systems Thinking

When making workplace changes one frequently encounters unforeseen problems. The world is so complicated, we don't know what to do. When we plan a change, employee or union resistance is greater than expected. An agreed change is never implemented. Changes don't work or have unintended consequences. Improvement in one area is of no value because of things that happen elsewhere in the organization. Problems are fixed, only to reoccur later in a different form. People don't behave as we expect or want them to, and when we don't understand all the complexity, we feel helpless. One can begin to comprehend the complexity only by understanding that the organization is comprised of highly interdependent parts and patterns of interaction, and changes in one part affect and are affected by other parts. The organization is a system, and systems thinking must prevail if we are to know what to do.

This chapter draws on the thinking and writing of others to briefly discuss some principles of systems thinking. It then applies that thinking to the circumstances of change in a unionized workplace to provide a framework for understanding why things happen as they do, and for thinking about what can be done to foster constructive change.

PRINCIPLES

"A system is an entity that maintains its existence and functions as a whole through the interaction of its parts."[1] A system is more than the sum of its parts. It functions as a whole and has properties not found in any of its parts. Its behavior depends on the total structure; on how the parts are connected and influence one another as well as what the parts are. For example, many parts of our natural environment work together to form our climate system. Cells and

organs work together to form our nervous system. And a business organization is an entity composed of many parts, including the people in it and their relationship to one another. Individuals working together create a whole, and their relationships and how they work together is as or more important than the talent or ability of any individual member.

A system may be composed of many sub-systems, or smaller systems that contribute to the whole. Climate is only part of the world's environmental system. Our nervous system is only part of us. And a business organization has many sub-systems that comprise a vast array of relationships and patterns that make up the whole. A labor union is a key sub-system of the business organization in a unionized workplace.

We are part of any system that affects us or that we are trying to affect. The authors of *Hierarchy Theory* note that "a systems approach involves including the observer, and human values, in the process of coming to terms with complex problems."[2] Our perceptions, beliefs, biases, goals, and aspirations all affect our ability to observe and interact with the systems of which we are a part.

Complexity of a system generally does not relate to the number of parts. Instead, a system is complex when the parts relate to each other in many different ways, change in many different ways in response to changes in other parts, or when small changes in the details of one part can lead to large changes in other parts or in the whole. In a business organization, adding employees with similar skills and interests in identical jobs does not make the system more complex. However, changes such as adding different lines of business or different governance concepts can increase complexity because they introduce new and different relationships and can cause parts of the system to react in different ways.

Complex systems have multiple levels of explanation, and what happens at the lower level can have a major effect on the upper level. The relationship between levels is key. From the viewpoint of a business organization, four key levels have been defined as follows:

- Events are defined as "who did what to whom."[3] Events are those activities that we most often react to and try to manage because they contribute directly to the purpose of the organization.

- Patterns of behavior "focus on seeing longer-term trends and assessing their implications."[4] They are the way key variables or people act over time.

- Systemic structure "is the pattern of interrelationships among key components of the system."[5] Structure might include the organizational hierarchy, work processes, employee attitudes and perceptions, product quality, how decisions are made, and many other factors.

- Mental models are "deeply held internal images of how the world works, images that limit us to familiar ways of thinking and acting."[6] They include assumptions, stories, and simple generalizations or complex theories that we carry in our heads. They affect how we perceive the world and how we react to our perceptions.

In *Beyond the Quick Fix*,[7] Ralph Kilmann describes a similar model that is also helpful in thinking about systems in a unionized workplace. He describes an "open system" model in which many systems exist, both within the organization and in the environment around it. These systems are in "dynamic equilibrium," and a change in one typically causes changes in others. This perspective, however, is two dimensional, while the world is really three dimensional.

Kilmann says the third dimension is below the surface and includes our unconscious psyches, tacit assumptions, and hidden cultures. When this depth is added to the open system model Kilmann's "complex hologram" results: a three dimensional model reflecting an integrated view in which the tangible structural relationships are underlaid by the intangible assumptions and cultural beliefs that affect what people do.

"Systems thinking is thinking in loops rather than in straight lines."[8] It is the ability to see the connections between the parts; the influence of one part on another and on the whole; the feedback resulting from the influence and the response to that feedback. Senge describes system thinking as "a discipline for seeing wholes. It is a framework for seeing interrelationships rather than things, for seeing patterns of change rather than static 'snapshots.' "[9] Interconnectedness is facilitated by feedback loops—the process by which a change in one part of the system influences other parts, which then change in ways that loop back to influence the original part. The feedback can reinforce the original change, creating more change in the same direction or balance the original change, leading to stability in the system.

An example showing different impacts of a change in a work system demonstrates two types of feedback loops. Assume an excessive level of overtime. This excess can cause poor employee productivity or high absenteeism because employees are overworked, tired, have a bad attitude, or simply can afford to lose a day's pay. Assigning more overtime intending to improve production actually further reduces efficiency or attendance, which exacerbates the original problem and is addressed by assigning additional overtime. And the cycle continues, as indicated in Figure 8.1.

On the other hand, if the increased overtime rate influences the employment system to hire more employees, the balancing effect of the hiring reduces the need for overtime and brings stability to the system as suggested by Figure 8.2.

These concepts provide a framework for a systems model of a unionized workplace: a complex entity composed of many interconnected parts and relationships at multiple levels, where changes in one part influence, and are influenced by, changes in other parts.

SYSTEMS MODEL OF A UNIONIZED WORKPLACE

The model described below requires a disclaimer. A union workplace is very complex. It has many structures, relationships, and mental models, and it is

Figure 8.1
Reinforcing Feedback Loop

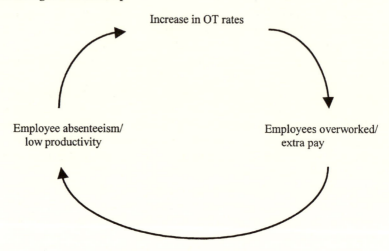

Increase in OT rates

Employee absenteeism/
low productivity

Employees overworked/
extra pay

continually adapting and changing on a day-to-day basis. Any model that can be reduced to writing does not do it justice. Nevertheless, a model that demonstrates various levels of the system, the relationships among levels, and the relationship among example elements within the levels, can be helpful in understanding how it works and evolves over time. The following is intended to do that.

Imagine three concentric spheres as a core with two adjoining layers. The core and each of the adjoining layers is composed of a number of closely related elements. Elements of the core are hidden from view from the outside, and even from most locations within the other layers, yet the core is necessary to hold the layers together. The elements of the outside layer are obvious for all to see. Between the two is the middle layer, which both separates the other two and holds them together. All are surrounded by an external environment that affects, and is affected by, the system. This system is illustrated in Figure 8.3.

A key feature of the system is that it is a whole that cannot be divided into parts. The interdependencies are too important. However, it is helpful for analysis and discussion to disaggregate the whole and view each of the three layers as a discrete sub-system composed of discrete elements. One can then look at the relationships within and among the different sub-systems, as a way of synthesizing the parts into a whole. The three sub-systems, and the relationships among them and among elements within them, are discussed below.

Management Sub-system

The external layer of the model represents the management sub-system: the part that management generally controls unilaterally and that is on the surface, obvious for all to see. When working properly, this sub-system allows the busi-

Figure 8.2
Balancing Feedback Loop

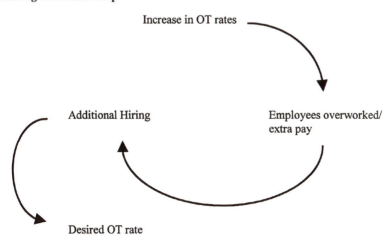

ness to function on "autopilot." It includes the many routine and non-routine events, tasks, actions, agreements, procedures, and decisions management uses to accomplish its organizational purpose. Although many examples could be cited, the illustration in Figure 8.3 includes the work to be done (selling the shoes, turning the valve, building the car), non-represented employee processes, supervisory processes, training, technology, and communication procedures. Each directly affects the others, and is affected by feedback from them. For example, training helps employees do the work, while doing the work obviates the need for training—or brings to light need for other training. The work to be done influences the technology required, but on the other hand, the technology used dictates the work tasks and required training. Non-represented employee and supervisory processes clearly affect, and are affected by, other elements of this or other sub-systems. We catch ourselves coming and going!

Labor Relations Sub-system

The middle layer represents the labor relations sub-system, which determines how labor/management issues are managed in the workplace. The elements of this sub-system are the processes that at the formal level govern the relationships among management, employees, and the union representing them and through which change is managed. The elements are unique in a union workplace and are a direct outgrowth of the legal obligation to bargain and live by agreements reached. They are as follows:

• Work processes are the processes for determining how work gets done and who does it. What tasks comprise a job? Does the supervisor autocratically make all the decisions,

Figure 8.3
Labor/Management System, Sub-system Model

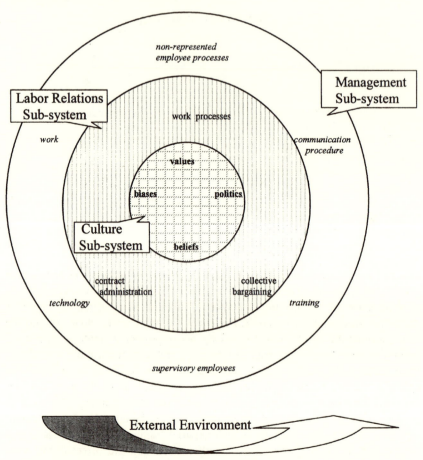

or are employees empowered to make many of their own? Are teams used? To what extent is the union contract and the union itself a factor?

- Contract administration processes are those processes that determine what the labor contract means and how it will be applied. The key aspects of this process typically are the supervisor initially interpreting the contract and taking an action putatively covered by it; the employee or union representative reacting; and if a disagreement exists, the parties following the grievance handling procedure. The results of the process are part of a feedback loop that will materially affect the supervisor's decision in the next similar decision.

- Collective bargaining processes are those processes for negotiating a labor contract, making changes in one, or addressing other issues where bargaining is required by law or the parties agree to negotiate. These processes may be utilized to negotiate an initial labor contract, negotiate a change during its term, or renew it after a contract has expired. They include the processes for arriving at agreement on disputes arising from the work and contract administration processes discussed above.

Each element of this sub-system affects and is affected by the other elements and subsystems. All must be synchronized and work together if any is to be effective.

Cultural Sub-system

The core of the model is the cultural sub-system: a key driver of what we do and how we behave. Elements of this sub-system are our values, beliefs, biases, political needs, and other deep-rooted influences derived from our history and experiences. These influences combine to create our mental models: our deep-seated internal images of the world around us and how it works, made up of "both the semi-permanent tacit 'maps' of the world which people hold in their long-term memory, and the short-term perceptions which people build up as part of their everyday reasoning processes."[10]

We usually are not aware that mental models exist, so without our knowledge they tend to limit learning and confine our thoughts and actions to those that are familiar. They frequently make life easier, as they provide internal guidelines to facilitate easy decision making and a predictable course of action. But they may lead to bad decisions, as they are based on perceptions that may not be the most accurate assessment of current reality but that nevertheless affect our sorting of available data, influence our judgment of which are relevant, and color our view of the data we do see as relevant.

Relationships

Each of these sub-systems represents levels within the overall system, but no level is discrete. Rather, each element of each sub-system can influence and be influenced by elements of the other sub-systems. For example, management beliefs can influence decisions relating to level of technology, which can require collective bargaining, which may affect the work to be done, which can affect work processes, which may become a political issue, which may affect management beliefs. These actions, influences, and reactions lead to a web of interconnecting relationships as demonstrated in Figure 8.4.

This web of interconnecting relationships—much more than the individual parts—creates the whole that is the unionized workplace. Each of the individual elements has identical or similar counterparts in a non-union organization, but the relationships are different, and they account for the uniqueness of a unionized workplace. Both horses and humans have bones, muscles, skin, blood, and brain, but they are very different animals because of the way the different elements are put together. And organizational systems are very different with a union than without one because of the relationships among the various elements.

Figure 8.4
Labor/Management System, Relationship Model

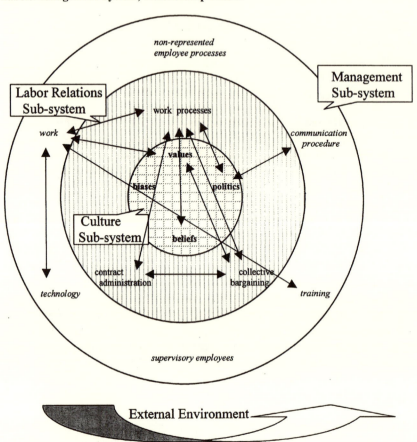

IMPLICATIONS FOR MANAGEMENT

Management has two key interests that relate directly to the systems model: its interest in insuring stability where needed, and its interest in making the greatest change for the least effort where doing so will enhance organizational performance. These interests present both sides of the same coin. On one hand, management must carefully manage the system to avoid actions in one part having unintended consequences elsewhere and upsetting desired stability. On the other hand, where significant change is desired, management must understand how to make it with the least effort and the least likelihood of unintended consequences. Managing these somewhat paradoxical needs requires management to engage in systems thinking. The sections that follow discuss some areas where such thinking is most important.

Mental Models

Labor relations is affected by mental models to a greater extent than most other fields. It has a long and rich history, filled with struggle and conflict, that has tended to polarize views on the basic "goodness" or "badness" of unions and management. Things that are dear to us all are at the heart of the relationship: money, economic well-being, and how we see ourselves. Tactics of both parties create strong feelings. And like in-laws, the parties cannot easily part. Such factors generate an environment where most people have strongly held views, right or wrong, about unions and management and how they should be dealt with. These are our mental models.

Four sets of mental models can affect management action and employee and union reaction:

- How managers perceive represented employees, unions, and the labor relations processes.
- How represented employees and unions perceive management and the labor relations processes.
- What represented employees and union leaders believe management perceives about them.
- What managers believe represented employees and union leaders perceive about management.

Mental models generally do not deal with facts. Rather, they deal with perceptions that may or may not be accurate and beliefs about perceptions that are even less likely to be true. But these perceptions and beliefs have a real impact on how the system works. In many cases, management perceptions about unions and represented employees, including its beliefs as to how each of them perceives management, are major considerations in deciding what to do and how to do it. One mental model may lead to condescending, essentially antagonistic micromanagement, while another model leads to respectful empowerment and involvement. Union and employee perceptions of management and their beliefs as to how management perceives them affect what they do, and in particular how they respond to management actions. One mental model leads to a cynical, mistrusting reaction regardless of the merits or intent of a management action, while another model accepts an action for what it is.

To optimize organizational performance management must operate from mental models—management's, employees' and the union's—that are based on reality. This requires identifying them, understanding them, and changing those that do not reflect reality. To succeed in this difficult task we must see ourselves as we really are and frequently change some deep-seated parts of ourselves that perhaps we previously haven't recognized or acknowledged: our long-held beliefs, perhaps our values, and certainly our biases. We must be willing to discard the old and learn the new, and we must behave in ways that begin to cause others—represented employees and union leaders—to reassess and possibly change their mental models about us.

Such a change process ideally is in collaboration with employees and union leaders, for mental models of all parties are interdependent, and all affect the entire system. If all parties acknowledge the impact of their mental models, are willing to assess them and consider change, and work together in a collaborative effort, progress can be rapid and far-reaching. However, even if unions and employees for political or other reasons are unwilling to join management in such a fundamental change effort, management can still assess its own mental models and begin to behave on the basis of more accurate ones. This alone will lead to better management decisions and implementation processes because they will be based more on fact and less on fiction. Equally important, however, the changed behavior of management will result in different influences on the other parties, which will in time cause their mental models to change. This can lead to a cycle of improvement in how the parties behave and see one another that can be highly beneficial, if perhaps slower and less wide ranging than where the union supports a collaborative change effort.

Whether a collaborative or unilateral approach is used, the key to change is to follow a thoughtful process for understanding what our mental models are, identifying gaps with reality, and changing those that need changing. A process based on the following is recommended:

- Identify those assumptions, beliefs, values and biases of the parties that drive their behavior but that heretofore have been implicit or not recognized. Bring those assumptions to the surface of consciousness and discuss them for understanding.

- Look honestly at the facts. Challenge the mental models against the facts and attempt to look at other relevant data without the bias imposed by history.

- Talk about the mental models and the data. Brainstorm other possible mental models among the parties and with outsiders with a different perspective or point of view.

- Agree on new mental models that are the most accurate available, based on objective consideration of the underlying data unbiased by old models, and begin to foster those throughout the organization.

- Test new models against future situations and be willing to change in the future if the data requires it.

This is a challenging process. We must find what we don't even know exists! Yet, we cannot change what we cannot identify. And there is no pat answer. Management, union, and represented employees have their own mental models that are a function of their particular history and current situation and that may or may not be justified by the facts. Understanding and changing these models can be facilitated by an analysis done solely by management or in collaboration with the union, as follows: Identify and write down patterns of management behavior relating to employees and/or the union that represent potential concerns. After identifying the behavior, construct a continuum or continuums of possible mental models that could be causing the behavior and decide where on that continuum management's mental models best fit. Then look at the facts and data to determine what mental models are justified and what, if any, changes are needed. Some examples are:

Behavior: management unwilling to really listen to union leaders

Continuum of management mental models:

union leaders represent the union	union leaders represent employees
employees don't need a union	employees believe they need a union

Behavior: management unwilling to show respect or take actions that could strengthen the union

Continuum of management mental models:

a strong union is a disadvantage	a strong union is an advantage

Behavior: management unwilling to share confidential information

Continuum of management mental models:

union leaders/employees not trustworthy	union leaders/employees trustworthy

Behavior: management unwilling to expand the role of represented employees

Continuum of management mental models:

limit scope of bargaining unit work	maximize employee contribution

Behavior: ineffective negotiations

Continuum of management mental models:

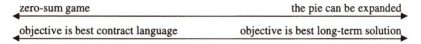

zero-sum game	the pie can be expanded
objective is best contract language	objective is best long-term solution

The continuum is not intended to suggest a movement from error to truth or from wrong to right. Rather, constructing a continuum helps challenge us to think honestly about where we are and expansively about what can be as we thoughtfully explore a broad range of possible mental models. We can then reach a dispassionate conclusion as to what is really causing our behavior, look at the data to determine if the causes are real, and begin to modify our mental models if appropriate.

One also can do a similar analysis of union leader/employee mental models, either in collaboration with the union or unilaterally on a "best guess" basis. Such analysis can foster empathy with their behavior and, more importantly, help develop a better understanding of how management and its systems contribute to union and employee mental models and subsequent behavior. A collaborative effort would put more emphasis on influences other than management actions that affect union/employee behavior. (They have responsibilities and room for improvement too!)

When considering employee/union leader mental models, managers should always remember that our own mental models filter the data we see and cause us to notice or credit only that which confirms our previously held beliefs. Therefore, management's own mental models can materially affect how it characterizes the employee/union behavior being considered and how it characterizes their mental models. For example, if we believe unions "are always protesting" then we will only see the grievances and never acknowledge all the management actions that are accepted without protest.

Changing inaccurate and counterproductive mental models is not an easy task. Fortunately, however, the process of identifying them and beginning an organizational conversation on the subject starts a learning process that facilitates change where it is needed. When changing mental models leads to constructive change in labor relations or management processes, a self-reinforcing cycle results that causes continuing reassessment of all our mental models.

The Union System

The NLRA requires management to recognize unions and deal with them in good faith concerning wages, hours, and conditions of employment. It is easy, however, for management to recognize a union in legal terms and yet fail to appreciate the breadth of its influence in the workplace. Systems thinking helps understand and address this failure.

The union itself is a system with sub-systems and elements very similar to those of the company. It has:

- A cultural system that is comprised of the same elements (e.g., values, biases, beliefs, and politics) as the company but which typically are very different from a substantive perspective.

- A labor relations sub-system in common with that of the company; that is, union and company are parties to the same contract administration and collective bargaining process, and the work of represented employees is determined by the company's work processes that typically are bargained by the parties.

- A union management sub-system that is the union counterpart of the company management sub-system and includes elements such as the union staff, union grievance procedure, union training, union communication procedures, union disciplinary procedure, and national offices.

Figure 8.5
Labor/Management System, Union System Model

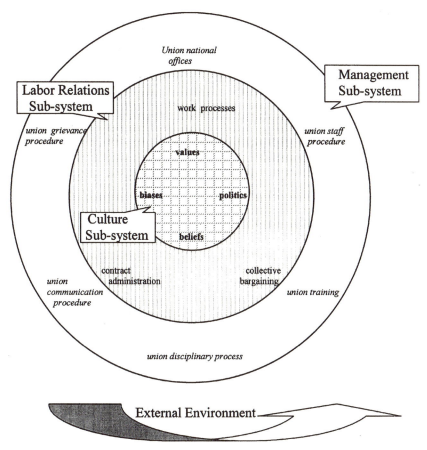

The union system is depicted in Figure 8.5. Since one labor relations system serves both parties, it is the formal interface between the union and company systems, and the channel through which essentially all elements in both systems are directly or indirectly connected. Because of this connection, actions by management affect not only employees; they can affect the union management or cultural sub-systems and have repercussions across the entire union system. The response to such actions can loop back into the company system through the labor relations sub-system. For example, a management mental model may cause a questionable work assignment by a supervisor, which is handled by the contract administration process, which becomes a political issue within the union, which gets the union national office involved, and on and on. The connections are too numerous to elaborate. But the point is that all management decisions should consider not only the impact on employees, but also the direct or indirect impact on the union and its leaders.

Systems thinking recognizes the many underlying reasons a union and its leadership have to resist company initiated change or otherwise influence company performance. From one perspective, the union represents the wishes of employees in their relationship with the employer, and union decisions are based on what is best for the people they represent. From a systems perspective, however, a union may have different or additional reasons for its actions. Pressures from within the union cultural or management sub-systems influence actions of union leaders in various ways and lead to decisions that may not be understandable from an employee perspective but are quite reasonable considering the mental models of the leadership or internal union management concerns. For example, a union leader may choose to resist a company objective to foster a better relationship because of long-held beliefs about management credibility, his relationship to the national union leadership, or internal union issues totally unrelated to the merits of the company objective. Or the union may resist a management wish to spread certain work among several jobs because of its mental model that increased job flexibility leads to fewer jobs. Management's challenge is to understand those underlying, systemic influences and respond to them appropriately.

And finally, systems thinking recognizes the extent to which management's behavior and attitude toward the union influence union behavior and attitudes toward the company. Companies who need unions get them, and they get the type they need because of systems influences and responses. Behavior is interconnected, and management-initiated actions and management responses to union actions give employees and unions feedback that strongly influences their behavior. Whether the issue is developing a trusting relationship, exercising power, or negotiating for mutual gain, management's actions are not a one-way street. Rather, in most cases they are part of a loop in which the union is a mirror that reflects management's actions back on itself. To improve on what it sees, management must change what it shows.

Synchronizing Systems

A clock will not keep time if the parts are moving at different speeds. A car won't move down the road if the wheels are going in different directions. A football team won't win if the linemen block in one direction and the back runs in another. And a business organization will not be as effective as it can be unless all elements are synchronized and working together. They must be governed by the same values, work for the same purpose, and function through processes that fit with each other. Further, even when all elements are aligned, the system will only work as well as its weakest link. No matter how good or effective much of the system is, its weakest or most out-of-sync part will set the standard and pull the remainder of the organization down, just like the new car that will not run because of a speck of dirt in the carburetor.

These concepts are not unique where employees are represented by a union. They are, however, particularly relevant in the labor relations sub-system in a unionized workplace (work processes, contract administration processes, and negotiation processes) where the elements are largely regulated by law or contract, are generally high profile, and frequently are the focus of power by either or both of the parties.

Consider a negative example that could develop as a manager attempts to improve productivity of her union-represented staff. She fosters collaboration, involves employees in open discussion, gets their input and involvement, forms teams, and in the end delegates more work to them and asks them to do work differently than in the past. Employees feel good and productivity is improving. But the union steward was not involved in the process. He gets his feelings hurt and claims one of the new work assignments violates a contractual work rule. He and the department manager cannot solve the disagreement, so he files a grievance for handling under the contractual grievance procedure.

Both parties want to ''win'' the grievance, so they adopt a legalistic approach, focusing on the narrow issue of whether the contract was violated rather than the real issue of how the company and union could work together to improve productivity and employee work life. The discussions to resolve the issue move from the people directly involved to more formal discussions between union leadership and company labor relations staff. There is posturing to set the stage for arbitration by a third party.

The company maintains there was no violation and the union asserts there was, so arbitration ensues. The arbitration process itself has little credibility with either party, as the arbitrator is selected from a panel based on past record, not on expertise in the case at hand. The parties believe there is a strong incentive on the arbitrator's part to balance his record to insure selection in future cases, so both parties feel in advance they are rolling the dice rather than working on a solution. Nevertheless, they proceed, agree on a very narrow definition of the issue, and the arbitrator hands down a yes/no decision. The individuals involved in the arbitration have only a superficial knowledge of the situation, so no real problem solving takes place. The manager and her subordinates miss the opportunity to learn from solving the problem. Dissatisfaction and hard feelings are created, cooperation goes away, and productivity levels out or declines, regardless of who wins the arbitration.

And the adversarial grievance process poisons an otherwise collaborative negotiation process. No matter who wins in arbitration, the real issue is not resolved and continues to fester until the contract expires and the disagreement is introduced into the negotiation process, where it causes conflict from the beginning. The most powerful party, speaking through negotiators who are far from the problem, forces the other to accept its position, probably after posturing and threats, and possibly after a strike or other coercive action. Again, the real problem is not addressed and depending on the relative power of the parties, the result may be an agreement contrary to the original intent or need of either party. Animosity created by the bargaining process causes managers to stretch the meaning of the agreement in future work assignments and the union to do whatever it can to resist the company's productivity initiatives, making collaboration at the department level even more difficult. And of course the union's principal vehicle for continued resistance is to look for an opportunity to file another grievance, thereby perpetuating the adversarial cycle.

In this example the adversarial grievance process was out of sync and the weakest link in the system. It poisoned positive work and negotiation processes and created a negative reinforcing cycle that will continue to detract from the desired work processes and impair the ability of the organization to get the work done. While the issue may have started on a collaborative note in the department, the lowest common denominator, the adversarial grievance process, took over and led to a downward cycle of adversarial dealings. This process is depicted in Figure 8.6.

The objective, of course, is to have all parts of the system in balance so that all elements are working together to reinforce desired results through a positive reinforcing loop as illustrated in Figure 8.7.

A corollary to the concept of the weakest link in the system setting the standard is that to improve the system, one must start with the weakest link, or if all are equal, bring them along together. For example, if work processes and the grievance procedure are reasonably collaborative but nevertheless need improving, while the negotiations process is adversarial in nature, one should start working to develop a more collaborative negotiation process as a way to improve the work processes—where the real money is. Doing otherwise would allow the negotiation process to begin a downward cycle as previously discussed.

A warning is in order. Addressing only part of the whole system can be misleading. For analytical purpose I have extracted one sub-system for a closer look, but in reality influences on and from elements of other sub-systems can have similar effects. For example, in the case cited above the mental models held by both management and union leaders about how grievance procedures or negotiations should be conducted or about union or company internal politics may be the real problem because they provide restraining forces that essentially prevent change. In such a case, one must go outside the sub-system and address mental models as a starting point. This brings us to the issue of leverage.

Leverage

Two frequently paradoxical needs of management, maintaining stability and creating change, were mentioned earlier. Stability fosters the predictability, trust, and longevity that employees, customers, and other stakeholders need. Fortu-

Figure 8.6
Out-of-Sync System

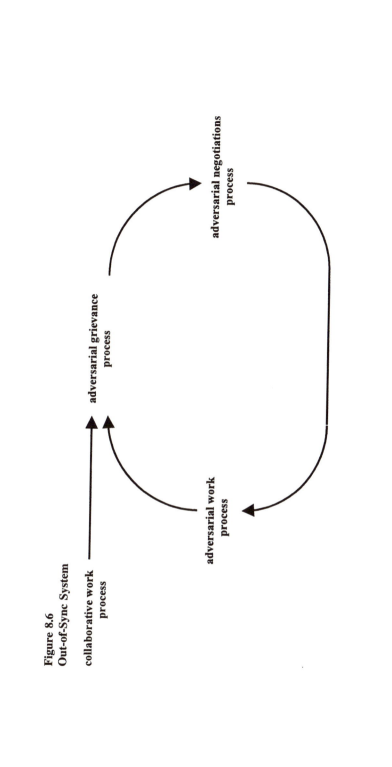

Figure 8.7
Synchronized System

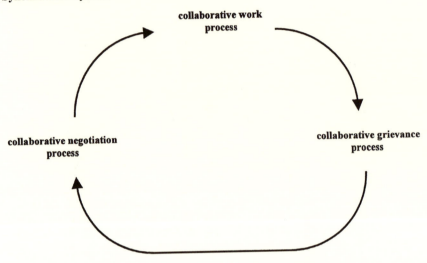

nately, most businesses are remarkably stable. Webs of relationships provide checks and balances that usually prevent issues such as differences of opinion, fluctuations in the power relationship, or individual erratic behavior from causing instability or having major detrimental effects across the whole. A union usually is a major factor in this stability, as its legal rights and the ability of employees to collectively resist change give it a unique ability to force stability, which can positively affect the organization.

But too much stability can lead to stagnation and decay, and the same elements and relationships that foster needed stability can also delay or prevent needed change. They create restraining forces that lead to equilibrium, and change requires overcoming the equilibrium with driving forces. The most efficient and effective driving forces are those that apply the principle of leverage.

O'Connor and McDermott describe leverage as follows: "Imagine a system as a web with many parts connected. Suppose you want to change the position of one part. When you pull on it directly, it seems to resist, but really the whole system resists. However, cutting a small link in another place may free this piece, like undoing a crucial knot in a tangle of string. You need to know how the system is made up to know which knot to undo."[11]

The principle has two dimensions: understanding where in a system the effects of a particular change will be seen and understanding where a small change can have a disproportionately large effect. The work assignment example discussed above illustrates both points. First, a change in the grievance procedure, or even the mental models supporting it, can lead to change in work processes because of the cycles of influence within the system. Second, the grievance process may be the place in the loop where a small change can have the greatest impact.

Change in the work process is likely to be limited to a single issue in a single department. A change to a more collaborative grievance process, however, is likely to be highly public, at a level in the organization that affects the whole, experienced on a recurring basis, and seen as representing the wishes of both senior management and union leaders. It can magnify the spirit of collaboration across the organization. This is leverage.

Leverage concepts apply in all businesses, but they apply differently where a union is present. Several issues are important:

- The system is more complex in a union workplace. It has more elements, relationships, and interdependencies because the union becomes part of the overall organizational system. This increases the options available for exerting leverage, but also increases the possibility of resistance or unintended consequences.

- The union is an entity that can exert organized countervailing leverage through the common labor relations system. For example, contract administration processes, negotiation processes, and associated legal requirements all provide the union with formal restraining forces that it can use to maintain the status quo across the entire organization.

- The union can also exert its leverage to foster positive change beneficial to management.

- The leverage available to the union is more powerful than leverage available to individual employees.

Because of this additional complexity and union leverage, management actions that in a non-union workplace might lead to positive change can be resisted, possibly causing unintended consequences if they are seen to affect the union system adversely. From a more positive perspective, the union can be a force for enhanced organizational performance if union and company systems are aligned to utilize the union's leverage. When considering and implementing change, therefore, management must understand the elements, needs, and relationships of both the company and union systems and foster an alignment that brings them together as a whole for their mutual advantage.

MANAGEMENT ACTIONS

Each of the implications for management discussed above suggested or implied various actions, yet the nature of systems thinking prevents attributing a particular action to a particular element, relationship, or concept. In a system, management actions taken for any of a number of reasons are likely to affect a number of areas or the whole. Accordingly, listed below are examples of endeavors systems thinking encourages management to consider. They are listed together here rather than in individual sections to avoid the implication that they stand alone or have impact in only one area, when in fact they cut across the organization and frequently concern relationships among various elements rather than specific elements. In this context, management should:

- Understand its mental models and change those not based on reality.
- Empathize with union and employee mental models and consider them in the decision process.
- Foster a collaborative review of management, union, and employee mental models where feasible.
- Acknowledge that management frequently does not understand the impact of its actions on the union.
- Take advantage of the fact that a union and its leaders have many opportunities to affect company performance.
- Behave toward union leaders as it wants union leaders to behave.
- Value stability, not only within the business organization but also among the union leadership.
- Emphasize changes where system-wide leverage is available.
- Seek to align company and union interests in order to use the leverage available to the union.
- Have the parties that created the problem involved all the way to the solution.
- Have labor relations staff become process facilitators first and management advocates only if necessary.
- Consider introducing mediation into the grievance process in an effort to solve problems rather than decide who wins.
- Solve problems by negotiations during the term of the contract rather than waiting for an open contract.
- Approach contract negotiations with a mutual gains objective.

Other examples could be cited. The common theme, however, is that management must view itself and the union as a whole with many related parts, understand that actions that affect one part affect the whole, and accept that these actions are primarily determined by the relationship among the various elements.

KEY POINTS

1. A unionized workplace is a complex system composed of many sub-systems and elements.
2. The union is a major sub-system in the overall system that comprises a union-represented workplace.
3. Systems thinking will facilitate constructive change if management will:
   - Examine the mental models that drive behavior and change those not based on reality.

- Acknowledge the union as a key part of the system.
- Synchronize all parts of the system.
- Use leverage to create desired change.

4. Management may foster constructive change by taking a number of actions that are driven by, and responsive to, several of the elements in the organizational system.

NOTES

1. Joseph O'Connor and Ian McDermott, *The Art of Systems Thinking* (London: HarperCollins, 1997), p. 2.

2. Valerie Ahl and T.F.H. Allen, *Hierarchy Theory* (New York: Columbia University Press, 1996), p. 11.

3. Peter M. Senge, *The Fifth Discipline* (New York: Doubleday, 1990), p. 52.

4. Ibid., p. 52.

5. Peter M. Senge, Charlotte Roberts, Richard B. Ross, Bryan J. Smith, and Art Kleiner, *The Fifth Discipline Fieldbook* (New York: Doubleday, 1994) p. 90.

6. Senge, *The Fifth Discipline*, p. 174.

7. Ralph H. Kilmann, *Beyond the Quick Fix* (San Francisco: Jossey-Bass, 1985), p. 8.

8. O'Connor and McDermott, *The Art of Systems Thinking*, p. 26.

9. Senge, *The Fifth Discipline*, p. 68.

10. Senge et al., *The Fifth Discipline Fieldbook*, p. 237.

11. O'Connor and McDermott, *The Art of Systems Thinking*, p. 19.

Chapter 9

Learning and Growth

This book presents ideas for improved, more collaborative relationships between management and unions. The problem is that they will not always work the way we want them to. Understanding concepts is one thing; actually applying them is another. What works one time will not work the next; what works in one place will not work in another place; and what works with one person will not work with another person. Even in a collaborative labor relations environment based on mutual values and common objectives, there will be disappointments, hurt feelings, and reversals. Such setbacks are inevitable in a relationship involving countervailing interests, rapid change, different accountabilities, issues of personal importance, and frequent person-to-person contact.

Making all parties happy all the time is not possible, and it should not be management's goal. To claim that it is will only lead to unrealized expectations, which are likely to trigger a decline in the quality of the labor/management environment. Instead, the objective should be to handle actions better than they were handled in the past and to continuously improve over time. This is not a small task in today's rapidly changing world. Accomplishing it requires most of the people in the organization to learn new concepts and practices, refine them by learning from their successes and failures, and maintain and expand them over time. The organization must learn, and management's challenge is to manage in a way that fosters that learning.

Much has been written about developing learning organizations, yet precisely describing one is difficult. Two basic concepts are critical, however. First, the organization must develop processes and collective skills that foster individual learning and also allow groups of people (frequently composed of represented employees, union representatives, and management) to reliably develop collective intelligence and ability greater than could be developed by the sum of the individuals. And second, it must insure that these processes and skills are sustained and grow over time. Applying these concepts in a unionized workplace is the theme of this chapter.

PRINCIPLES

In *The Living Company* Arie de Geus describes a river as a metaphor for a living organization.[1] The following paraphrase of that metaphor provides an excellent image for a management/union relationship that learns and grows over time: Life-giving rain falls to the earth, but what happens to it depends on the character of where it falls. If the raindrops end up in a cavity or a hole, they become a puddle. They remain where they are. When more rain falls the puddle grows and expands its size and influence but stays in the same place and retains its same character. It has a very short life span. Cars drive through it and splash the water out, and when the sun shines and the temperature rises, the water evaporates and the puddle disappears. All that is left is a mess; mud for awhile and then ugly, sun-baked ruts in the earth's surface.

In contrast, if the raindrops flow to a river they become part of an ongoing community. Unlike a puddle, a river is a permanent fixture. It may swell and shrink, move faster and slower, but it does not disappear. Within the stability is continuous change. The drops are continually on the move. Some drops of water disappear into the sea, but others are added; the drops are not destroyed, but are carried forward. While the river is always there, it is never the same; one cannot step in the same river twice. New drops succeed the old ones, and they in turn become an integral part of the river for awhile and then are carried out to sea. No drop is dominant. Rather, all together they form a self-perpetuating community with component parts that enter and leave, providing a built-in continuity.

Instead of stagnating and dying like a puddle, a management/union relationship based on collaboration should emulate the rainfall that becomes a river. Just as a river is more than a collection of raindrops, an organization and a relationship must be more than the sum of its individuals. Like the first rainfall, initial training and learning are required to begin improving performance. But the training must fall on a receptive environment and become part of a whole capable of regenerating itself and perpetuating the improved relationship. And just as the river always requires continuing rainfall to live, the organization must provide training on a continuing basis and learn from its successes and failures. The organization must learn.

On Organizational Learning by Chris Argyris, *Organizational Learning II* by Argyris and Donald Schön, and *The Fifth Discipline* by Peter M. Senge are recommended reading for a more in-depth discussion of organizational learning than is appropriate here. However, the following briefly reviews concepts that are particularly relevant for developing and maintaining a learning, collaborative relationship in a unionized workplace.

Learning may be individual or organizational. Individuals learn in many ways: by exercising their own intellect, trial and error, success and failure, and being taught by another. What they learn is held in their own minds and also is an organizational resource if the individuals are part of an organization and choose to use their learning for organizational purposes. But when the individuals leave, their knowledge is lost to the organization, like a puddle that receives rain and then dries up. For the living continuity of a river the knowledge and learning must be attributed to the organization.

Organization learning exists when an aggregation of the learning of all the individuals in an organization creates a monolithic entity with its own impersonal capacity to know, act, think, or remember. This leads to "processes within an organization that give rise to patterns of activity seen, in the aggregate, as the organization's knowing, thinking, remembering, or learning."[2] For example, we might say "the company" investigated the grievance and granted the request, or "management" took a particular action. In each case, individuals actually took the action, but we view them as impersonal actions of the whole. Similarly, we must view organizations as a whole as capable of learning.

In *Organizational Learning II* Argyris and Schön note that "an organization may be said to learn when it acquires information (knowledge, understanding, know-how, techniques, or practices) of any kind and by whatever means."[3] In *The Fifth Discipline* Peter Senge describes a learning organization as "an organization that is continually expanding its capacity to create its future."[4] He observes that survival or adaptive learning is necessary, but is not enough. Rather, amassing of knowledge must be joined by generative learning that enhances the capacity of individuals to create.

Argyris and Schön state that information becomes organizational knowledge only if two conditions are met. First, organizations must function as "*holding environments for knowledge*" in the minds of individuals who make them up; in the organizations' files, records, and data bases; and in the physical objects such as tools, products, and working materials that individuals use as references and guideposts in their day-to-day business. Second, the organization must "*directly represent knowledge*" in the sense of strategies or "theories of action" for performing complex tasks. Such knowledge "may be variously represented as systems of beliefs that underlie action, as prototypes from which actions are derived, or as procedural prescriptions for action," and may include "values that govern the choice of strategies and the assumptions on which they are based."[5]

Organizational learning takes place when individuals encounter a problem and inquire into it on behalf of the organization. Finding a mismatch between expected and actual results, they engage in a process of thought and action that leads to restructuring of their theory of action and modification of their behavior. When these changes become embedded in the holding environment, organization learning has occurred.

Two types of learning must occur. Single loop learning "changes strategies of action or assumptions underlying strategies in ways that leave the values of a theory of action unchanged.''[6] It is concerned primarily with effectiveness of the existing organization: how to do better what has always been done, better meet existing objectives, and cause the organization to live within its existing values and principles. Double loop learning, on the other hand, leads to a change in the values behind the theories of action. It supports more fundamental change, as it creates new understandings of conflicting demands, sets new priorities, or changes norms in addition to fostering change in the strategies and assumptions addressed by single loop learning.

An effective organization must encourage both single loop and double loop learning. But many of our theories of action make double loop learning difficult. Argyris describes a theory of action used by most individuals as including the following: ''(1) strive to be in unilateral control, (2) minimize losing and maximize winning, (3) minimize the expression of negative feelings, and (4) be rational.''[7] (Amazingly similar to the beliefs of many parties in a labor/management relationship!) These theories of action lead individuals to behavior that includes advocating their own views without encouraging inquiry, attempting to unilaterally save face, and other behavior that tends to limit double loop learning. To foster such learning, individuals must become aware of the theories of action that are inhibiting their learning, see how the systems they maintain foster these theories, discover new theories of action, and introduce them into the organization. Valid information, free and informed choice, and internal commitment are necessary for this to happen.

While much learning is implicit within the organization, identified education activities are also necessary. Conventional training is a starting point. In a learning organization, however, training should not rely on a teacher to describe a problem, solve it, pass the solution on to the students, and administer a test to determine effectiveness. Rather, as Argyris observes in *On Organizational Learning*, the purpose of education is ''for organizational and system diagnosis, renewal and effectiveness.'' To accomplish this requires education that ''(1) focuses on individuals in team systems and (2) it occurs where the problem is located, (3) is learned by the use of actual problems, and (4) is tested by the effectiveness of the actual results, and (5) is controlled by those participating in the problem (aided by the educator as a consultant).''[8]

Training is of no value unless behavior changes, and identified ''lookbacks'' are important for insuring change of behavior and continual learning. In *Hope Is Not a Method*, Gordon Sullivan, former Army Chief of Staff, and Michael Harper describe a lookback process used in the U.S. Army. They refer to Senge's description of ''adaptive'' and ''generative learning,'' and note that both are necessary in a learning organization. They argue that ''Generative learning is not about amassing a body of knowledge so much as it is about amassing a body of experience, interpreting that experience, and changing behavior as a result.'' Further, ''A structured, open process of sharing information about events is the basis for this kind of learning.''[9] To foster such learning the Army has developed the "After Action Review," a structured feedback process involving several layers of command. The process is intended to enhance learning from both training activities and actual operations by after-the-fact dialogue that builds trust, leads to mutual planning and preparation, and improves subsequent performance. The process closely examines the following:

- What happened?
- Why did it happen?
- What should we do about it?

If the process is successful, people not only learn, but also become engaged as leaders with a shared responsibility for the success of the entire effort.

ORGANIZATION LEARNING IN A UNIONIZED WORKPLACE

A model for effective individual and organizational learning within the labor/management relationship can be fashioned utilizing the concepts discussed above. It begins with an environment conducive to organizational learning: one that fosters individual learning, allows groups of people (composed of represented employees, union representatives, and management) to reliably develop intelligence and ability greater than what could be developed by the sum of the individuals, and insures that these processes and skills are sustained and grow over time. Within this environment, individual and group learning experiences should be provided and various activities jointly assessed after the fact. An organization based on this model will have an expanded capacity to survive and create its own better future. To develop one, management must:

- Create a holding environment for knowledge.
- Walk its talk.
- Foster learning that leads to fundamental change as well as increased efficiency and effectiveness.
- Conduct individual and group educational activities where needed to increase the capacity to act and close the gap between actual and desired performance.
- Insure lookbacks to build trust, foster dialogue, and plan for improved performance in the future.

Each of these endeavors will be discussed in more detail below.

Create a Holding Environment for Knowledge

Opportunities for learning abound within every organization that is willing to tap the intellectual capacity of people at all levels and take advantage of the many situations where learning is implicit in the work. Employees or groups of employees observe what works well. They also experience surprises or problems, inquire into them, think about them, and make corrections if appropriate. In both cases, the individuals involved learn from their experience, but this learning is ephemeral unless the organization captures it, holds on to it, and replenishes it: unless the organization has the characteristics of a river. And management has a number of opportunities to build these characteristics.

Hiring Practices. Organizations are made up of individuals, and management must hire the right individuals to develop and hold the knowledge required for organizational learning. Learning must be part of the job, so employees who are able and willing to absorb the knowledge that is available must be hired. Hiring such people is not a certain task, but it can be facilitated by a number of actions.

Frequently management must rethink and clearly articulate what is expected of potential employees. It often has a limited view of the opportunities inherent in certain jobs as well as the capability of people who might be interested in them. In this situation, hourly paid and other employees frequently represented by a union are likely to be selected for their ability to do the specific technical or manual tasks associated with a particular job or group of jobs. They are hired for their task experience or their physical ability rather than their ability and motivation to learn, grow, and create. This leads to a situation where learning opportunities are missed or are limited to individual employees for the period of their employment tenure. To address this shortcoming, employers must expect employees not only to do specified tasks but also to demonstrate skills such as communicating, relating to others, solving problems, growing themselves and their jobs, and creating new improvement opportunities. These expectations must become part of the job and must be clearly articulated to insure they become hiring standards.

Having articulated expansive expectations, job roles, and hiring standards, management frequently must revise its hiring procedures to increase the likelihood of selecting individuals who meet those standards. Procedures should assess candidates' ability to handle expanded jobs, including their ability and willingness to communicate effectively, solve problems, interact with fellow employees, work in teams, and appropriately challenge the status quo. Many techniques are available for making such assessments.

A diverse work group is required to optimize organizational learning. True learning requires challenge of the status quo in areas such as beliefs, values, assumptions, experiences, and mental models. This type of challenge is not likely in a homogeneous work force where all employees are basically alike and cannot see potential learning opportunities or appreciate the value that differences or change can bring. On the other hand, a work force composed of individuals from different backgrounds and cultures, having different experience, talents, beliefs, and values is more likely to explore the differences and learn from them.

The union and represented employees should be deeply involved in the employment process in order to optimize the opportunity for attaining such a work force. This type of involvement is not common. As a general rule, unless special circumstances pertain (like use of a union hiring hall or preferential rehiring of laid-off employees), a union or employees it represents have little say about which employees are hired. Management hires employees, the union represents them, and current employees work with them. In this situation those employees who know most about the job, who frequently must teach the new employees, and who must work closely with them on a day-to-day basis have no say in who is hired. Nor do union representatives, who will be directly involved in addressing work or personal problems incurred by the new employees. This approach does not foster the type of teamwork, collaboration, and mutual support needed for organizational learning. On the other hand, if union representatives and individual employees are educated in appropriate employment practices and are involved in designing and implementing a hiring process, assessing prospective employees, and making hiring decisions within established legal and business parameters, a different environment is created. Better qualified employees are likely to be hired because those involved in the process really understand the needs and requirements of the job. More importantly, fellow employees and the union will understand why certain employees were hired, have an ownership in them, and be committed to their success. In this situation, they are more likely to offer the encouragement and help to new employees that can lead to success, continuity, and organizational learning.

Organizational Files. A second opportunity for creating a holding environment for learning arises from the fact that knowledge may "be held in an organization's files, which record its actions, decisions, regulations, and policies."[10] In a unionized workplace, where practices of the parties can bind them in the future, files and related records are critically important, but can be a two-edged sword. They are necessary as an organizational memory when the organization is too complex or the turnover too great for face-to-face conversation among employees to adequately perpetuate learning. On the other hand, files raise potential concerns.

The first issue arises from the fact that typically the union keeps its own files—its own independent institutional memory—covering many of the same events or actions covered by management's files. And not surprisingly, the two frequently do not tell the same story. Each party's files reflect its assessment of relative importance, its biases, and its selective memory. This can lead to good-faith disagreements between management and the union concerning what really happened in the past, what the learnings were, or how current policies or labor agreements should be interpreted. Such disagreements probably can never be eliminated. They can be minimized, however, by the company and union jointly maintaining and publishing an agreed record of those actions or decisions that merit a record. (It should be remembered, however, that highly structured documentation of what each party said can discourage innovation and exploration of various options.) Where a record is appropriate, getting agreement on what it will say tends to foster organizational learning by making current disagreements obvious, providing an opportunity for the parties to resolve them in real time, and narrowing the area for future disagreements. If disagreements nevertheless arise in the future, the parties at least have a common starting point for resolving them.

The second potential issue is a function of the common law of labor arbitration. Evidence of past practice may be introduced in arbitration for the following purposes: "(1) to provide the basis of rules governing matters not included in the written contract; (2) to indicate the proper interpretation of ambiguous contract language; or (3) to support allegations that clear language of the written contract has been amended by mutual action or agreement."[11]

Files and records of past actions help establish past practice, and where company and union records are reasonably consistent, they tend to insure stability, predictability, and continuity concerning the issues covered. But practices, regardless of whether or not they are documented, also tend effectively to become part of the labor contract and require maintaining the status quo unless both parties agree to a change, creating a situation that prevents organizational learning and improvement.

True organizational learning requires the ability to try things and experiment without being bound by prior practices or creating binding practice for the future. Where a binding practice already exists, management and union must agree before a change can be implemented. Looking to the future, however, where there is a past practice concern associated with a particular change, the parties should agree in advance to the extent to which certain actions will be considered binding and maintain such agreement as part of their organizational file. This will help preserve the right to try new things without being bound to continue them forever. This might be done by agreeing to a trial period—each party having the right to revert to the previous practice—or other procedures for trial activities.

Physical Objects. The third area for holding organizational knowledge is the physical objects employees use in their day-to-day work. These objects may guide action, suggest a particular behavior, or help in thinking through issues. For example, time clocks in the work place may imply lack of trustworthiness and therefore sanction untrustworthy behavior. Presence of distinctive uniforms or hard hats may suggest a bureaucracy that impedes communication and joint effort. Many perks and status symbols intended to be incentives for management performance have the reverse effect on employees who are not eligible for them. On the other hand, physical objects can be powerful objects for learning. Open doors suggest communication. Easily accessible workrooms with flip charts or chalkboards imply joint problem solving. Universal availability of computers, telephones, and other appropriate equipment tell employees they are expected to solve problems. A clean, safe work environment is the starting point for production of quality products.

To foster organizational learning management must minimize those objects that discourage and maximize those that encourage learning. Although management has primary control over the physical objects in the workplace, union leaders may have the best information as to how they affect the behavior of employees. Further, in most cases changes that facilitate learning and improved performance are in the best interest of employees. Therefore, changing physical objects to improve organizational learning and performance is an ideal area for collaboration and mutual gains for employees, union, and management.

Walk the Talk

Senge describes theories of action from two perspectives: espoused theories (what we say) and theories-in-use (theories that actually lie behind what we do).[12] He notes that organizational learning does not take place if there is an unrecognized gap between the two—if we say one thing but our actions obviously are based on another. Managers may publicly endorse collaboration, for example, but unless their behavior is collaborative they haven't really learned. To learn they must recognize the gap and change their behavior. If management says one thing and does another, cynicism quickly develops among employees and the level of trust rapidly declines. Managers are accused of hypocrisy and of attempting to manipulate the work force.

This need for consistency between what we say and what we do is important in all parts of our business, but it is especially relevant in building collaborative efforts with unions. Much historical management behavior, combined with their own mental models, makes it difficult for employees and unions to believe in the sincerity of management collaborative initiatives in the first place. If, in addition, management talks about collaboration but fails to deliver, the organization will not learn how to be more collaborative but instead will become more cynical and mistrusting. Accordingly, before attempting collaborative changes, management must insure the presence of the resources and the will to continue the effort for the long term. As previously discussed, tying changes to a bottom-line business need is an effective mechanism for insuring such continuity. Closely related is the need to insure that senior management supports the change. Without the profile and power of senior management, employees and the union will quickly conclude that the company does not mean what it says, and the organization will not learn to deal effectively with change.

Foster Learning that Leads to Efficiency, Effectiveness, and Fundamental Change

Single loop learning is concerned with efficiency and effectiveness; with doing a better job in attaining current goals and objectives. It results when changes are made within the range set by existing values and norms. Effective single loop learning is critically important throughout the business, including in the labor/management relationship. We must continue to improve the way the work is done, the contract is administered, complaints are handled, and other day-to-day activities are managed.

But transformational change, such as major revision of the labor/management relationship or other broad, fundamental change, requires the reflection and inquiry that lead to double loop learning: learning that leads to changes in the underlying values and norms of the organization. For example, assume a management has set out, with or without explicit union agreement and support, to develop a more collaborative labor environment in which employees are allowed to contribute all they can and union leaders are treated with respect and dignity. This quickly leads to practices that do not conform with the company's norms, and perhaps its unstated values. Employees are making more decisions and unilaterally changing the way they do their jobs. Grievances are being resolved in the field rather than around the grievance table or by arbitrators. Union representatives are working on training program design formerly handled exclusively by the training department. Such new practices are likely to conflict with long-held corporate norms and mental models that are common in management/union relationships, such as management striving to be in unilateral control and to minimize losing and maximize winning. Management faces conflict between new practices and its comfortable norms, and it cannot have both.

To deal with such conflict, management must be aware of its long-held mental models and norms, recognize that they conflict with the new practices, and be willing to challenge and reconsider them. It must reflect on whether its values are based on truth or expediency and whether its norms are preventing productive change. Values must not be lightly disregarded, but they must be challenged. Those fundamental human values that give life to and perpetuate the organization must be reaffirmed, but those that arose almost by default and no longer apply must be changed. Management also must weigh the value of the old norms—for example, of predictability and control—against the value that transformational change can add in terms of new and better ways of doing the business. The old norms should be retained if they are too fundamental and valuable to discard. But if there is value in changing to new practices, then the norms must be reconsidered and reprioritized to make them compatible with the desired practices.

Unions, of course, also have similar mental models and norms that may impede change and must be dealt with. There is no easy formula for dealing with them or for causing the union to engage in double loop learning. At a minimum, however, management must:

- Acknowledge the existence of union norms and values and attempt to empathize with them.

- Be open and honest about management objectives and concerns.

- Provide the union an opportunity to change without the risk of severe consequences to it, perhaps using trial periods as previously discussed.

Conduct Educational Activities to Close the Performance Gap

Learning from working is less risky, more cost efficient, and probably more effective than other processes for employee education and organizational learning. Unfortunately, however, even though people learn from doing, gaps inevitably appear between actual and desired performance. Where gaps exist because of lack of knowledge or understanding, on-the-job learning must be supplemented by specifically designed interventions. These interventions should be as close to the "real thing" as possible. To the extent feasible, they should be with groups or teams of people who work together and address real workplace issues.

The union and represented employees should be consulted and provided an opportunity to influence and participate in the development and implementation of education programs for represented employees. They are closer to the work than many managers or training staff and frequently have a better understanding of what is needed. Involving employees who do the work in planning their training provides them additional opportunities and motivation to learn, and involving the union fosters a synergy that can improve the quality of the training and encourage union leaders to support participation by employees they represent. Management, union, and employees have a strong mutuality of interest in training, so they should work together to create better opportunities. This working together can in turn be a learning laboratory for exploring how the company and union can collaborate on more difficult issues in the future.

Training in connection with transforming the labor/management relationship to one that is more collaborative requires special note. While the need for training and the priority of various types must be decided on a case-by-case basis, the following should normally be considered, in the order indicated.

Job Training. The top priority for all of us is to do our jobs properly and safely. The work is central to the reason businesses exist, and if individuals or organizations fail to understand their jobs or have the skills to do them, little else in the business matters. While a collaborative union relationship can and should help solve many job and business problems, it must be based on a foundation of fundamental operating competence. If it isn't, the resulting deficient organizational performance and poor results will overwhelm the labor relations effort. Employees will understand the futility of the effort and become cynical and uncooperative, and senior management will not have the patience to see the effort through.

Business Training. Business training includes a broad range of educational efforts that are not specifically related to work tasks or labor relations but that have an impact on both. It includes education in how to work together and addresses areas such as communication, team skills, problem solving, and leadership. It also provides a basic understanding of issues such as the economic and competitive realities of the business, customer needs and issues, financial requirements, and shareholder expectations. Such training is necessary for all employees, represented and non-represented alike, as a prerequisite to attaining true labor/management collaboration. Without it employees typically do not have the understanding of the business necessary to motivate them to work with management or the skills necessary to do so.

Such training is a lot like that typically seen in manager and supervisor development programs. If management's goal is to have employees see the broad picture, manage their own jobs, and contribute with their intellect, they will need skills similar to managers and supervisors. In addition, providing supervisors and the employees they supervise with the same type of training, preferably together, helps develop a mutual empathy that can foster a more collaborative relationship between them.

While this discussion has focused on employees, it is clear that union leaders, whether or not employees of the company concerned, need the same understandings and skills. Accordingly, they should be involved in such education efforts whenever feasible.

Labor Relations Training. Changing the relationship between labor and management requires training a substantial number from both groups in philosophy and skills in areas such as joint problem solving, mediation processes, mutual gains bargaining, and other collaborative efforts. Such training can, however, present a dilemma. On one hand, the extent of change typically needed requires understandings, behaviors, and skills that most individuals and organizations do not possess. To have a chance of success, large numbers of individuals—management, union representatives, and employees—must be trained. On the other hand, such a training program can be costly, even though the results may be uncertain, nebulous, and long term. More importantly, high profile training can create expectations that may be difficult to deliver. If expectations, whether or not realistic, are not quickly met, represented employees, supervisors, and managers are likely to become disenchanted and fail to support the effort, or even sabotage it. Employees may bring political pressure on union leaders to get out of the apparently futile effort, and senior management may put similar pressure on those managers who are directly involved. This can escalate with disastrous results.

Cost of training can at times be minimized with computer-based and other non-traditional learning processes. But management must accept that change requires education and learning, and that providing these will cost money. They must be viewed, like so many other costs, as an investment for the future: money spent now for an expected return later with associated and hopefully understood risks. Management must make its own assessment of the cost/benefit relationship as part of its business decision whether to attempt to transform the labor/management relationship.

The expectation issue can be dealt with in two ways. First, labor relations training should be integrated closely with various types of business training whenever feasible. The two are closely related, and if labor relations training is not broadly touted as such, expectations will not be escalated. Second, action training, where participants learn from doing, involves less risk and is more likely to succeed than instructor training. In such training, groups frequently work with a trainer/facilitator to address real problems in a team setting. Where the issues involve mandatory subjects of bargaining or topics covered by the labor contract, the union and company must agree in advance on questions such as the approach to be taken, who the trainer/facilitator will be, what issues will be addressed, and the number and selection of participants. In addition, they must agree on the authority of the group engaging in the process; that is, will its solution bind the parties or is it a recommendation that will be subject to collective bargaining by a different group and subsequent approval by each party.

Action training has several advantages. It provides instant feedback and continual inquiry and learning, thereby minimizing the risk of thwarted expectations. Further, if a problem or problems are solved in a mutually satisfactory way it provides an example of success that can foster future collaborative efforts. For this reason, to the extent they can be isolated from broader systems, meaningful but "easier" issues probably should be addressed first, with success on these laying the groundwork for addressing tougher issues.

Do Lookbacks

Arie de Geus argues that strategic planning has had few successes and that rather than trying to follow a rigid strategy or steer a predetermined course, a management should at each decision point do the next right thing. In pursuing improvement, "the living company takes one step at a time. Each decision is followed by an action, and then new observations about the effect of that action, and then another step tomorrow. . . . Before each new step, it looks up and decides where to put its foot in the light of the conditions of the moment. There are no maps and no final destination."[13]

Kanter discusses "logical incrementalism" in which strategies emerge from an iterative process summarized as "action first, thought later; experience first, making a 'strategy' out of it second."[14]

Similarly, a detailed plan for implementing change in a unionized workplace, whether operational change or transformational change to a more collaborative union/management relationship, is not likely to work. Essentially everything is dependent on the actions of people, who frequently are operating in an emotionally charged environment where they are even less predictable than normal. Moving to a new relationship involves such fundamental change that the past cannot be used as a predictor of the future. Unstated and unknown values and beliefs frequently affect actions. Company or union politics can change in short order with dramatic effects on collaborative efforts. Under these circumstances, de Geus's advice is particularly compelling. The parties must follow the "cycle of seeing, concluding, deciding and acting"[15] and try to do the next right thing.

Ideally, management and the union representing its employees can work together to establish processes for productive incrementalism. In doing this they should involve as many individuals as possible in informal learning from their own and other's actions as a normal part of their day-to-day work. After the processes are set, however, both management and union leaders must let go. They must allow supervisors and departmental stewards to solve their own problems or allow joint committees to do their work and steer their own course without interference from management or union leadership. Mistakes will be made, but in the proper environment they will lead to the type of organization learning being sought.

Although this informal, distributive approach to learning has great value, certain situations require more. A more formal lookback may be needed where the effort is substantial or unusually significant, or the number of people involved is large. Sullivan and Harper describe the Army's After Action Review, which can be used as a model for a structured lookback at labor relations activities, as including the following elements:

- Identifiable event, with associated standards.
- Identifiable players.
- Knowledge of what happened (ground truth).
- Non-threatening environment.
- Willingness to take personal risks in order for the team to learn and grow.[16]

In the labor/management relationship, lookbacks can be of great value in assessing and learning from particular events, such as an education initiative, a joint committee, the renegotiation of a collective bargaining contract, a plant closure, or employee layoffs. The review should involve both company and union leaders at the level appropriate to focus on a discrete event and benefit from the potential learning. What actually happened should be carefully assessed and compared to what was intended in an open environment conducive to real dialogue that can lead to both single loop and double loop learning. Such learning will provide the basis for the next collaborative action and hopefully is the beginning of a cycle of improvement that benefits all involved.

KEY POINTS

1. Disappointments, hurt feelings, setbacks, and reversals are inevitable in a labor/management relationship.

2. Individuals, and the organization itself, must learn and grow from the problems that are encountered and mistakes that are made.

3. To foster organizational learning and growth, management must:

   - Create a holding environment for knowledge by involving the union and represented employees in hiring the right people, in maintaining a record that provides an organizational memory, and in managing the physical objects of the workplace.

   - Insure its actions are consistent with its words.

- Foster single loop learning that addresses efficiency and effectiveness and double loop learning that addresses the underlying values and norms of the organization.
- Offer job training, business training, and labor relations training, in that order, to close the gap between expectations and performance.
- Do lookbacks with union collaboration to build trust, foster dialogue, and plan for improvement in the future.

NOTES

1. Arie de Geus, *The Living Company* (London: Nicholas Brealey, 1997), p. 125.

2. Chris Argyris and Donald A. Schön, *Organizational Learning II* (Reading, Mass.: Addison-Wesley, 1996), p. 5.

3. Ibid., p. 3.

4. Peter M. Senge, *The Fifth Discipline* (New York: Doubleday, 1990), p. 14.

5. Argyris and Schön, *Organizational Learning II*, pp. 12–13.

6. Ibid., p. 20.

7. Chris Argyris, *On Organizational Learning* (Cambridge, Mass.: Blackwell, 1992), p. 26.

8. Ibid., pp. 78–79.

9. Gordon R. Sullivan and Michael V. Harper, *Hope Is Not a Method* (New York: Random House, 1996), pp. 193–194,

10. Argyris and Schön, *Organizational Learning II*, p. 12.

11. Frank Elkouri and Edna Asper Elkouri, *How Arbitration Works*, 3rd ed. (Washington, D.C.: BNA, 1973), p. 389.

12. Senge, *The Fifth Discipline*, p. 202.

13. De Geus, *The Living Company*, p. 185.

14. Rosabeth Moss Kanter, *The Change Masters* (New York: Simon and Schuster, 1983), p. 290.

15. De Geus, *The Living Company*, p. 188.

16. Sullivan and Harper, *Hope Is Not a Method*, p. 197.

Chapter 10

Mutual Trust

Trust is an elusive concept, based largely on perceptions and feelings. Francis Fukuyama has defined it as "the expectation that arises within a community of regular, honest, and cooperative behavior, based on commonly shared norms, on the part of other members of that community."[1] Robert Bruce Shaw defines trust as a "Belief that those on whom we depend will meet our expectations of them."[2] In an effective management/union relationship, trust is an unwritten and usually unspoken contract, based on the beliefs and values of the parties and demonstrated through their actions and behavior, that allows each of the parties to believe in the honesty, integrity, reliability, and justice of the others. Trust is an issue among those who have influence over things that are important to one another. Consequently, all those who can influence the labor/management relationship are essential parties to the contract. Each must be trustworthy and also trusting of the other parties, although one rarely finds complete trust or complete distrust. The purpose of this chapter is to share thoughts on developing and sustaining such trust in a labor/management relationship.

PRINCIPLES

Trust is a fundamental requirement in any effective relationship. In a business enterprise it is necessary for those attributes of human capital that provide a competitive advantage, such as innovation, effectiveness, or efficiency. The absence of trust increases the cost of doing business because it increases adversarial activity and the direct and indirect costs associated with warranting transactions among people. The potentially increased transaction costs are a particular concern in a unionized workplace, where the presence of a union introduces an additional party with significantly different roles and interests. The presence of this additional party leads to increases in the number, formality, and potential controversy of transactions. The company and union engage in formal negotiations where personal credibility is paramount, and they frequently use force to cause the other to grant concessions. They enter into explicit contracts that frequently are subject to differing interpretations and disagreements, and the union has the ability to influence employees to exploit or not to exploit these disagreements. Examples of increased transaction cost resulting from lack of trust in a unionized workplace abound:

- Voluminous contracts are negotiated and maintained to limit management discretion.

- Grievance/arbitration procedures are maintained because the union doesn't trust management to administer the contract fairly.

- Disputes are settled with win/lose arbitration because employees and the union don't believe they are being treated fairly.

- Inefficient, restrictive work rules are maintained to address fear of layoffs and preserve employment.

- Needed changes are delayed or prevented because the union and employees don't believe management's version of the implications.

- Strikes occur over the union's felt need to cover a lack of trust with contract or because the union believes management doesn't mean what it says and will back down under pressure.

As these examples suggest, law and contract provide guidelines for handling most labor/management transactions. Relying too heavily on them, however, is dysfunctional rather than effective or efficient, and the opportunities available in the labor/management relationship cannot be optimized unless law and contract are supported by trust. Ryan and Oestreich note in *Driving Fear Out of the Workplace*, "When work demands something more than quick handoffs of individual efforts, the ability to follow explicit directions, and rudimentary communication, then trust becomes a vital and very smart business strategy."[3] The authors of *The Transformation of American Industrial Relations* note that the success of workplace reform efforts over time "depends on the ability of the organization to reinforce and sustain high levels of trust."[4] Trust is particularly important for a collaborative labor/management relationship for a number of reasons.

- For synergy to exist, each party must trust that it will get more from the relationship than it can see on the surface.

- Effective collaboration requires an ability to work together that is not constrained by worries about the trustworthiness of the other party.

- Employees and the union will bring their hearts and minds to the relationship only when they trust their management and their management trusts them.

• When coercive power is used, trust must provide the stability and predictability necessary to prevent major organizational damage.

The Parties

The labor/management relationship is based on the reciprocal attitudes among three parties: the company, the union, and represented employees as a group. But trust is largely personal and individual and cannot exist for the parties apart from the individuals who make them up. Therefore, a trusting relationship in a union workplace must be discussed in the context of five parties: the company, the individual representatives of the company, represented employees, the union that represents them, and the leaders of that union. While the parties are closely related, each plays a different role in the relationship, and each engenders trust differently. All must work together to create an environment of trust.

The individual management representative who deals with employees and unions may be a supervisor dealing one-on-one with employees, a manager or labor relations specialist dealing with employees or union officials, a senior manager dealing with groups of employees or union leaders, or an outside attorney or consultant. Whichever the case, employees and union leaders view them as individuals and perceive them as trustworthy or not independent of how they view the company. Employees may feel good about their company but genuinely dislike and mistrust their boss; or genuinely like and trust their boss whom they see as an anomaly in a bad company. In a trusting environment, representatives of management as individuals deal fairly with those with whom they interact, tell the truth, and exhibit the capacity and willingness to deliver on their promises. All do their part in fostering trust in the company and its institutions.

Trust in the company is a function of the aggregate of the trustworthiness of its individual managers and institutions over a significant period of time. When there is trust in the company, employees perceive the group of managers, supervisors, and other corporate spokespersons as trustworthy. They see them as speaking with a common voice and in matters of principle acting consistently with each other and with corporate institutions over time. Employees feel they are treated fairly as compared to other employees and generally accepted standards of treatment. Employees and the union understand certain parameters for management behavior, and generally can anticipate what "they" will do in a particular situation. This trust is not necessarily based on agreement or friendship, but rather on the knowledge that the company, regardless of who is speaking for it, will act fairly and do what its representatives say it will do.

Represented employees in a trusting relationship must behave in the same trustworthy way as company representatives: deal fairly, tell the truth, and be able and willing to deliver on their promises to their employer, their union, and fellow employees. Their promise to their employer includes their explicit commitments but also their implicit representation that they are qualified for their job, that they will do the job or jobs for which they were hired to the best of their ability, and that they will abide by reasonable rules appropriately established by the company. Delivering on promises to other employees and the union is also necessary. For example, employees must respect the rights of other employees, refrain from individual action proscribed in the union setting, and be subject to appropriate rules and disciplines of their union.

Individual union leaders may range from the national president to the steward on the shop floor. Like company representatives in a trusting relationship, they must deal fairly with those with whom they interact, tell the truth, and exhibit the capacity and willingness to deliver on their promises. They frequently must exhibit this behavior while taking unpopular stands that result in intense political and other pressure from the employees they represent. Further, they must meet the needs and expectations of employees they represent while fostering trust with management.

Requirements for "the union" as an institution in a trustworthy relationship are essentially a mirror image of those for the company. The union must be credible and have a reputation for trustworthiness locally and on a national scale. Further, its leaders, from local to national or international, must be trustworthy over time and must behave consistently with each other and with the institutions of the union.

Thus, each party is different and brings different things to the relationship. But certain common threads suggest that for trust to exist all parties must be consistent over time in matters of principle, be truthful and deliver on their promises, deal fairly with one another, and show one another respect.

The Challenge

Trust is a two-way street. To develop a trusting relationship, each party must demonstrate over time that it can be trusted and also show that it trusts the other parties. Which comes first? Is trust always earned and never freely given, or does one freely give trust first in order to win it from another? The answer probably varies from case to case, but in a union workplace management typically gets the worst of both worlds. It must earn a reservoir of trust before it gets any from employees. On the other hand, to earn that trust, it must demonstrate by its actions that it trusts employees and the union before those parties have earned it and before they are willing to trust management!

Building and maintaining trust can be especially difficult in a union environment. Employees are likely to split their loyalty between the company and the union, and union leaders may try to enhance their power by questioning or challenging the credibility of management and its representatives. This challenging is frequently made easier when employees and local union leaders are in place for the long term while managers move in and out. One misstep, misunderstanding, or failure to follow through can destroy credibility that has been built over years.

Notwithstanding the difficulties, management can determine the future of the relationship and can by its own actions create an environment conducive to mutual trust. While management cannot create morals or ethics where they don't exist or make union leaders trustworthy in all cases, it can create an environment where employees and the union become more trustworthy. It can build long-term trust by changing itself and its behavior when needed, concentrating on the relationship with employees and the union, and taking actions within its power that foster trustworthy behavior in others. This leads to reciprocal behavior and the emergence of completely new characteristics within the relationship. The remainder of this chapter will discuss what management can do to make itself, employees, and union leaders more trustworthy.

BUILDING MANAGEMENT TRUSTWORTHINESS

Unions and employees decide whether to trust management on the basis of what they hear management say and what they see it do. To develop and sustain trust, managers and management must insure that what they say and do meets the following minimum standards:

- Their words and actions are based on clearly communicated core values.
- They are honest in all they do and say.
- They treat employees with fundamental fairness.
- They show respect for individuals and for the union as an institution.

These standards will be discussed in the following sections.

Core Values

Management frequently is advised to adopt and communicate a core ideology for the enterprise. These principles often include a statement of mission or purpose that addresses why the organization exists, a vision of what the organization seeks to be, objectives or strategies for getting there, and clearly understood core values. Many reasons are offered for establishing such principles: providing a common sense of direction, gaining employee commitment and focus, creating a sense of purpose that brings people together, developing a collective sense of what is important, aligning efforts of the work force, providing a tool for employee self-realization, establishing strategic priorities, and other similar objectives.

All of the guiding principles are important for an effective organization, but core values is the critical one for establishing mutual trust. Peter Senge notes in *The Fifth Discipline* that "Core values answer the question 'How do we want to act, consistent with our mission, along the path toward achieving our vision?' A company's values might include integrity, openness, honesty, freedom, equal opportunity, leanness, merit, or loyalty. They describe how the company wants life to be on a day-to-day basis, while pursuing the vision."[5]

Fukuyama has noted that "As a general rule, trust arises when a community shares a set of moral values in such a way as to create expectations of regular and honest behavior. To some extent, the particular character of those values is less important than the fact that they are shared."[6]

Core values provide enduring guidelines for the behavior of people within the organization. They guide the choices we make, indicate which matters are to be given most attention, and allow employees and the union to reasonably predict what management will do in a particular circumstance. They are key to the mutual trust required for an effective collaborative relationship.

Building trust requires consistency and predictability over the long term. The mental models that affect what union leaders and employees hear and see management saying and doing, and are often the basis of mistrust, are accumulated and reinforced over a long time period. To gain trust management must demonstrate trustworthiness consistently for long enough that union leaders and employees choose to change their mental models about management. Doing this requires continuity that can only be present when management actions are guided by clearly understood core values.

Values must be well understood by all parties, whether they are formally communicated or part of the stories and myths that describe the organization. Further, to be credible, management must be seen to be guided by them. Managers must speak with a common voice and behave with a consistency that validates their values and allows employees and union leaders to reasonably predict how they will act in a particular situation. This predictability must be sustained over time, even in the face of dramatic business and process changes and pressure to compromise in the interest of solving immediate problems. Compromising a value builds an expectation of another compromise and makes it easier. Soon, employees and the union don't know what to expect, and credibility and trust are gone.

Employees and union leaders understand that issues based on strong core values are not negotiable. An example of the opposite is a flaw that has been suggested in former President Bush's management style: "Because he sends out no clear signals, everyone believes everything with Mr. Bush is negotiable. He is paralyzed by his own pragmatism."[7] The same can apply to management behavior in the workplace. Management must be clear over time what it will not change and must maintain these positions even when the cost is high. Short-term pragmatism must not give way to longer-term interests. Short-term costs that can be clearly calculated must not prevail over longer-term value that is more nebulous. For example, a company that values a flexible work force must maintain positions consistent with that value in contract negotiations, even when compromise would result in union pay concessions that may reduce costs in the short term. Management must from time to time give up something big for something that seems small at the time.

One view of predictability is "tell me what the rules are, don't change them, and enforce them rigidly and consistently over time." This approach provides predictability and allows employees and union leaders to know what to expect. It also, however, prevents change, stifles initiative, and leads to a stagnant organization incapable of competing. Thus, management's challenge is to foster flexibility, experimentation, and change while maintaining an environment where employees and union leaders know what to expect on matters of importance. This means providing a stable foundation from which future actions can reasonably be predicted. This foundation is the value system of the organization.

Core values are important from both a process and a substantive viewpoint. From a process perspective, broadly understood core values provide a basis for predictable behavior that all parties can depend on, regardless of what the values are. For example, the Mafia has certain principles that its members presumably understand and can depend on, for better or for worse. While the principles may be abhorrent to most of society, they nevertheless foster a clear trust in the sense that members understand the rules and the consequences of violating them. Likewise, core values within a company, whether liked or disliked by employees, or whether good or bad for the business, provide a level of dependability that is essential for mutual trust. For example, an employer might have a strongly held value opposing union security measures in a contract, believing they limit individual employee freedom. The union no doubt would disagree strongly, but if it is understood as a strong management value, continuing fights over the issue are less likely because the union would understand their futility.

Although the existence of well-understood core values provides an important sense of predictability, if their substance is abhorrent to employees or otherwise inappropriate they will not support a relationship based on trust. The substance determines what we say and do, over time. Management's actions both confirm the existence and validity of its values and provide a basis for employees and the union to judge its trustworthiness. While core values will vary from company to company, from a substantive viewpoint, they should at a minimum include honesty, fairness, and respect, as discussed in the following sections.

Honesty

Telling the truth and doing what we say we will do are necessary for a trusting relationship. Robert Dilenschneider noted in *On Power* that in any power transaction, "truth is the mutual version of reality with which the engaged are willing to live in order to get something done. In any sustainable world, the truth is anchored in the facts, but its real operational force ensues from being cemented in trust. If getting things done is the goal, reliability is crucial, and reliability is just not possible without a common understanding of what constitutes the truth.''[8] Management and its representatives must tell the truth, and employees and union leaders must believe what they hear. Both aspects are critical.

Telling the truth seems simple enough: just the facts, accurate and complete. Black or white. A moral and ethical management that does not intentionally misstate facts or give false testimony, as is assumed in this book, should have no problem being honest in a black-and-white world.

But we don't live in a world where everything is so clear. A black or white view of truth would probably work if the world were machinelike, static, determined, and backward looking. But we live in a world that is open, changing, interconnected, living, and defined largely by relationships rather than facts. In this world most issues of truthfulness arise when management honestly thinks it is telling the truth, and the hearers (employees or union) honestly believe it is not. Four situations of this type are discussed below. They are all situations where the parties can be assumed to be behaving in good faith, but questions as to management's truthfulness lead to a decline in trust.

Withholding Information. How management communicates, rather than what it says or does, can create doubt about its veracity. For example, when management tells only part of the story or withholds information that could be detrimental to its position, doubts are created not only as to what is missing but as to what has been said. "If we believe that others are sharing the full extent of their knowledge on issues of importance to us, we begin to trust them and their motives. If instead we believe they are not sharing appropriately and that they know more than they are saying, we usually become suspicious.''[9]

Communicating primarily with formal and highly disciplined processes that place tight parameters around what is said and limit the opportunity for questions frequently appears to be a process for withholding rather than sharing information. For example, while communicating in writing or with set presentations may at times be necessary, doing so can leave many questions unanswered and appear to be guarded. Preventing access to certain company personnel or experts by insisting that all communications with the union be through designated labor relations specialists and that communications with employees be through the chain of command can also raise negative inferences. Such behavior can give the appearance of a cover-up and cause employees or union representatives to doubt the veracity of management even when it is being truthful.

On the other hand, an environment of openness where only truly confidential information is withheld fosters a belief in the honesty of managers and the company. In this environment employees and management are encouraged to engage in open, unrestrained discussion of issues, and the union has direct access to the best sources of information and expertise available. Employees and their union having access not only to information management believes they need but also to what they want and believe they need creates a self-correcting environment. Management is sure to take extra precaution to fully and truthfully represent the facts because it knows it is subject to challenge. And employees and union are more likely to believe what is said because they can check the facts for themselves, and frequently will do so.

Even in such an environment of openness, from time to time some information must be withheld. Where for legal, confidentiality, or business reasons management is unable or unwilling to share certain information, it should clearly divulge the existence of the information and discuss why it cannot be shared rather than pretend it doesn't exist. Legal and confidentiality reasons for nondisclosure usually are well understood and accepted. If management decides to withhold information for purely business reasons, the likely effect on trust should be recognized and balanced in the decision process.

Predicting the Future. Sharing beliefs about what will or will not happen in the future can also lead to concerns about veracity. Frequent travelers will no doubt identify with this dilemma. A scheduled flight is late. The airline posts a delayed departure time. But the plane doesn't leave until much later. If the airline posted its best estimate at the time of the delayed departure time and further delays were encountered, was it being truthful? How certain of the future must it be before posting a new time? Most travelers are probably not forgiving and assume the airline is either negligent or manipulative. In similar situations the union and most employees are not forgiving of management either.

Situations frequently arise where it is helpful for management to advise employees and the union of what it expects, but doesn't know, will happen in the future. For example, if employees are concerned about layoffs and management has no plans for any and honestly believes none will be required, it may wish to say so. Or a management resisting a union proposal for restrictions on its right to reduce staff may wish to advise the union truthfully that it has no plans for layoffs and doesn't believe any will be necessary. In both examples, statements about the future might solve a short-term problem, but they are dangerous. If circumstances change, management could either be constrained to debilitating inaction or face charges of lying if it does act. Former President Bush learned this when he promised no tax increases and subsequently increased taxes. Yet qualifying statements intended to leave flexibility for uncertainty and future changes frequently aren't heard; and if they are, they tend to be heard as hedges intended to hide the truth, casting doubt on the main point being made. Therein lies the dilemma. There are no easy solutions, but thinking about several simple guidelines can be helpful.

- Don't refuse to address relevant issues. Remember that failing to address an issue can be seen as withholding relevant information, regardless of whether any pertinent information actually exists.

- Don't be afraid to say "I don't know." Employees and the union appreciate the honesty, sincerity, and vulnerability conveyed by this admission if it is true.

- Share facts, not forecasts. Sharing beliefs about what will happen in the future can be dangerous. However, extensive sharing of existing facts sufficient to allow others to draw their own conclusions or make their own judgments can meet their needs without making or implying commitments that may be difficult to live with.

- Remember that actions are judged against what is heard and not what is said. Therefore, if it is necessary to share a prediction about the future with qualifications, be sure the qualifications are clear, unequivocal, and easily understood.

Communicating Inconsistently. Lack of consistency among management spokespersons can also cause mistrust. Inconsistency, or the appearance of it, can arise in many ways even when all believe they are being truthful. Company spokespersons can speak from different perspectives or time frames; one can generalize and another offer details; they can reach different conclusions based on the same facts; or someone can just fail to get the message. The problem is exacerbated if employees or union leaders shop their questions to try to get preferred answers, perhaps presenting slightly differing questions each time they are raised.

Argyris has observed that inconsistency is more likely when the spokespersons are from different levels of the organization because the nature of the information required by managers at higher levels is different from that needed by those at lower levels. He notes:

The top, who are distant from the point of action, require information that is abstract, objective, in which the logic is explicit, and in which the data can be compared and tracked. The first line or local level use data that is concrete, subjective, in which the logic is tacit, and in which the data cannot be compared or tracked. These information characteristics produce worlds with different views about what is effective and what is just. The relevant parties, using the logic inherent in the information they use, create conditions of misunderstanding and distancing from each other.[10]

There is no magic formula for eliminating inconsistency. Communicating broadly in writing obviously can provide consistency on the issues addressed and is appropriate in many circumstances. Such communication is generally time consuming and impersonal, however, and can be ineffective in bringing about understanding and commitment.

Individual managers can go a long way to insure they do not foster inconsistent communication if they avoid meddling in areas better addressed by others. This is particularly important for the senior person. Managing by walking around and frequent open discussion with employees can be very effective, but senior managers must recognize that what they say will be compared in great detail to what other managers and supervisors are saying and doing. Furthermore, employees and the union may expect them to be able and willing to answer any question or address any issue they raise. Such questions of senior managers may be good-faith queries, but they also may be attempts to appeal an answer previously received from a supervisor. Whichever the case, senior managers should carefully consider their answers and resist the temptation to respond to most hypothetical questions or where an inconsistency could result. They must be willing to acknowledge that certain issues are outside the realm of their day-to-day involvement and are best delegated to more junior managers or supervisors.

Most importantly, managers should not talk to employees; rather, they should engage them in dialogue. Where employees or the union have an opportunity to question, react, and fully understand a statement from management, different perspectives are more likely to become obvious and the perception of inconsistency reduced. Such dialogue can be effective in planned or ad hoc, person-to-person meetings. Electronic channels also provide a very effective mechanism for dialogue, as they allow management to fully consider what it says and then communicate thoroughly and uniformly to all or most employees.

Failing to Follow Through. Failure to follow through on promises creates unfulfilled expectations and casts doubt on the veracity or capacity of the person making them. Where trust exists, employees and the union can depend on management fulfilling its commitments, whether they involve matters the union wants or matters they want management to refrain from.

The need to follow through on clear, legally binding commitments is obvious. Fortunately, unilateral abrogation of such contracts rarely happens, if for no other reason than because the union has a mechanism for enforcement. Even trying to do so would obviously create mistrust, but it would be so outside the realm of good faith that it is not dealt with here.

More difficult issues arise where management (or an individual manager) has stated that it will or will not do something, but there is not a legally binding agreement and the union has no effective enforcement mechanism. When circumstances change, new information becomes available, a heavy work load and changing priorities take precedence, or a new manager with different views takes over, there may be pressure to renege. Management's mettle is tested. The easy answer, of course, is to avoid such situations. When they happen, however, two considerations—ethics and business pragmatism—should usually lead to the same response. Integrity demands the promise be fulfilled if possible or an agreeable revision negotiated, even though the union may have no power to enforce the original promise. Business pragmatism will usually lead to the same conclusion when viewed over the long term. If the promise is not fulfilled, the costs associated with loss of trust arising from the thwarted expectations are likely over the long term to outweigh the benefits from abrogating the commitment.

Good-faith misunderstandings about what management actually committed to are more common and perhaps raise more difficult issues. Such misunderstandings can arise concerning the meaning of a legally binding contract or unilateral management promises.

Disagreements involving legally binding contracts are probably simplest because typically a grievance-and-arbitration procedure anticipates such a possibility and provides an agreed mechanism for resolving it fairly. In this situation, even if the union disagrees, management's position is not likely to destroy trust if it is honest and not outrageous or part of a pattern of "hedging" on agreements. On the other hand, if management continually administers the contract aggressively in its favor or makes interpretations not supported by reasonable evidence, trust will suffer whether or not it ultimately prevails in arbitration.

When there are disagreements as to the meaning of a unilateral promise, arbitration may or may not be an effective recourse for the union. To the extent that the union does not have recourse against an action it believes is contrary to management's promise, it is at a power disadvantage. These situations present real dilemmas for management, since any action seen as exploiting this disparity will cause lack of trust. Should management stand by its view of what happened and suffer the consequences for trust or "give in" to the union or employee's position? Each case must be decided on its own merits, considering the core values of the organization, the evidence describing the misunderstanding, and the consequences of various resolutions. Some additional points to consider are:

- Avoid personalizing the disagreement. Attempt to solve the substance of the issue without pointing fingers at the individual or individuals who may have caused or are raising the misunderstanding.

- Engage in open dialogue with those involved in an honest attempt to resolve the issue, acknowledging any fault on the part of the company spokesperson.

- Try to solve the problem, rather than argue about the superficial aspects of what was or was not said.

- Where informal resolution fails, use mediation or other problem-solving processes to attempt to solve the problem.

- Agree as a last resort to use arbitration. If the matter is arbitrated, frame the issue in terms of deciding whether there was a commitment and if so what the commitment was, rather than relying on technical legal arguments to escape a recognized commitment.

The discussion above envisioned management's failure to deliver on a promise of benefit. In addition, however, management's failure to stand behind a position employees or the union do not like when faced with their pressure to change can be equally damaging. Two types of reasons for changing positions pursuant to the union's request or pressure may exist, and an important distinction must be made between them.

Changing a position in ways not inconsistent with core values and in response to a changed understanding of facts or reasoned arguments aimed at solving a problem can enhance trust. This type of response is a natural result of the synergy of ideas advocated in a countervailing collaboration relationship.

On the other hand, giving in to pressure from employees and the union may gain short-term peace, but over the long term will create an environment where management cannot be depended on. Giving in creates an incentive to resist unpopular management positions rather than attempt to work together for mutual gains. Union leaders become reluctant to support management because of concern it will reverse its position and discredit them. Over time, the union "winning'' one case increases the likelihood of a challenge in the next, resulting in a downward spiral of trust. All this suggests that before taking positions with employees and the union, management should carefully balance the need and value of the position against the impact on employees and their likelihood of resisting. Management should only take those unpopular decisions if the potential gain is worth the risk and it is prepared to take the heat.

Fairness

Robert Bruce Shaw notes in *Trust in the Balance* that

at the most basic level, we assume that those we trust will not deliberately take advantage of us. In other words, trust requires that those in whom we place our faith remain responsive to our needs, even in the face of potentially conflicting pressures. Trust, therefore, requires that we . . . show that we understand and are responsive to the needs of others.[11]

Management must deal fairly with both employees and their union if it is to be trusted. This book, however, will not attempt to describe what fair treatment means for employees generally. That question is beyond its scope. Instead, the paragraphs that follow discuss two fairness issues that are unique to union workplaces: how represented employees are treated as compared to non-represented employees and whether the union and its leadership are treated fairly.

For trust to prevail in a unionized workplace, represented employees must be treated fairly as compared to non-represented technical, clerical, supervisory, or managerial staff. This does not mean all groups must be treated the same. Circumstances may require different treatment in areas such as pay, hours, and conditions of work, and the union may have negotiated differences they believe are in the best interests of the employees they represent. In such cases, represented employees may fare better or worse than others, presumably for objective reasons. All things considered, however, group differences of these types are not likely to be of concern because they are obvious and usually subject to negotiation and agreement. The issues are clear enough that both management and union play effective roles in insuring fairness.

The concern about unfair treatment typically involves individual actions that management fails to see or manage, over which the union has little or no control, that arise when represented and non-represented employees subject to the same policy are treated differently for no objective reason. For example, non-represented clerical staff may be treated more leniently in absence from work or disciplinary matters; more lenient performance standards may exist for non-represented supervisors than for represented employees; represented employees may not have an equal opportunity to attain promotions to jobs outside the bargaining unit; or management may take a harder line with represented employees in discharge matters. In these types of cases, represented employees may be treated consistently among themselves and fairly by almost any absolute standards but unfairly relative to non-represented employees. This treatment may exist because of favoritism among non-represented staff, biases against unions, or the feeling that represented employees get better treatment in other areas and the advantages should be evened out. Whatever the reason, a pattern of such disparate treatment can lead to a system that is seen as fundamentally unfair and in which trust cannot exist.

Treating "the union" fairly is an issue because power is such an important aspect of the relationship. Companies are nearly always more powerful than the union representing their employees when power is broadly defined. This places management in an advantaged position in the ongoing relationship and provides many opportunities for exploiting the power disparity and treating union leaders unfairly. Use of coercion is frequently the most problematic, but trust issues can also arise in connection with exercise of less coercive powers such as management's ability to exercise its management rights or control resources and information. Power is more subtle in these areas but is no less significant in establishing or destroying trust. Management can use its advantaged position to cast the union in a bad light, embarrass union leaders, or put them to a significant disadvantage in their bargaining role. It also can demonstrate fairness by actions such as the following:

- Giving union leaders fair and timely access to information, regardless of whether it is legally required.
- Giving the union credit where it is due.
- Not interfering in union politics.
- Not unreasonably using the right to direct the work force to interfere with the union accomplishing its role.
- Avoiding inappropriate direct dealing with employees.

Respect

Respect for individuals and the union as an institution is closely related to fairness but goes a step beyond. Fairness is reflected in the substance of our actions; in what we do without regard to how or why we do it. We may treat people fairly for purely pragmatic or economic reasons that have no relation to respect. Respect is based on how we feel and why we do what we do. It is reflected less in what we do and more in how we do it.

A number of factors in a unionized workplace can foster a lack of respect. Managers and decision makers frequently have a different level of formal education than union-represented employees. Managers may be paid better and have more authority and freedom in the workplace than employees generally. This can lead to different lifestyles and interests, which can cause unthinking, insensitive people among both managers and represented employees to develop an "attitude" and show little or no respect for individuals in the other group. With regard to the union itself, employers frequently would prefer not having their employees represented by a union. Managers may object to unionism generally or have concerns that the presence of a union impinges on management discretion and increases costs. A key role of the union is to challenge management, which can easily lead to lack of respect if management is not receptive or if the challenge is not handled well. Further, some union leaders do not engender respect for themselves and the organization they represent. All these factors combine to create a situation where managers may fail to exhibit respect for the union, union leaders, or employees they represent.

Respect has two dimensions: how one feels, and how the feelings are demonstrated. Arguably, the two can be separated, although over the long term one probably cannot show respect without also feeling it, and one cannot feel respect without showing it.

Developing a feeling of respect for other parties involves internal, highly personal considerations that depend to a great degree on the extent to which the other party earns respect. Managers must do their part, however, by looking inside themselves and assessing the mental models that color their views of union leaders and employees. Some thoughts for doing this and enhancing a feeling of respect are:

- Honestly examine beliefs and mental models. Throw out those that don't square with reality.
- Develop an in-depth knowledge of the work others do and what it requires.
- Get to know employees and union leaders on a personal level. It is easier to respect a friend.
- Remember that even if you don't want a union, your employees do.
- Empathize. See things through the eyes of employees and the union, and share in their emotions and feelings.
- Give them a chance to earn respect. Unions and employees can make a real contribution only if they are allowed the freedom and flexibility to do so.

Feeling respect is of little value in developing trust and fostering a collaborative relationship unless it is demonstrated. Ways of demonstrating respect are, for the most part, personal and obvious. However, some areas managers should give particular attention to in the union/management relationship are:

- Willingly give unions and employees credit where it is due.
- Involve union leaders and employees as key participants in external and social activities.
- Be willing to show vulnerability—both your personal vulnerability and the company's—without suggesting weakness or lack of commitment.
- Meet in employee or union offices or workplaces when feasible.

- Eat together.

- Trust their judgment and be willing to share information with them beyond that required by the bargaining obligation.

- Help union leaders solve their problems. While management must not interfere with the internal business of the union, it frequently is in a position to appropriately do or say things that can help union leadership with their internal problems. Doing so in a balanced and collaborative way can demonstrate real respect for union leaders and their institution.

BUILDING TRUSTWORTHINESS IN OTHERS

The last section discussed ideas for building management trustworthiness. This section recognizes that for collaboration to work employees and union leaders must also be trustworthy. They must wrestle with the same dilemmas involving honesty, integrity, reliability, and justice as management, and like management, their actions may or may not always demonstrate trustworthiness.

John O. Whitney notes in *The Trust Factor: Liberating Profits and Restoring Corporate Vitality* that we must deal with three types of people: "those who would cheerfully cut our throats," "those who would like to cooperate but do not know how," and those "whose goals may be incongruent with ours or those of the enterprise."[12] Unfortunately, employee groups and unions, like other segments of society, have a few individuals of the first type. Bad people do exist. Attempts to bring these individuals around are wasted effort, and such individuals must be dealt with accordingly. Fortunately, however, most individuals we deal with do not have such malevolent intent, and it is a mistake to base our actions for the entire group on the assumption that they do. Most people want to be trusted, and management can help them be more trustworthy.

Management cannot take responsibility for the integrity and behavior of employees and union leaders; not as a group and certainly not for every individual in the group. It can, however, create an environment where the best and most trustworthy tendencies are more likely to win out, and when this happens, the level of trustworthiness of the group is increased. Robert Bruce Shaw notes in *Trust in the Balance*:

In many ways, organizational trust begins and ends with the actions of leadership. Indeed, trust is based on the caliber of leadership within a firm or team. To better understand trust, we can start by examining the personal attributes and behavior of an organization's current and past leaders. Highly credible leaders can, through the sheer impact of their individual influence, overcome distrust and create a trust-based environment.[13]

Fukuyama confirms this view and begins to address how management can make employees and the union more trustworthy:

Figure 10.1
Management-Initiated Cycle of Distrust

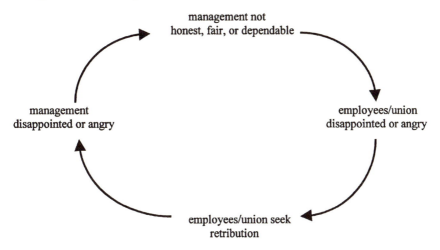

Just as the general level of trust varies greatly among societies, it can also change over time within a society as the result of specific conditions or events. Alvin Gouldner argues that reciprocity is a norm that is shared to some degree by virtually all cultures: that is, if person X does a service for person Y, that person Y will then feel grateful and seek to reciprocate in some manner. But groups can enter into a downward spiral of distrust when trust is repaid with what is perceived as betrayal or exploitation.[14]

The idea of reciprocity and a spiral of trust or distrust is fundamental to the objective of building trustworthiness in others, and systems thinking helps understand how these concepts work and how managers can help employees and union leaders to be more trustworthy. In systems terms, reality is not made of straight lines. Instead, it is composed of circles or loops of cause/effect relationships called feedback processes. These processes are in reality reciprocal flows of influence that are both cause and effect. We all are part of this process. We influence what happens and are influenced by it, and all of us are at least partially responsible for the actions of others with whom we are in contact.

In a management/union relationship this loop of influence can cause a downward spiral in the level of trust. The cycle can begin anywhere and works generally as indicated in Figure 10.1 when management is not trustworthy.

When employees or union leaders fail to exhibit trustworthiness, the cycle appears as in Figure 10.2.

These situations build over time, with bad behavior on the part of one party leading to bad or worse behavior by the other. The spiral can only be reversed if one party takes the initiative to break the cycle. Either party can do so, but management is the party with the most resources and best position to take needed actions. To reverse the cycle and build trustworthiness it must act counter

Figure 10.2
Employee/Union-Initiated Cycle of Distrust

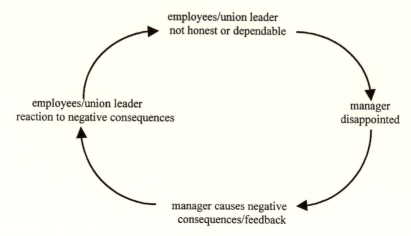

to the influence it is receiving and take action that the union and employees will respond to positively rather than negatively. Doing so may require an initial leap of faith, but the actions that are counter to the negative influence can be quite small at first and commensurate with the risks involved. Over time, as the response becomes positive and reinforcing feedback takes over, larger actions may be introduced, all building to major improvement. This sequence can be illustrated as suggested in Figure 10.3.

To start a cycle of improvement management must assess how to initiate actions that are counter to the influence being received. It must consider why employees and union leaders are not trustworthy, and identify what influences they are reacting to that management can change. Stated differently, management must look at itself through the mirror of its employees and union leaders and identify those areas where its acts or shortcomings are influencing employee and union behavior. The reasons will vary from case to case, but more common ones are:

• They are responding in kind to actions by management that are not trustworthy.

• They are reacting in frustration to the company exercising its disproportionate power. This can happen during an open contract, but is less likely because the union's power may equal or exceed the company's at this time. Frustration is probably more common during the contract period when the management may have the unilateral right to take actions employees and the union disagree with and against which they have little recourse.

• They don't believe management will respond appropriately to trustworthy behavior.

• They are acting as management's behavior suggests they are expected to act. For example, management actions demonstrate it has no confidence in them, and they don't

Figure 10.3
Trust Improvement Cycle

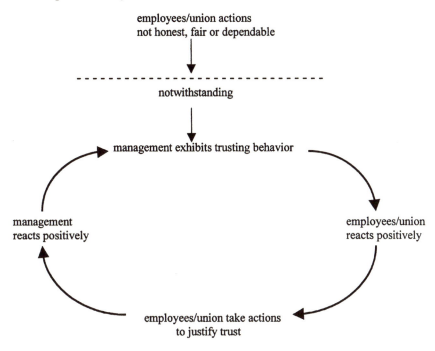

disappoint. It's interesting how so often managers teach employees and union leaders how to be untrustworthy and then are surprised when they get the message.

- They don't have the ability or training to deliver on management's expectations.

The corollary, of course, is what management can do to break the cycle of mistrust and begin an improvement cycle that leads to employees and union leaders being more trustworthy. It can, for example:

- Always act in ways that are completely trustworthy. If misunderstandings arise, openly discuss and freely admit fault if it exists. Don't blame the union leadership.
- Find low-risk ways to show more trust than past behavior or mental models justify. Initially this may involve changes of small consequence or agreements that a disappointed party has the right to revert to the way things have been in the past.
- Acknowledge and reinforce positive actions on the part of employees and union leaders.
- Be willing to share confidential information with union leaders.
- Give union leaders maximum advance notice of, and maximum involvement in, changes to be made during the contract.
- Hire capable employees.

- Provide information, education, and training necessary to insure that both employees and union leaders are able to deliver on expectations.

A final note: be prepared to deal effectively with disappointment. Management can break cycles of mistrust, but it isn't easy and failures and disappointments will occur. Doing so must become a key part of the organizational learning journey.

TRUST IN A POWER RELATIONSHIP

Power is an important aspect of countervailing collaboration that should be acknowledged and accepted by the parties. While use of coercive power to force compliance may be ineffective or even counterproductive, the threat of coercion seems to be an aspect of the management/union relationship that will continue to exist into the foreseeable future. Therefore, a discussion of trust would not be complete without some discussion of the implications of the exercise of coercive power, for it is here that the strain on trust is probably greatest.

Coercive power typically becomes an issue when there is a major disagreement. For example, management may want a major change but employees and the union don't; or employees and union want more, while management wants to give less. Each party is trying to impose its will on the other, frequently by causing economic hurt. Self-interest prevails. Emotions rise. Anger takes over. In this environment, trust can easily become a casualty and almost always suffers when strikes and similar activities occur. Following are some recommendations for maintaining trust when the parties are involved in the exercise of force.

- Acknowledge the legitimacy of coercive power from the beginning. The language of the countervailing collaboration philosophy is intended to do this. While disagreements may occur as to just when or how force is appropriate (e.g., when does the company have the right to unilaterally impose a change), there should never be disagreement on the fundamental proposition that use of force is a legitimate tool for each party.

- Convince employees and union leadership that whatever management is trying to obtain is really needed. If they are convinced, the likelihood of resolving an issue is increased and the need for force may go away. If it doesn't, force is better understood.

- Follow the rules. Rules of conduct exist even for war among nations. The company and union should agree on rules of conduct for strikes, for example, and both parties should adhere to them.

- Don't let the disagreement become personal. The disagreement should be between ideas, beliefs, and institutions. Keeping it there enhances the chances of maintaining trust on a personal level.

- Let there be no surprises. Don't trade off the long-term, strategic value of a trusting relationship for the perceived advantage of surprise in negotiations or in a power conflict. This, of course, requires honesty throughout the entire process. If a company interest warrants use of force, make this clear from the beginning.

- Don't abuse management's power. For example, management should not attempt to penalize the union for unsuccessful collective actions by extracting punitive concessions in negotiations, insisting on positions for the purpose of embarrassing union leaders, or voluntarily granting something employees want after it has refused to agree to a union proposal for it.
- Don't threaten use of coercive power unless you plan to use it if necessary.
- Do not compromise the values of management. This means do not compromise them in the exploitation of a position of power, and do not sell out to avoid short-term pain when the union has the power.
- Have the person who holds the power exercise it. The senior operating manager, and not subordinate staff specialists, should personally explain why force is necessary and management's commitment to using it.

KEY POINTS

1. In a unionized workplace trust must exist among the company, the individual representatives of the company, represented employees, the union that represents them, and the leaders of that union.
2. Management is likely to be seen as trustworthy if:
   - Its actions are based on its core values and are reasonably predictable.
   - It tells the truth and matches actions with its words.
   - It deals fairly with employees and the union.
   - It shows respect for individuals and the union as an institution.
3. Management can cause others to be more trustworthy by taking actions that break the cycle of mistrust and begin a cycle of trust.
4. Use of coercive power puts a strain on trust, but when acknowledged as legitimate and exercised appropriately the effect can be minimized.

NOTES

1. Francis Fukuyama, *Trust* (New York: Simon and Schuster, 1995), p. 26.
2. Robert Bruce Shaw, *Trust in the Balance* (San Francisco: Jossey-Bass, 1997), p. 21.
3. Kathleen D. Ryan and Daniel K. Oestreich, *Driving Fear Out of the Workplace*, 2nd ed. (San Francisco: Jossey-Bass, 1998), p. 44.
4. Thomas A. Kochan, Harry C. Katz, and Robert B. McKersie, *The Transformation of American Industrial Relations* (New York: Basic Books, 1986), p. 175.
5. Peter M. Senge, *The Fifth Discipline* (New York: Doubleday, 1990), p. 224.
6. Fukuyama, *Trust*, p. 153.
7. Robert L. Dilenschneider, *On Power* (New York: HarperCollins, 1994), p. 41.
8. Ibid., p. 30.
9. Shaw, *Trust in the Balance*, p. 63.
10. Chris Argyris, *On Organizational Learning* (Cambridge, Mass.: Blackwell, 1992), p. 47.
11. Shaw, *Trust in the Balance*, p. 83.

12. John O. Whitney, *The Trust Factor: Liberating Profits and Restoring Corporate Vitality* (New York: McGraw-Hill, 1994), p. 6.

13. Shaw, *Trust in the Balance*, p. 105.

14. Fukuyama, *Trust*, p. 226.

Chapter 11

The Power Paradox

The story of unionism is a story of management power, union countervailing power, and the rise and fall of the two over time. Early property owning industrialists frequently used their personal power to protect their own property from competition and financial pressures by holding wages down, cutting costs, and taking other actions that were at their workers' expense. Individual workers had little power, and their alternatives were to accept the demands of their employers or join with others in collective action against them. By the end of the eighteenth century they increasingly chose the latter course and early trade unions came into being.

Early trade unions, primarily encompassing skilled crafts, waged blunt attacks on employer actions of the time. Their demands, frequently addressing basic issues such as wage levels, apprenticeship programs, and union security were enforced by their willingness to strike if necessary.

Such actions led employers to seek ways to increase their power. They formed employers' associations for the purpose of holding wages down and destroying labor combinations, and they asked the courts to declare worker organizations illegal conspiracies in constraint of trade.

Unions responded by seeking to organize more non-union groups and form organizations of unions on a city-wide or national basis that allowed for broader joint action and pursuit of significant political agendas. Union power ebbed and flowed during the 1800s, with their bargaining power and economic gains flourishing during times of economic prosperity and all but disappearing during periods of economic depression. Continuing efforts to increase union power led to formation in 1886 of the American Federation of Labor, a consolidation of skilled worker unions, and in 1935 to the Congress of Industrial Organizations, a federation of workers primarily in the mass production industries.

Union power was further enhanced by passage of the Wagner Act in 1935 that, among other things, placed specific restrictions on what employers could or could not do and established secret ballot elections as the method for determining whether a union would represent employees. During World War II unions were granted equal representation with management on the War Labor Board, the institution that adjusted collective bargaining disputes during this period.

The 1947 passage of the Taft-Hartley Act amended the Wagner Act to give greater protection to employers and individual employees by outlining six "unfair" union practices. This tended to level the playing field from a legal viewpoint and provided the framework for current labor relations.

Relative power continued to ebb and flow, with union power reaching its low point in the 1980s and 1990s as increasing foreign competition drove managements to take stronger stands for major change. Union membership continued to decline, with the percentage of the private work force belonging to unions dropping by more than half to about 10 percent by 1997. The decline was exacerbated by President Reagan's breaking of the air traffic controllers' strike in 1981, followed by union setbacks in the United Auto Workers seventeen-month strike against Caterpillar and the Newspaper Guild action against the *Detroit Free Press* and *Detroit News*.

Is there evidence of a shift back to more union power in the late 1990s? Early reports concerning the 1997 Teamsters' strike against UPS suggested the union was the winner, signaling that the decline in union strength had bottomed out or perhaps union strength had begun to increase. The 1998 United Auto Workers strike against General Motors reportedly cost the company $2.2 billion and slowed the pace of that company's restructuring. But there are differing views as to which parties won in these cases, and many view them as one-off actions that do not indicate a trend. Strikes involving 1,000 or more workers in 1998 were at the lowest level since World War II, and union membership remained stagnant. The fact remains, however, that regardless of the power balance across the labor movement, power and its use remain an important issue at the individual company level.

Use of power will no doubt continue on both sides, as managements insist on their right to make changes they believe necessary for the business, unions resist, and the parties resort to power to resolve the resulting issues. The institutional framework in which labor/management relations take place permits, or perhaps encourages, use of power, and there is no reason to believe its use will materially decline in the foreseeable future. Management must be prepared to use its power, for it will be subjected to power and it has an obligation to stakeholders to use power as necessary to manage the business in their best interest. At the same time, it has an obligation to stakeholders, including employees, to understand all facets of the power it holds and to use all of them in a balanced and fair way as appropriate for optimizing corporate objectives. The purpose of this chapter is to foster such use of power.

PRINCIPLES

Power is someone or some group "imposing its will and purpose or purposes on others, including on those who are reluctant or adverse."[1] Or it is the "ability to get things done,"[2] "the ability to get people to do things,"[3] or "the potential to influence others for good or evil."[4] These brief definitions answer the what—the ability to make things happen—but don't address the types of power, where one gets it, or how it is used.

Galbraith addresses these issues as follows:

- "Condign power wins submission by the ability to impose an alternate to the preferences of the individual or group that is sufficiently unpleasant or painful so that these preferences are abandoned." It "wins submission by inflicting or threatening appropriately adverse consequences."
- "Compensatory power, in contrast, wins submission by the offer of affirmative reward—by the giving of something of value to the individual so submitting."
- "Conditioned power, in contrast, is exercised by changing belief. Persuasion, education, or the social commitment to what seems natural, proper, or right causes the individual to submit to the will of another or of others."[5]

Galbraith also suggests that the sources of power are personality, or personal power; property, or the ability to change the will of another by purchase; and organization, or the uniting of groups of persons for a common purpose.

In *The Power Principle*, Blaine Lee lists three types of power almost identical to Galbraith's:[6]

- Coercive power is based on fear and is the power to influence behavior by doing something to someone.
- Utility power is based on what people can do for each other and is the power to influence behavior by doing something for someone.
- Principle-centered power is based on honor extended to one from others and is the power to do things with another.

Lee maintains principle-centered power is clearly the most desirable, followed by utility power and coercive power, both of which have many drawbacks.

Dilenschneider takes a slightly different approach. He asserts that competence and ideas are the foundation of power and that several evolving modalities or tools of power are based on this foundation. These are not seen as evolving from wrong to right but as transitional and directional. They are as follows:[7]

- Intimidation versus voluntarism—From fear, threats, and momentum to motivating others to want to do what one wants.
- Belligerence versus mediation—From physical aggression or litigation to listening for the truth.

- Order-giving versus empowerment—From autocratic command to providing access to the actual right to decide.

- Decree versus consensus—From a single decision maker to everyone helping make the same roster of decisions.

In *The Power of Influence*[8] Tom Lambert cites Galbraith's discussion of power and then provides a more detailed list of types of power we wield in the workplace to get people to do what we want. He lists:

- Resource power where I control resources others value.
- Information power where I have access to information others need or desire.
- Position power where I hold a powerful position in the social or business hierarchy.
- Proxy power derived from my friends in high places.
- Reward power where I can reward those who comply with my wishes.
- Sanctions power where I can punish those who don't comply with my wishes.
- Expert power derived from my knowledge and expertise.
- Personal power where people do as I wish because they like me and want to model their behavior on mine.
- Status power where others defer to my status or position in the group.
- Charisma power derived from my personality, vision, enthusiasm, and/or charm.
- Favor power where I build a bank of favors and call them in when I need compliance.
- Technical power where I influence behavior with knowledge and skill.

A few key points emerge from these models. Power is the ability to make things happen. Different types or sources of power fall within one of three general types: forcing, buying, or persuading. These concepts provide a backdrop for consideration of labor/management power.

POWER IN A UNIONIZED WORKPLACE

The term "power" has been used in different ways in the labor/management relationship. One definition has been "the ability of one party to achieve its goals in bargaining in the presence of opposition by another party to the process."[9] Another is "the capacity of a party to produce an agreement on its own terms."[10]

Charles S. Loughran notes in *Negotiating a Labor Contract* that the bottom line in any negotiation is bargaining leverage, which "can be gauged by *the relative willingness of each side to incur the consequences of not reaching an agreement.*" He discusses the following sources of employer bargaining power:

- Employer's Financial Condition
- Anticipated Demand for Product(s) or Service(s)

- Ability to Supply or Service Customers
  - —Product or Service Inventory
  - —Farming Out/Contracting
  - —Operating Struck Facilities
- Mutual Aid or Mutual Assistance Pacts

Loughran lists the following sources of union bargaining power:

- Recent Levels of Employment Hours and Earnings
- Strike Fund
- Availability of Government Subsidies
- Alternative Employment Opportunities[11]

Thus power can be defined as the ability of one party to force its will on the other: management by unconstrained use of its managerial and economic might and the union by engaging in punitive job actions as deemed necessary. But power is much broader. It involves much more than the ability of management and the union to impose their will by threats and coercion.

A broader definition of power starts by questioning the objective of power use. Compliance is the objective in the conventional view. In this situation, one party wishes to do something or have the other party do something, so it uses its power to get the other to comply with its wishes. Management attempts to use its power to overcome the power of the union to resist management initiatives or to impose union initiatives. If successful, the union and employees comply with management's wishes. While compliance may be important in any labor/management relationship, it is a limited objective when attained by forcing or purchase.

Thinking more broadly, and in the context of the labor/management change model, management's objective goes well beyond compliance. Its objective is to focus all available resources on fulfilling the purpose of the organization. It must, therefore, use all its power to that end and also focus the power of its employees and the union on the same objective. Such confluence of power is necessary to bring together the talent and energy of all the parties in order to provide the best chance of accomplishing the purpose of the organization. Unlike the more limited objective of attaining compliance, this objective requires use of all the power of all the parties.

Three types of power held by all parties to the labor/ management relationship can be described, based generally on those suggested by Galbraith and Lee.

- Coercive power is the power to require or force one's will without willing agreement by the other parties.
- Utility power is the power to buy what one wants.

- Collaborative power is the power in the hearts and minds of all parties to accomplish common objectives.

Each of the three parties—management, employees and the union—has different types of power, but all can be placed in one of the three categories. Reasonable people can differ about how types of power are best categorized, but such analysis provides a discipline that is helpful in addressing how to best utilize management power. Accordingly, following is an analysis of the power of each of the three parties in the labor/management relationship, followed by some brief observations about the relationships among them.

Management Power

Coercive Power.

- Capital power is the inherent power derived by management from the investment in the business. Management made the decision to invest capital under its control, decided what business to invest it in, and continues to make major investment and divestment decisions. Over the long term such decisions are at the heart of whether a continuing business and employment relationship exists.

- Management rights power flows directly from the investment decision and the reserved rights doctrine, which holds that, absent a union, implied terms of the unwritten contract of employment give the employer absolute discretion over terms and conditions of employment that are within the law. Anti-discrimination statutes, state court decisions, labor contracts, and past practice have made substantial inroads in management rights. Notwithstanding these limitations, employers generally have retained the legal right to direct the work force and to exercise discretion over a broad range of subjects not covered by law or contract. This legal right to implement a change, frequently over the union's objection, is an important power. It is further strengthened by the "work now, grieve later" concept, which requires employees to comply with orders of management and seek a determination of appropriateness after the fact, except in rare cases such as the likelihood of imminent danger.

- Bargaining power is the ability of management to impose its will on the union/employees during an open contract, when it has the legal right to do so. Threats, belligerence, and intimidation may be factors in this situation, but "Holding other things constant, . . . the simplest measure of bargaining power is the amount of strike leverage each party holds."[12] From management's perspective, strike leverage is a function of its ability to minimize the cost of a strike as compared to the union's ability to maintain one over a period of time. Management can minimize cost by activities such as stockpiling production, maintaining operations with supervisors or temporary replacements, hiring permanent replacements, and maintaining positive customer relations.

- Disciplinary power is the power vested in management to take appropriate punitive measures to enforce its rules and regulations. This power may be limited by contract, but management generally has the right to take action and the employees/union may subsequently protest through the arbitration procedure.

Utility Power.

- Financial power is the ability of management to buy what it wants in the negotiating process. The company may choose to purchase union and employee agreement where its contract prevents unilateral change or where the company has the right to implement a change but the union has the right and power to resist it through collective action.

- Resource power is the ability to draw on key persons, information, goods, or services that will help the company prevail in the negotiating process. For example, management can draw on staff resources to gather and prepare data or to prepare a negotiating strategy that will help insure that it effectively utilizes its other types of power.

- Reward power is the power to reward people who do what management wants done. This is different from the financial power, noted above, used in the negotiation process to purchase agreement. Reward power contemplates rewards under management control that can influence individual behavior, such as positive feedback, public recognition, and promotions to non-represented jobs.

Collaborative Power.

- Position power is derived from management's leadership role and its responsibility for the overall success of the enterprise. Managers have the license to make requests, and their job titles and location in the organizational hierarchy influence others to listen and comply. Therefore, management is positioned to drive the overall relationship, initiate action, and cause things to happen.

- Information power exists when management controls access to information that is necessary for accomplishing organizational goals or relevant to the employment relationship. Management typically controls much information that is not generally available to employees or the union, such as information about individual employees, company performance, industry developments, business plans, and benefit plan performance. Such information can be a source of utility power in the bargaining process. More importantly, however, much of the information management controls can be used to affect the ability or inclination of employees to do their jobs and to maximize their contribution to organizational success.

- Expertise power is derived from the special skills, knowledge, or expertise that management has or has access to that can be used to accomplish organizational goals. Such expertise may exist in the managers themselves, non-represented technical employees, outside consultants, represented employees, or others under the control of management. The effect of this power can be expanded if it is passed to and utilized by employees throughout the workplace.

- Appraisal power is based on the ability of management to give feedback to employees about the efficiency or effectiveness of their efforts. If properly handled, such feedback informs employees of what needs to be done and encourages them to do it. Appraisal power addresses the implicit, internal motivation of people who draw satisfaction from a job well done.

Employee Power

Coercive Power.

- Legal power is the ability of employees to resist management actions or enforce their will by relying on state or federal laws such as those proscribing discrimination or requiring a minimum wage, overtime pay, or minimum health and safety standards. This power exists regardless of whether or not employees are represented by a union.

- Contractual power is the ability to enforce, typically through arbitration if necessary, the terms of a negotiated contract covering wages, hours, and conditions of work. The extent of power, however, depends on the ability of the union to negotiate an effective labor contract and enforce it through arbitration if necessary. If a union has negotiated a comprehensive contract it is willing and able to defend, employee contractual power is great. Conversely, if the union is unable to negotiate or enforce such a contract, employee contractual power is lacking.

Utility Power. Employees as individuals have little utility power. An implicit aspect of their employment contract is the obligation to exercise their best efforts under the terms and conditions laid down by the employer. Thus, following the rules and optimizing their individual work contribution are generally minimum expectations and not available to buy anything. Employees may withhold utility through actions such as slowdowns, sick-outs, or work to rule in order to resist management's will or to enforce their own. However, such actions typically are illegal or in contravention of labor contracts.

Collaborative Power.

- Information power exists when employees have access to information that is important for accomplishing organizational goals. They have unique access to information that ranges from personal information about themselves and others that can materially affect morale and job performance to information about work processes that is not generally available to supervisors and managers. Employees' effective use of such information, including communication to management when appropriate, is critical to effective organizational performance.

- Expertise power is derived from the special skills, knowledge, or expertise of employees that are relevant to accomplishing organizational goals and that frequently exceed those possessed by management. Power exists in employee willingness to effectively and efficiently utilize this expertise or to share it with others in the best interest of organizational goals.

- Instrumental power, as defined by Lee in *The Power Principle*, is the power of a "can-do person, who has the capacity to get things done, mobilize others, get a group moving, or take needed action."[13] Individual employees have frequent opportunities to exercise initiative and leadership if they choose to do so. The ability to make this choice gives them significant power to affect organizational performance.

- Relation power is derived from the ability of employees to affect the behavior and performance of others with whom they work. For example, in integrated work systems the willingness of workers to openly communicate directly affects the ability of others to perform. Employee ability to control such relationships gives them the power to materially effect organizational performance.

Union Power

Coercive Power.

- Legal power is primarily the ability of a union to force management to comply with the National Labor Relations Act. For example, unions can use the law to force employers to bargain, prevent anti-union animus or discrimination, and enforce its contracts with the employer. It is important to note, however, that the Act addresses process and not substance. It gives unions the right to negotiate and enforce contracts, but other sources of power determine the substance of the contracts. These other sources may include the legal power to cause enforcement of environmental, safety, or other similar laws, perhaps as part of a corporate campaign intended to intensify government monitoring or cause customers or investors to withdraw their support.

- Contractual power is basically the same power described for individual employees. A union's contractual power is greater than an individual's, however, because it has the power to negotiate the contract in the first instance and to make final decisions regarding enforcement actions.

- Punitive power is in two forms. First, it is the ability of unions, typically through actions of employees they represent, to punish companies for actions with which they disagree. Vehicles for this punishment include activities such as strikes, boycotts, inside games, and corporate campaigns. Second, it is the ability of the union to punish its own members in order to maintain discipline within the ranks. This punitive power may be exercised in an informal manner or through formal procedures contained in the union constitution, and it may be required to maintain discipline among employees who collectively are taking punitive action against a company.

Utility Power. Unions, like individuals, have limited utility power as compared to employers. Although they do have the ability to reward employees through political appointments or other favors, it is not their role to pay wages and benefits, so they cannot purchase agreements by bringing money to the negotiating table. They do, however, have the following sources of utility power:

- Resource power, similar to the definition for management, is the ability to draw on key persons, information, goods, or services that will help the union prevail in the negotiating process.

- Concession power is the union's counterpart to the company's financial power. When the company wants a concession in negotiations it may buy it with financial or other economically significant offers. Absent an ability to do this, a union may choose to buy a company concession or agreement by conceding a benefit negotiated previously and contained in the existing contract, such as doing away with work assignment constraints or reducing benefit levels. This is a power that unions use very reluctantly and usually only as a last resort, but it is one way unions have to buy agreements or management concessions.

Collaborative Power.

- Information power is basically as described for management and individuals. Union leaders frequently have unique access to information that is valuable to the business, such as information relating to needs, desires, and morale of employees; what is really going on in the workplace; the current rumors; and information regarding competitors. Considering such information can substantially improve the decision process, and the union's control of it allows union leaders to affect the quality of decisions being made.

- Relation power is derived from the ability of the union to affect the behavior of employees in the bargaining unit. A union's ability to discipline individual members for failing to conform with union rules and initiatives can be a major factor in its ability to use coercive power to force its will on management. Union leaders, by the way they characterize and deal with management, can also materially affect the attitude and behavior of employees toward their work and management. If union leaders are positive about company initiatives in day-to-day contact with employees they represent, those employees are more likely to adopt similar attitudes that can enhance organizational performance.

Observations

It is now possible to make certain observations about the power of management, individual employees, and unions. First, while it is a helpful analytical tool, such categorizing of power oversimplifies the situation. The types of power listed are important, but in many cases other sources of power also exist. Further, types of power were placed in discrete categories on the basis of how they are frequently used, when in fact they are interdependent parts of a system in which they are used in different ways, sometimes simultaneously. Categorizing is valuable because it helps management think about when and how each type of power is currently being used and how it should be used to attain organizational objectives.

Second, companies and unions do not have the level of independence generally contemplated by many power models. Lee notes in *The Power Principle* that:

Independence is the hallmark of utility power. While coercive power relies on dependence and submission, utility power relies on freedom. Those involved in a transaction are independent—they can walk away from the deal if they don't like what's happening. And just as they are free to leave, they are also free to stay. In fact, if you are not free to walk away, you are not free to choose to stay. In that case, you are operating in the world of coercive power.[14]

Companies and unions are not independent. Companies cannot walk away from the relationship because the law prohibits their doing so, and unions cannot walk away because doing so would be self-destructive. Both parties know they must continue to work together, and they know the use of coercive power is always possible. In fact, the presence or threat of coercive power is in a real sense its use. Thus, the use of pure collaborative or utility power is generally polluted by the environment in which the parties cannot walk away and either party may ultimately choose to use whatever coercive power it possesses to resolve an issue in its favor.

A short-term exception may exist when one party proposes a change in an existing contract during its term. In this case, the contract prevails unless the parties agree to a change, coercion is not legal or appropriate for either party, and either party may discontinue the discussions at any time. Thus, while a contract is in force, utility or collaborative power can work with little coercive overlay. Even in this case, however, either party may be haunted by the fact that when the contract term expires, the other party may legally use coercion to address the issue. Thus, all types of power are relevant for all change issues, and management must optimize the use of all three for the best long-term results.

Third, the parties are not of equal, or even approximately equal, power. Managements who have made major concessions due to fear of a strike, who have just been "defeated" in a strike action by a powerful and well-disciplined union, or who manage entities that are highly labor intensive and cannot be operated during a strike could disagree. For example, in the General Motors and American Airlines actions discussed earlier the unions had great coercive power through their ability to impose huge financial losses in a very short time. But in the broader context—in the context of the ability to make things happen in the organization—management has superior power. It has the coercive power to require a multitude of operational actions on a day-to-day basis (if not larger changes in the face of a strike), substantial utility power where employees and union have very little, and collaborative power derived from its leadership role and unique access to information. The implications of this disparity are significant for the type of relationship that can exist between company and union, and for management's obligation to take the lead in using its different types of power in ways that best benefit the organization.

POWER PARADOXES

The paradoxes of power appear on the surface to be self-contradictory, but in fact they help us understand how the various types of power can best be used.

The Paradox of Unintended Results

The exercise of coercive and utility power frequently has unintended results that are self-defeating, as their use for a positive purpose frequently has negative results. Galbraith[15] has noted that

We may lay it down as a rule that almost any manifestation of power will induce an opposite, though not necessarily equal, manifestation of power. Any effort to bend people to the will of others will encounter in some form an effort to resist that submission. On the relative effectiveness of these opposing forces depend the extent and effectiveness of the exercise of the original power.

He cites "the classic struggle between employer and employee, capital and labor" as illustrative of the point, noting the Carnegie Homestead Works strike of 1892 and the great labor conflicts of the 1930s as examples.

Lee notes that coercive power, while perhaps necessary in a genuine emergency or in cases of danger, generally does not work over the long term. Relationships are poisoned, learning is subverted, resistance is fostered, and spirits are broken. Significantly, he notes that "The coercive leader must be all-seeing, because his eyes alone are committed to success. The responsibility for accomplishing the task is his alone. Others only do what they are told, what they are forced to do, what they are made to do. They only do it when someone is standing over them, physically or figuratively. They comply because they have no other option."[16]

Dilenschneider expresses a similar view when asserting that "Today, power is paradoxically at odds with the instinct to control."[17] Even if true control can be attained, which is doubtful, we are in a world of change that requires great flexibility, and those who invest the time and energy in a search for absolute control are thrown off balance when the world around them changes and they cannot adapt.

Thomas Gordon in *Leadership Effectiveness Training* notes that we tend to ignore what the use of coercive power actually does to people and their relationships, and he outlines several typical reactions:

Reduction in Upward Communication

Apple-polishing and Other Ingratiating Reactions

Destructive Competitiveness and Rivalry

Submission and Conformity

Rebellion and Defiance

Forming Alliances and Coalitions

Withdrawing and Escaping[18]

Although use of utility power does not create quite the negative backlash of coercive power, it also has a dark side. Lee acknowledges that utility power often gets us what we want but states, "Although it feels better than the force and fear common in the world of coercive power, it is still temporary and conditional: if the situation changes in any way, your power could evaporate. In utility-centered relationships, everything is always up for grabs."[19] Thus, use of utility power leads to an attitude of "what have you done for me lately," as we all tend to rather quickly forget what we were paid, while remembering for a long time what we sold.

The Paradox of Power Sharing

Collaborative power is of limited use if management tries to hold on to it. As Dilenschneider notes, "One of the cornerstones of power in the 1990s is that those who know how to use real power know how to share it effectively."[20] This is because ideas and knowledge, the foundations of power, are essentially collaborative and constantly changing, which means that to retain power, and certainly to see it grow, we all must continue to learn from each other. We must give our ideas and knowledge—our power—to others, and receive and use theirs in return. Such sharing of ideas and knowledge, which leads to learning and increased power, is the essence of collaboration.

Because power is relational and comes from many sources, it is not a zero-sum game. Sharing collaborative power with employees and union leaders allows a synergy and commitment that leads to a net gain in available power. Therefore, management must leave behind old ideas focused almost exclusively on coercive power, and grant unions and represented employees power in operational decisions and other matters where learning, growth, and mutual gain are possible.

The Paradox of Effective Use

The third paradox is that "power must be used effectively in order to successfully surrender that power to others."[21] Things don't just happen, and simply letting go of power does not mean that others will pick it up and use it properly. New and different uses of power must be encouraged, given direction, and rewarded if they are to be effective. This requires strong management leadership.

The need for strong leadership is particularly true in a union setting, where a management that wants to engage the hearts and minds of employees by surrendering power to them may meet unusually strong resistance. Employees and the union are likely to believe that any change violates their contract or is a threat to their jobs. Union leaders may see empowered employees as more independent and with less need for a union. Or some managers may be reluctant to share power because of fear the union may take, expand, and use those powers against the company's interest.

In this situation, management may need to negotiate new contract language to allow more worker involvement, or develop a relationship with union leaders that encourages them to foster enhanced worker participation. It must exercise forceful leadership to insure the business purpose is clearly understood and to provide direction for employees who are exercising new powers. It also may need to provide education and training opportunities that show employees how to use their new power. Whatever the case, management must use its power to deal with employees and the union in order to effectively share its collaborative power with employees.

EXERCISING POWER IN LIGHT OF THE PARADOXES

A management that is seeking more than mere compliance with its directives and is instead trying to engage the hearts and minds of employees and gain the support of the union representing them must deal with these paradoxes on a day-to-day basis. Following are some ideas for doing this.

Avoiding Unintended Consequences

To avoid unintended consequences management must understand and antici- pate the reaction each type of power is likely to engender. The types of power were discussed earlier. Employee and union reaction to the various types of power may vary along a continuum represented by the following:

- Active resistance, where employees and/or the union resist change through actions such as the grievance procedure, inside games, picketing, strikes, or boycotts.
- Passive resistance, where employees, with or without support of their union, use in- formal, individual actions to attempt to resist management change.
- Coerced compliance, where employees comply with management's directions reluc- tantly and only because they have no effective or practical ways to resist.
- Willing compliance, where employees willingly do what they are told but nothing more.
- Reactive support, where employees react positively to management's directives and do all they reasonably can to support them.
- Proactive support, where employees share the organization's objectives and use their own initiative to support them.

Management's objective must be to emphasize those aspects of its power that are most likely to lead to union and employee responses in the supportive area of the continuum. While one cannot precisely state what specific response will result from use of particular types of power, one can predict with virtual cer- tainty areas along the continuum within which response to a particular exercise of power will fall. Figure 11.1 demonstrates this.

One may disagree about exactly where on the continuum the response to a particular type of power is most likely to fall, but it clearly demonstrates the paradoxes. Use of strong coercive power is most likely to lead to unintended results in the form of strong active or passive resistance, and the most that can be hoped for is compliance. Utility power is essentially neutral and likely to cause little resistance but can lead to compliance and perhaps some reactive support. Only collaborative power, which requires forceful leadership and shar- ing, is likely to garner true employee support and engagement in that higher order of work that is necessary for success in a competitive world.

On its face the Action/Response Continuum suggests avoiding coercive and utility power in favor of collaborative power. But life isn't that simple. The

Figure 11.1
Action/Response Continuum

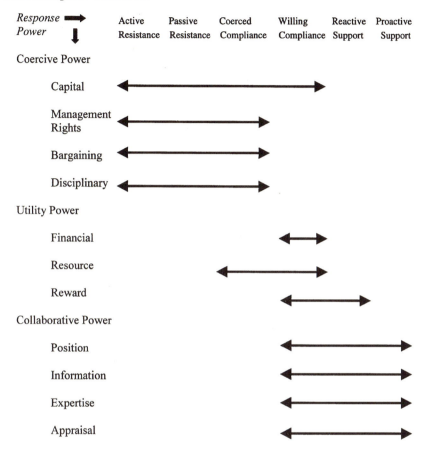

Response ➡ *Power* ⬇	Active Resistance	Passive Resistance	Coerced Compliance	Willing Compliance	Reactive Support	Proactive Support
Coercive Power						
Capital	◄─────────────────────────────►					
Management Rights	◄──────────────►					
Bargaining	◄──────────────►					
Disciplinary	◄──────────────►					
Utility Power						
Financial				◄──►		
Resource			◄──────────►			
Reward				◄──────►		
Collaborative Power						
Position				◄──────────────►		
Information				◄──────────────►		
Expertise				◄──────────────►		
Appraisal				◄──────────────►		

National Labor Relations Act requires bargaining with the union, and the NLRB considers whether give and take (use of utility power) actually happened as an indicator of whether the parties have complied with the law. Further, difficulties and disagreements will occur, mutually beneficial arrangements are not always possible, and the parties cannot walk away, so it is unrealistic to expect them to abstain completely from the use of coercive or utility power. Thus, management should not do away with such power, or fail to use it under any circumstance. Doing this would destroy its credibility and abrogate its responsibility. Rather, management should use the full range of its power to foster the most constructive response feasible but give priority to those types of power most likely to garner a supportive response.

Unfortunately, this priority is frequently not the case. In open warfare, adversarial, and often even in accommodating relationships, management uses its coercive power first, and if that doesn't work it then uses its utility power and finally its collaborative power. In such cases management unilaterally decides what it wants and then simply announces what it intends to do. The announcement may be fashioned as a proposal if bargaining is required, but if there is disagreement after appropriate bargaining the result is determined by the coercive powers of the parties. The company uses its capital, management rights, and/or bargaining power to force its will; and the union and employees resist by exercising their legal and contractual power or resorting to punitive use of the various pressure tactics available to them. The matter is determined by law, decree, bluff, threat, pressure, and/or intimidation.

If coercive power is not available or doesn't work, management then tries to use utility power to purchase what it cannot get by coercion. It engages in trading things of value, attempting to get the most for the least by narrowing the negotiation to what it will take to solve management's problem. But use of utility power is not independent of coercive power because the parties are not independent. Each party considers not only the relative value of the items to be traded but also the ability and willingness of the other party to use coercion to get its way and the risk of losing if a deal isn't struck. While the parties may exchange utility through bargaining, the context remains one of coercion, and the best response management can realistically hope for is compliance.

Finally, if both coercive and utility power fail to resolve an issue, the parties give up on the formal processes and resort to collaborative power. They use informal dialogue, education, and collaboration to address the ''real'' problem and do the right thing to meet the needs of both parties. In this situation, however, collaboration follows the previous failures and must address not only the original issue but also all the issues arising from the company's power play and the union's resistance to it. Even when the original issue is resolved, the impact of the attempted use of coercive power and the reaction to it is likely to remain. If so, compliance, not true support, is the result.

Countervailing collaboration uses the same types of power, including coercive and utility power. It recognizes that the purpose of a union is to harness and use the collective power of employees, which is largely coercive and that only the most naive employer would fail to be prepared to respond to this. To deny the existence and potential use of coercive power would cast serious doubts on the truthfulness, credibility, or competence of management.

Countervailing collaboration, however, gives priority to those types of management power most likely to attain a supportive response; that is, collaborative power derived from its position of leadership and the information and expertise it possesses. Management does not deny the existence or potential use of all types of power but initially emphasizes those types of power most likely to engender the response it wants within the interdependent context of the management/union relationship. To obtain a supportive response, management must use its collaborative power first in an effort to arrive at a solution that employees understand, buy in to, and view as in their best interest. If this doesn't work, the give and take of bargaining (use of utility power) may be required to enhance the possibility of an acceptable resolution or perhaps because it is a required legal step. Management must use its information, expertise, and other resources to obtain the most mutually beneficial bargaining outcome that is feasible within the context of the relationship where use of coercive power is a potential.

Finally, if management needs to use coercive power, it should do so as a last resort. Countervailing collaboration adopts the perspective noted in *Bargaining: Power, Tactics, and Outcomes* that use of coercive power is acceptable but

Punitive tactics are antithetical to bargaining if overused, used too early in the bargaining, or used indiscriminately. Punitive tactics are to be adopted only when all else fails (Tedeschic and Bonoma, 1972), and the only justifications for punitive tactics are the failure of the opponent to support the normative framework and the depletion of other options for influencing the opponent.[22]

Sharing Power with Union Leaders

The collaborative power of union leaders can help the organization in two ways. First, union leaders can contribute their information, expertise, and ability. They often are employees or former employees who have an excellent knowledge of the business, and typically they are close to the pulse of the work force. Thus, they are an excellent source of information and knowledge necessary to manage effectively. Second, union leaders can use their influence to focus the collaborative power of employees on company objectives. They are the informal thought leaders among the work force and the go-betweens in the management/ employee relationship on many subjects. Union leaders cannot or will not use their power to help the company, however, unless they are presented with opportunities, are working from the same information and expertise as management, and have an incentive to do so arising from a feeling of ownership in success of the enterprise.

Management's best hope for providing the opportunities and ownership necessary to focus union power on company performance is to share its collaborative power with union leaders. This sharing of power will encourage union leaders to direct their considerable collaborative power toward management objectives when they understand the need and see a mutual benefit. This, in turn, frequently leads to a synergy that enhances the overall result.

The key to empowering union leaders is in sharing problem-solving and decision processes with them. Unions are elected because employees want more influence with management, and employees expect their union leaders to have and use that influence. Unless management shares its decision processes through collaboration, the only opportunity for union influence is through use of its legal rights, using coercion if necessary: after management announces plans, the union can react, resist, and attempt to force a change. The union can have a more collaborative effect, however, if it is given an opportunity. To provide this opportunity, management can delegate its right to make certain decisions to union representatives in areas where they have equal or better information and a mutual interest in success. For example, management might ask union leaders to select employees for participation on a team addressing a business issue, or it might have a union member in the lead role in a joint accident investigation.

More importantly, however, management should involve union leaders in the decision process as often as feasible, even where it is unwilling to give up the right to make the final decision. To do this, management must provide union leaders the opportunity to be in the room when the decision is made, so they can provide meaningful input, argue their case, and understand the decision on the spot. If this is not feasible, management should inform union leaders in advance and give them an opportunity to provide legitimate input that is considered in the final decision.

This sharing goes well beyond bargaining. In conventional bargaining, management does not involve the union in permissive areas, and in mandatory areas it decides on its position and attempts to buy acceptance. The union has no input or influence on broader financial or entrepreneurial issues and limited influence on workplace concerns because it is only involved in the final stages of the decision on mandatory subjects. On the other hand, where collaborative power is shared, union leaders are involved in discussions broader than wages, hours, and conditions of work. They are involved in early discussion of management needs and in formulating how those can be best met. This will be discussed in more detail in connection with discussion of mutual gains bargaining.

Some examples of specific activities that share power and involve the union in the decision process are:

- Having union leaders select employee participants on teams and other ad hoc work activities. Union leaders are likely to have more information and make a better selection; and certainly employees and the union are more likely to support the activity if the union picks the participants.

- Openly sharing all nonconfidential information the union leadership wants or could want. Early exposure to such information can only increase understanding and the likelihood of support.

- Discussing with union leaders in advance and in detail those management decisions of a broad, entrepreneurial nature where bargaining is not required. Increased understanding and consideration of the potential impacts on employees and the union can reduce the motivation to resist and foster support.

- Inviting union representatives to participate in joint investigation of issues such as safety incidents or potential disciplinary cases. Common understanding of the facts is more likely to lead to agreement about the consequences, and even if there is no agreement, reduce the scope of the potential conflict.

- Having functional experts and line decision makers, rather than labor relations experts or lawyers, involved directly with union leaders in problem solving and bargaining discussions. This allows better, more direct communication and an opportunity for union leaders to directly impact the decision makers.

- Involving union leaders or represented employees in the hiring process. This involvement will vary from case to case and can include actions up to deciding who will be hired, subject only to review to insure all legal requirements are fulfilled. When this happens, union leaders' workplace experience can lead to hiring of employees most likely to succeed, and union leaders will have more ownership in the results.
- Having union leaders participate as ex-officio members of management teams.

We have discussed ways for management to multiply its power to make positive things happen in the workplace by sharing its power with the union. Such actions reduce resistance and increase the likelihood that union leaders will support management's direction. A proviso is in order, however. The ultimate decision in most cases must be retained to management, subject to the union's legal right to bargain and resist as it sees the need. Management's accountability was discussed in detail in an earlier chapter, and it must not be abrogated through sharing of power. Hopefully the parties can agree on the union's role, but at a minimum each party's position must be absolutely clear to the other. Even if the union asserts more rights, if there is clear agreement to disagree the parties can work collaboratively toward solutions and, if they fail, resort to coercive power without violating the trust and integrity of the process. But if the positions of the parties relating to the process of decision making are not clearly understood in advance, discussions are likely to become hostile and lead to a total disintegration of the relationship of trust that is so critical.

Using Management Power to Empower Employees

Management can multiply its power for positive change by exercising its leadership to empower employees. Its objective is to get employees to support management actions and use their initiative to foster success of the enterprise. While sharing power with union leaders is a way of encouraging this support, the best opportunities lie in the direct relationship between managers, supervisors, and represented employees; and in how supervisors allow or encourage employees to use their power.

Much has been written about how to empower employees by actions such as involving them in decisions that affect them, expanding their role, utilizing teamwork, and giving them the freedom to engage their hearts and minds. This book will not cover such matters. Rather, it will address the paradox that management must effectively use its power in order to give it away. Management must exercise strong leadership in dealing with the union to get its support and in dealing with employees to assure their involvement. It must also have the power and self-confidence to deal with possible downsides of employee empowerment in a union setting.

The union must be involved in essentially all efforts to empower represented employees because of the threat such empowerment imposes to union leaders. Empowered employees may be inclined to take actions not supported by the union or endorsed by the labor contract, and they may be difficult for union leaders to control or influence. In addition, bargaining with the union, and perhaps its agreement, is required before most empowering changes can be made, as nearly all actions that empower employees are likely to involve work duties that are mandatory bargaining subjects and covered by contract. Involving union leaders can alleviate their concerns about what employees are doing and cause union leaders to see a self-interest that may reduce their resistance to actions that empower employees. If bargaining is required, the stage is set for use of collaboration to resolve the issue. Whatever the case, strong management leadership will be required for management to effectively share power with employees.

Without due caution, changes that empower employees can be a one-way street in a union environment. Once the change has been made retraction may be difficult because of employee and union leader expectations or the potentially binding implications of past practice. This should not be a problem, as expanding the opportunities for employees to contribute is hardly something management is likely to want to retract. There may be cases, however, where management is unsure about likely results and would like to make a change on a trial basis. In this situation, the parties should agree, perhaps in writing, that the change is for a specified period and either party has the right to revert to the previous status.

KEY POINTS

1. Three types of power are important in a union workplace: coercive, utility, and collaborative. Each may be exercised, in varying degrees, by management, employees, and the union.

2. Interdependence among management, employees, and their union requires integrated use of all types of power.

3. Three paradoxes of power are important.

   - Use of certain types of power does more harm than good.

   - To take advantage of certain types of power one must give it away.

   - Management must use power to give it away.

4. To effectively address the paradoxes, management must give priority to those sources of power most likely to garner a supportive response and share its power with employees and their union.

NOTES

1. John Kenneth Galbraith, *The Anatomy of Power* (Boston: Houghton Mifflin, 1983), p. 2.

2. Robert L. Dilenschneider, *On Power* (New York: HarperCollins, 1994), p. 2.

3. Mitch McCrimmon, *The Change Master* (London: Pitman, 1997), p. 191.

4. Blaine Lee, *The Power Principle* (New York: Simon and Schuster, 1997), p. 7.

5. Galbraith, *The Anatomy of Power,* pp. 4–6.

6. Lee, *The Power Principle,* pp. 15–16.

7. Dilenschneider, *On Power*, pp. 134–144.

8. Tom Lambert, *The Power of Influence* (London: Nicholas Brealey Publishing, 1996), pp. 120–122.

9. Thomas A. Kochan, and Harry C. Katz, *Collective Bargaining and Industrial Relations*, 2nd ed. (Homewood, Ill.: Irwin, 1988), p. 53.

10. Samuel B. Bacharach and Edward J. Lawler, *Bargaining: Power, Tactics, and Outcomes* (San Francisco: Jossey-Bass, 1981), p. 37.

11. Charles S. Loughran, *Negotiating a Labor Contract*, 2nd ed. (Washington, D.C.: BNA, 1992), pp. 31–42.

12. Kochan and Katz, *Collective Bargaining and Industrial Relations*, p. 54.

13. Lee, *The Power Principle*, p. 83.

14. Ibid., p. 81.

15. Galbraith, *The Anatomy of Power*, pp. 74–75.

16. Lee, *The Power Principle*, p. 69.

17. Dilenschneider, *On Power*, p. 36.

18. Thomas Gordon, *Leader Effectiveness Training* (New York: G.P. Putnam's Sons, 1977), pp. 159–165.

19. Lee, *The Power Principle*, p. 93.

20. Dilenschneider, *On Power*, p. 22.

21. Price Waterhouse Change Integration Team, *The Paradox Principles* (Chicago: Irwin, 1996), p. 136.

22. Bacharach and Lawler, *Bargaining*, p. 108.

Chapter 12

Mutual Gains Bargaining

Mutual dependency between a company and its employees is a premise of this book. A company cannot succeed unless employees commit their energies to meeting its economic objectives and management is committed to the welfare of its employees. Employees cannot attain long-term employment and income security unless the company succeeds and shares its success with them.

In a unionized workplace, collective bargaining is the process for determining what employee energies will be devoted to the enterprise and what share of the company's success they will receive. To maintain a competitive advantage, a company must optimize the amount by which the value of the employee contribution exceeds the cost of this contribution. In the short run this can be done by extracting more contribution from employees or by reducing their share of the results. But this will not work over the long run. Over time, employee contribution will stabilize or decline because employees have no incentive to keep it up, and competitors will engage in similar efficiency measures that lead to reduced margins. Obtaining a long-term advantage requires mutual gain for all parties: more contribution by employees, which leads to better results for the company, and better treatment of employees, which provides a reason for their continually improving contribution. The negotiating process must foster such mutual gains.

Effective bargaining improves employee contribution in ways that go beyond improvements attained by concessions on work rules, broader job descriptions, or other such changes. Employees whose needs are being met are more committed and more willing to go the extra mile than those whose needs are not adequately addressed. The dialogue, involvement, and trust present in effective bargaining improve management's understanding of employee needs, allowing it to make better choices to positively address employee concerns and minimize the destructive personal conflict that degrades individual and organizational performance. When this happens, employee effort increases. More importantly, effective bargaining can create a synergy that makes the whole bigger than the sum of its parts. It engages union leaders and brings their knowledge, ideas, and beliefs to the decision process where effective dialogue tables them for solving problems. The process provides a sense of empowerment that encourages union leaders and employees to take constructive initiatives and leads to more effective implementation of decisions. All these factors combine to expand the ultimate result.

Effective bargaining can benefit employees and their union in several ways. First, they have a clear interest in the success of the enterprise, as their livelihood, standard of living, and personal self-esteem are all jeopardized if the company fails and enhanced if it succeeds. Bargaining that helps the company also helps employees and union leaders by providing them additional opportunities for improved wages, benefits, and conditions of work. Such opportunities are enhanced when management shares the value of the larger whole resulting from the synergy. Although the parties may disagree on the size of each share, an effective bargaining process provides each with a better understanding of the needs of the others and a fair process for doing the division. This understanding tends to minimize destructive conflict and allow each party to gain enough to justify the effort and risks associated with the process.

Bargaining is required by law, leads to an agreement governing the parties' relationship, and provides a framework for the give-and-take necessary for collaboration: it is the fulcrum on which the entire labor/management relationship turns. Therefore, a process of negotiations that expands the size of the whole and finds productive ways of dividing it is critical to a collaborative relationship. Developing and maintaining such a process is not easy, particularly against a background of adversarial bargaining practices, but it can be done. This chapter outlines some principles and practical ideas for such a process.

PRINCIPLES

The NLRA defines bargaining as the parties meeting at reasonable times to confer in good faith with respect to wages, hours, and other terms and conditions of employment. This definition leaves ample room for a zero-sum process in which one party wins and the other loses or for a more collaborative, mutual gains process in which the parties try to expand the size of the whole and then divide it equitably. The mutual gains process requires theoretical underpinnings that are different from a zero-sum process. They are best articulated as a combination of three concepts:

• Concepts of interest-based negotiations, as presented by Roger Fisher, William Ury, and Bruce Patton in *Getting to Yes* and Fisher and Scott Brown in *Getting Together*.

- Concepts of discussion and dialogue, as presented by Peter Senge in *The Fifth Discipline* and further elaborated by various writers in *The Fifth Discipline Field Book*.
- Concepts of constructive conflict management, as discussed in *Using Conflict in Organizations*, edited by Carsten De Dreu and Evert Van Vliert.

Interest-Based Negotiations

Negotiation is a means of getting what we want, and the outcome of any negotiation is affected by the bargaining approach and the relationship between the parties. Although two or more parties are necessary for a negotiating relationship, one party can change the relationship by changing how it behaves; and management's power base gives it the primary ability to change the negotiation process in a labor/management relationship.

Study of *Getting to Yes* and *Getting Together* is recommended for anyone interested in improving a negotiating process. These books present interest-based negotiations as a process where the parties work together to understand the underlying issues and interests of the parties and find the best solutions for all concerned. This approach is in lieu of processes where each party decides what is best for it and then attempts to buy or force that solution. The objectives of interest-based negotiations are to "produce a wise agreement if agreement is possible," "be efficient," and "improve or at least not damage the relationship between the parties."[1]

Position bargaining, which involves successively taking and then giving up a sequence of positions, rarely accomplishes these objectives. The parties typically lock themselves into their positions and pursue them rather than the underlying concerns, frequently leading to unwise agreements that are not implemented according to either party's wishes or understanding. They are likely to take extreme positions that make reaching agreement difficult and inefficient, and because each negotiation becomes a test of wills, anger and resentment frequently result.

An alternative, principled or interest-based negotiations, is much more likely to lead to a wise agreement. Four points define this approach to negotiations.

"Separate the People from the Problem."[2] Two types of interests are present in every negotiation: substantive interests that can lead to cognitive, content-based conflicts and interests in the relationship among the people involved that can lead to affective, or personal, conflicts. The different types of interests often are overlooked and become entangled. One party may take a hard line on a matter of substance because of a personality conflict with a member of the other party, and conflicts may be addressed by trading a concession on one type of interest for a concession on another type. But if the parties' true interests are being addressed, the two types must be kept separate and dealt with on their own merits. Relationship problems must be dealt with directly using techniques designed to address personal conflict. Substantive concessions will not work. They will not buy friendship, respect, or credibility—or solve the relationship

issues at the root of the problem. Rather, they "may do nothing more that convince the other side that you can be taken for a ride."

"Focus on Interests, Not Positions."[3] "Interests define the problem. The basic problem in a negotiation lies not in conflicting positions, but in the conflict between each side's needs, desires, concerns, and fears. . . . Such desires and concerns are *interests."* Interests are what cause one to decide on something, as contrasted to positions, which are what one decides on. Interests can be reconciled more easily than positions because several possible positions can exist for each interest, and frequently interests that do not conflict lie behind conflicting positions. Instead, compatible interests may lie behind conflicting positions; and compatible or shared interests can lead to a common solution. Agreement may be possible precisely because interests are different but compatible, and opportunities are enhanced for both parties to come out ahead.

"Invent Options for Mutual Gain."[4] Working together to invent a variety of options for addressing the interests of the parties is more likely to lead to an acceptable solution than each party developing, advancing, and defending its own solution. The parties should use techniques such as brainstorming to separate inventing options from criticizing or deciding among them and to broaden the number of options beyond those easily generated by an individual. Each party should try to walk in the other's shoes in order to advance options that the other can more easily accept. Processes such as these can increase the likelihood of attaining mutual gains by exploiting the synergy of the parties to expand the size of the whole. They also overcome four major obstacles to development of effective options: "(1) premature judgment; (2) searching for the single answer; (3) the assumption of a fixed pie; and (4) thinking that 'solving their problem is their problem.' "

"Insist on Using Objective Criteria."[5] Conflicting interests that are difficult to resolve are to be expected in any negotiation. Deciding such issues with coercive power is not likely to produce solutions that are the best for either party over the long term. Conversely, bringing standards of fairness, efficiency, scientific merit, or other objective considerations to bear on a problem increases the chance of producing a final package that is wise and fair. Criteria such as market value, precedent, scientific judgment, professional standards, efficiency, costs, what a court would decide, moral standards, equal treatment, tradition, or reciprocity may be used as standards. When applying them, the parties should remember three basic points:

1. Frame each issue as a joint search for objective criteria.
2. Reason and be open to reason as to which standards are most appropriate and how they should be applied.
3. Never yield to pressure, only to principle.

Dialogue and Discussion

Dialogue and discussion are key factors in the quest for team learning, and they are uniquely applicable to mutual gains bargaining, a process in which a team of people tries to learn together how to address their individual and mutual interests.

"There are two primary types of discourse, dialogue and discussion," and "their power lies in their synergy, which is not likely to be present when the distinctions between them are not appreciated."[6] In a discussion, subjects of common interest are taken apart and analyzed from the perspectives provided by those involved in the discussion. The objective of discussion is normally to win by having one's views prevail and be accepted by the group, and its ultimate purpose is to make decisions. Productive discussions lead to a conclusion or course of action.

In dialogue, on the other hand, different perspectives are presented in order to discover an entirely new perspective. "During the dialogue process, people learn how to think together—not just in the sense of analyzing a shared problem or creating new pieces of shared knowledge, but in the sense of occupying a collective sensibility, in which the thoughts, emotions, and resulting actions belong not to one individual, but to all of them together."[7] "The purpose of a dialogue is to go beyond any one individual's understanding. 'We are not trying to win in a dialogue. We all win if we are doing it right.' In dialogue, individuals gain insights that simply could not be achieved individually. . . . In dialogue, a group explores complex difficult issues from many points of view."[8] While decisions and actions are often the focus of discussion, they are only a by-product of dialogue.

Senge, citing quantum physicist David Bohm, identifies three basic conditions that are necessary for dialogue:[9]

- "All participants must 'suspend' their assumptions." Assumptions are inherently nei-ther good nor bad, but they are part of who we are and what we believe. Therefore, we must not throw them out, suppress them, or avoid them. Instead, we must be aware of our assumptions and the impact they are having and not act on them immediately but hold them up for examination.

- "All participants must regard one another as colleagues." Colleagueship does not re-quire agreement or sharing of the same views. Instead, the real power of colleagues is in their ability to exploit the synergy of their differences. This can happen when the parties are willing to see each other as friends and work together for the insight and clarity that dialogue can bring.

- "There must be a 'facilitator' who 'holds the context' of dialogue." A facilitator helps people maintain ownership of the process and keeps the dialogue moving.

A balance of discussion and dialogue is necessary for team learning to occur and for successful mutual gains bargaining to take place. An effective bargaining team must clearly distinguish between the two and move back and forth between them, using dialogue to develop insights that expand the size of the whole and discussion to come to decisions as to how it will be divided.

Constructive Conflict Management

Conflict has been variously defined as "the process that begins when an individual or group feels negatively affected by another person or group," as involving "opposing, divergent interests" or "incompatible activities," and as "an awareness by the parties involved that there are discrepancies, or incompatible wishes or desires present."[10] "Cognitive conflict pertains to conflict of ideas in the group and disagreement about the content and issues of the task" while "affective conflict exists when personal and relationship components within the group are characterized by friction, frustration and personality clashes within the group."[11] Affective conflict can exist among any individuals or groups and certainly can be present between management and union representatives. It generally is counterproductive, reduces organizational performance, and must be dealt with. Dealing with affective conflict, however, is not the purpose of bargaining. The primary purpose of bargaining is to deal with cognitive conflict.

Cognitive conflicts are not necessarily good or bad. Such conflicts between management and employees or the union will occur: they are not breakdowns of the system but are central to what an organization is. They should not be ignored or suppressed, but rather should be managed constructively within the bargaining process to minimize possible damage and gain advantage where possible. *Using Conflict in Organizations*[12] outlines a series of studies supporting the view that conflict can be positive for organizational performance if it is among parties with similar values and is managed in an atmosphere of respect and trust. Benefits suggested by the studies include:

- Making the system more open and adaptable to change.
- Calling attention to serious issues that otherwise might go unrecognized; serving as a "whistleblower."
- Causing periodic reevaluation of the status quo.
- Increasing self-exploration and awareness; causing us to look at ourselves.
- Fostering continuous organizational learning.
- Improving quality of decisions by:
  —Avoiding "group think."
  —Challenging illusions of invincibility and too many concessions to the "boss."
  —Generating more new ideas.
  —Combining and integrating varying ideas into a problem-solving mode.
  —Bringing multiple perspectives to the decision process.
  —Causing evaluation of underlying assumptions.

To gain such benefits, management must engage the union as a vehicle for surfacing conflict, understanding it, and focusing it on organizational performance. This relationship must be managed to minimize affective conflict through trust and respect, and to capture the potential synergy of cognitive conflict. *Using Conflict in Organizations* suggest two possible approaches:

The *one-best-way perspective* states that, compared to avoiding, accommodating, compromising, and forcing, problem solving is the most constructive mode of conflict management because it always serves the joint welfare best. . . . In contrast, the *contingency perspective* contends that the answer regarding what is effective can only be given in the light of situational realities, and that each mode of conflict management, even forcing, is appropriate under some circumstances.[13]

Unfortunately cognitive conflict is not always resolvable with dialogue, discussion, and problem solving. Even the most genuine, honest, good-faith efforts to collaborate in addressing an opportunity or solving a problem sometimes fail. When these difficult disagreements and conflicts arise, the legal rights and powers of the parties will be factors in the ultimate resolution. While there is no single best way to think about using such power, the contingency perspective suggests a situational approach.

The world is too complex to rely on one approach, and problem solving mixed with forcing is necessary in many circumstances. The parties must acknowledge up front that difficult conflicts will arise and that ultimately each party may choose to rely on its legal rights or its right to exert lawful pressure on the other party; that doing so, while unfortunate, is acceptable and is not a breach of trust; and that such instances are not a basis for destroying the collaborative, synergistic nature of the relationship but do have consequences that must be managed.

MUTUAL GAINS BARGAINING IN A UNIONIZED WORKPLACE

The basic standard for management/union bargaining is set by the NLRA, which prohibits an employer from refusing to bargain collectively with the representatives of its employees and prohibits a union from refusing to bargain with an employer. Although the law leaves the parties considerable flexibility to determine what bargaining procedures to use, management and unions have tended to perpetuate what has been approved by the NLRB and courts, is understood and accepted by employees, and has worked in the past. They have generally preferred maintaining the status quo to exploring new processes that are inconsistent with past practice, that increase the risk of new misunderstandings, or that could be seen to shift the balance of power.

Because of this inertia of the status quo, one can describe with a reasonable degree of accuracy a bargaining model that has been broadly used for many years. It is position bargaining, based on the ''carrot-and-stick'' methodology as discussed in *Bargaining: Power, Tactics, and Outcomes*: ''the bargaining process can be construed as a mixture of inducements (carrots) and sanctions (sticks). Inducements consist of provisional offers and counteroffers—tactical concessions—that reduce the difference between bargainers on an issue, while sanctions are grounded in punitive capabilities that permit bargainers to threaten and damage each other.''[14]

One can also construct a more collaborative bargaining model that emphasizes mutual gains, based on the principles enunciated above. The purpose of the remainder of this chapter is to describe such a model and contrast it with position bargaining where doing so is helpful. Two notes of explanation are in order to start:

- The process is discussed primarily in the context of periodic renegotiation of an expired contract because such bargaining is more discrete, predictable, and comprehensive than interim, ad hoc negotiations. However, "evergreen" bargaining that addresses issues when they arise during the contract term is highly recommended, particularly given the current trend toward longer contract terms. The principles discussed for renegotiating a contract apply to ad hoc bargaining as well.

- The discussion generally presumes the company, union, and employees all endorse and support collaborative bargaining, when in fact such processes themselves must be negotiated and a union may be unwilling to agree to participate in them. Union agreement to cooperate is desirable but not required for positive results. Where a union is unwilling to formally agree to a collaborative process, it may nevertheless be willing to engage in collaborative bargaining practices on an informal, case-by-case basis, which opens up most of the opportunities that collaboration offers. Even when a union is unwilling to participate in informal, case-by-case collaborative practices, unilateral company use of many of the ideas presented will pay dividends. Human nature is predictable, and people tend to respond positively to positive treatment. Management actions can build credibility and over time lead to reciprocity and a willingness to engage in more collaborative activities.

Thus, collaborative bargaining practices work for both contract renewal and ad hoc negotiations and regardless of whether the union agrees to participate. The following sections present ideas for operationalizing such practices.

Developing a Collegial Relationship

A number of factors, such as history, economic forces, or relative power, affect bargaining results. Among the most important, however, is the personal working environment among those participating in the process. While agreement on all issues or personal friendship is not necessary, a special chemistry and a relationship based on trust is needed.

Separating people from the problem and regarding each other as colleagues are key underpinnings for collaborative bargaining. The goal is an environment where acknowledged peers, working together in an atmosphere of openness, trust, and respect, focus on substantive issues rather than issues of personality. Colleagueship is particularly important in collaborative bargaining where the parties are working together in a search for new answers. Their willingness to explore the unknown introduces personal vulnerability and mutual risk that is well beyond that commonly seen in position bargaining.

Management holds the key to establishing a collegial relationship with union leaders, but such a relationship cannot be developed overnight or turned on and off at management's whim. It must be maintained over time, across the entire workplace, and in day-to-day relationships as well as formal bargaining. To foster colleagueship managers must maintain the highest personal credibility over time. They also must demonstrate respect for union leaders as individuals and for the union as an institution at the bargaining table and in day-to-day intercourse. When credibility and respect are buttressed by sincere efforts to get to know union leaders in a way that mutual empathy is possible, reciprocal behavior leading to true colleagueship is likely to follow.

Colleagueship implies seeing each other as co-workers and friends. The parties should not attempt to develop an especially close personal relationship, as this could be seen as compromising the objectivity necessary for hard bargaining, and perhaps could in fact confuse each party as to its own accountabilities and self-interests. Instead, a balance of friendship and objectivity can help both parties deal with the uncertainty and increased vulnerability required for collaborative bargaining. Such colleagueship can be fostered by actions such as the following:

- Learn more about each other's personal lives: families, personal interests, likes, dislikes, and other issues that can lead to mutual empathy. Management and union leaders typically are more alike than different. This learning process can begin with formal team-building type exercises and evolve to informal social situations of various types.

- Look for community, political, or charitable activities that the parties can work together on or mutually support.

- Jointly communicate on issues of mutual interest.

- Visit union leaders in their offices and hold meetings on the union's territory as well as the company's.

- Find occasions to have meals and/or refreshments together, both during bargaining and on a day-to-day basis.

- Support the union on its initiatives whenever possible.

- Include union leaders in meetings with important outside visitors.

- Do not embarrass the union as an institution or any of its leaders personally.

- Address affective conflict and other personal issues in a timely and appropriate fashion, either outside the bargaining process or as a specifically identified issue within the bargaining process.

- Participate in joint training and other non-threatening collaborative activities.

Colleagueship among those at the bargaining table provides the lubricant that makes synergy and agreement possible. Equally important, a collegial relationship among a few leaders sets an example for others across the organization that can foster a transformation of attitudes in the workplace.

Pre-negotiation Planning and Preparation

Collaborative bargaining must start at the preparation stage. The process is different from that used in position bargaining, and comparing the two provides a helpful perspective.

Position Bargaining. In position bargaining, the parties do thorough planning and preparation independently, well in advance of any significant joint discussions. Typically the labor relations staff is assigned initial responsibility for management. Its members decide on management "demands" by reviewing grievances and arbitration cases, surveying managers and supervisors, recalling conventional wisdom, and identifying "red herrings" that are important to the union and can be used for trading in later stages of negotiations. They then consult with supervisors and others in an attempt to predict the union's demands. Proposed company demands and predicted union demands are then reviewed with senior management, where the most likely bargaining issues are identified and parameters are set for further preparation. Staff gathers both economic and noneconomic data, reviews available information about competitors and recent industry settlements, and compiles additional information deemed relevant. Based on this information, it develops specific arguments for its demands and in opposition to anticipated union demands. It may also develop tentative solutions to potential issues and draft tentative contract language. All this is placed in a bargaining data book, which is a basis for further discussions with senior management, where bargaining goals are set and the chief spokesperson is delegated the authority to represent management.

Union preparation is typically along similar lines. Union leaders solicit input from their constituency, gather information from outside sources, and request certain information from the company. Management may object to providing the information, leading to the first disagreement of the negotiations. Based on all the information available, the union formulates its demands and reviews them with the union membership. To enhance the union's bargaining leverage, the membership may give the union bargaining committee advance authorization to call a strike if necessary to obtain the demands.

These simultaneous but independent processes prepare the chief spokespersons for discussion at the bargaining table and ensure that they take positions that management and union members have authorized. But the process has the following downsides:

- It establishes a "win-lose" mind set from the beginning, as each party typically is preparing to "beat" the other.
- It builds frequently unreasonable expectations among both supervisors and employees that often are difficult to deal with after negotiations are completed.

- It sets the stage for disagreement where there shouldn't be any. The parties typically are interested in the same types of preparatory information but are likely to use different or conflicting sources, ask different questions, or emphasize different data, all of which can lead unnecessarily to disagreements. Resolving these disagreements may detract from the more important effort of resolving substantive issues.

- It limits the options and opportunities for solving problems. When company labor staff involves senior management and union leadership reviews with the membership, views as to solutions become solidified. This is especially true when negotiating authorities are established, as authority to do certain things or make certain concessions usually excludes other options. While either spokesperson can go back for changes, this may be viewed as not politically feasible.

Mutual Gains Bargaining. Independent preparation before the parties meet should be less rather than more in mutual gains bargaining. Collaboration cannot start at the bargaining table but must exist throughout the entire process of seamless movement from preparation through bargaining. Starting collaboration at the beginning means using joint processes for gathering information, analyzing data, and deciding on which issues are to be addressed in later stages of bargaining.

The joint processes must be designed to meet the needs of the particular situation. They may involve only members of the respective bargaining teams or may be expanded to include supplemental teams of managers and employees who are closer to the issues considered important. Typically, however, they would include the following:

- A joint steering committee to oversee the entire process.
- Joint workshops for learning as well as for identifying issues and making joint decisions.
- Procedures for involving a broad group of represented employees, supervisors, and managers as and when appropriate.
- Joint teams to research and analyze issues.

Using such a collaborative process means that vulnerability and risk begins at the preparation stage, as the lawyer's adage to ''never ask a question unless you know the answer'' is violated from the beginning. Both parties must be prepared to deal with the unexpected. In theory this is not a problem if the parties are honestly seeking improvement and are prepared to openly deal with the truth. As a practical matter, however, too many unknowns and surprises can be difficult for the parties to deal with, so uncertainties should be minimized as much as possible without destroying the freedom of thought and action that is the purpose of collaboration. To do this, both parties must know what to expect of the bargaining process; that is, while the substance and results may be unpredictable, the actual process for raising and dealing with issues should contain no surprises and should circumscribe the areas where substantive surprises can occur. If the parties are significantly changing their negotiating process, they should as part of their pre-negotiation preparation be clear on a protocol covering the new one, including both the preparations and actual bargaining. The protocol should be in writing if feasible and cover elements such as:

- Bargaining principles.
- Purpose and scope of negotiations.
- Information sharing procedures.
- Tentative timetable and schedule.
- Procedures for constituent communications.
- Authorities of management and union representatives.
- Use of a facilitator.
- Procedures for appropriate confidentiality.
- Media relations procedures.
- Preparation and use of record of the proceedings.
- Other matters deemed appropriate.

It addition, either as part of the protocol or by separate agreement, the parties should agree on any issues that are not to be included in the collaborative process. For example, if the parties are subject to company-wide, industry, or pattern bargaining, collaborative bargaining at the local level will need to be limited to issues the parties can meaningfully address.

The Negotiation Process

For many company/union relationships, adoption of a mutual gains bargaining process represents a cultural transformation from a long historical practice of position bargaining. Therefore, comparing the two approaches is helpful.

Position Bargaining. As a general rule, position bargaining is a structured, reasonably predictable process that is driven by practice and custom. While the details may vary from company to company and from year to year, most position bargaining involves elements along the following lines, in more or less the order indicated:

- The parties conduct a series of meetings in a formal setting, with the union representatives aligned on one side of a rectangular conference table and the company representatives on the other.
- Management makes an opening statement, addressing the big picture and attempting to set the tone for the negotiations. This statement is followed by a union statement or response.

- The union presents its bargaining agenda, usually in the form of specific proposals or demands. Discussions are held in which the management bargainers seek to understand and clarify the proposals and the union attempts to justify them.

- Management presents proposals for contract changes that address its concerns. Union representatives seek to clarify and understand the management proposals, and the management spokesperson attempts to justify them.

- Between meetings, each party evaluates the other's proposals and determines its response.

- Each party responds to the other's proposals, attempting to signal its position in "negotiation speak" without implying any commitments or revealing its bottom line.

- The parties make a succession of offers and counteroffers intended to make their positions somewhat more favorable to the other. If the union rejects a management proposal but refuses to make a counterproposal, management may make back-to-back offers.

- Difficult issues are resolved by trading proposal for proposal. All proposals and offers, and most discussions, are recorded and may be used as evidence if disagreements as to meaning of the agreement arise.

- Management makes its "last, best and final" offer. The union accepts the offer, continues working under the existing contract, or threatens to strike or take other action to force management to improve its offer.

- In a last-ditch effort to avoid a strike, the parties engage in off-the- record meetings where they go beneath the bargaining positions and explore the "real" problems and issues in a problem-solving mode.

This type of process gets agreement. It has resulted in thousands of satisfactory labor contracts over the years. Where a high level of antagonism or mistrust exists between the parties, this or a similar approach may be the only bargaining option the parties are comfortable with. Even in a genuinely collaborative effort, some aspects of position bargaining may ultimately be necessary and appropriate where the parties have sincerely explored all options and yet have been unable to agree.

Notwithstanding its use in various situations, position bargaining has several negative effects. Prepared opening statements and presentation of previously approved demands tend to prevent dialogue and limit opportunities to explore the broad range of possible solutions necessary to solve difficult problems. They create a win-lose atmosphere where each party keeps score based on the relative number of proposals accepted, withdrawn, conceded, or compromised. Trust declines and the ultimate agreement does not feel good to either party if it is based on compromises that miss the real issues or coercion that imposes the will of the strong on the weak. Whoever "wins" may ultimately lose because the bad feelings lead to poor implementation. If the company wins it may be unable to attain the secondary result it is seeking because of continuing employee and union resistance. If the union wins, the company's implementation may be lacking as compared to expectations. Grievances and arbitration frequently are used to determine what the parties really agreed to.

Mutual Gains Bargaining. Adopting a collaborative bargaining process after a history of position bargaining—even cordial, non-adversarial position bargaining—represents a major change in the company/union relationship. It introduces uncertainty where there has been predictability, freedom where there has been constraint, and messiness where there has been neatness. And it is very hard work for all concerned. But it is also management's best chance for cashing in on the advantages that diversity of thought can bring to bargaining and that a union can bring to creating a more productive work force.

The parties may move to collaborative bargaining in a few major steps, or the process may evolve over time as the parties take a succession of next, logical, incremental steps. Whatever the case, a process along the following lines is the objective:

- Most bargaining is in a workshop setting, around groups of round tables, with union and management representatives interspersed.

- A facilitator leads a discussion of the issues the parties previously agreed would be subjects of negotiation. The parties agree on the order in which they will be addressed and that all exchanges will be off the record unless agreed otherwise.

- The parties problem solve each issue, attempting to determine what is right rather than who is right. They use a flip chart to facilitate dialogue and capture progress but not to create a record for interpreting any future agreement. All members of both negotiating teams actively participate in problem-solving activities such as:

  —Clarifying the issues and problems.

  —Identifying the needs and interests of all parties relating to the issues being addressed.

  —Reviewing results of joint data gathering and analysis.

  —Brainstorming possible solutions.

  —Assessing the options identified in brainstorming against the needs and interests of the parties.

  —Deciding on which option(s) best meet the needs of the parties.

- If an option is acceptable to both parties, a draftsman develops a written "proposal" that can then be formally accepted by each party, perhaps after further discussion relating to details and language. All "agreements" are tentative until confirmed by the respective constituencies.

- If the parties cannot develop options for resolving a particular issue that are mutually acceptable standing alone, they discuss tradeoffs and compromises. This is facilitated by either party floating "supposals" (a very helpful term that to the author's knowledge was coined by members of the Oil, Chemical, and Atomic Workers International Union): informal, non-binding "what ifs?" that allow a better understanding of what tradeoffs may be possible. The subsequent give-and-take is similar to position bargaining, but because of the preceding dialogue, options, and supposals, it is more likely to result in an agreement acceptable to all.

- If all else fails, the process reverts to position bargaining, with management making a "last, best, and final" offer and the ultimate decision being determined by the relative coercive power of the parties. It is unfortunate when this happens, but it should not be considered a failure of the process. Rather, the parties must recognize it as a legitimate step if good faith attempts at a more collaborative approach have failed.

As with a collaborative pre-negotiation process, the collaborative bargaining process is under less control than position bargaining, and it exposes vulnerabilities and creates risks for both parties. Minimizing these risks to the extent feasible without destroying the synergy of the process is important and is the key objective of the bargaining protocol discussed above. Minimizing the process risks in this way should allow the parties to concentrate on innovative ways to address important substantive issues.

Role of the Spokesperson and Bargaining Team

Both company and union have the right and responsibility to select who will represent them in the bargaining process and what the authorities and responsibilities of those representatives will be. The representatives selected by the parties determine what bargaining process will be used, and they are a major factor in whether it will succeed. Therefore, who is on the bargaining team and what is expected of them are considerations of major importance. The composition and role of management bargaining teams differ between position and collaborative bargaining.

Position Bargaining. Management bargaining teams and roles of their members will vary from company to company. Where position bargaining is the practice, however, the number of participants is likely to be limited in order to maintain discipline within the team and confidentiality of management plans and strategies. A management bargaining team might include the spokesperson, a person with a broad knowledge of the likely issues if the spokesperson doesn't fill that role, a notetaker, and someone to draft contract language. It may also include additional persons who are on the team because of custom or because they want to be and have the authority to insist on it. The spokesperson is the central focus, and the role of other team members is generally to advise and support the spokesperson behind the scenes but be seen and not heard in sessions with union negotiators.

The spokesperson's role may be that of a "talking head" who simply communicates positions and arguments developed and decided by others. More frequently, however, the spokesperson is the "head negotiator," who manages all aspects of the negotiation process and is the primary or only spokesperson for management at the negotiating table. Typically the spokesperson is a labor relations specialist or attorney who does not have direct authority for the issues being bargained. The spokesperson's roll in position bargaining includes the following:

- Managing all pre-negotiation planning and preparation.

- Recommending bargaining parameters and authorities, and getting approval from executive management.

- Managing development of objectives and strategy for the bargaining as a whole and specific plans for each session. Many session plans would require agreement by the union negotiators, in which case a pre-session, off-the-record executive session with the union spokesperson might be held.

- Controlling and guiding management input to the bargaining process. The management spokesperson is expected to maintain direction and discipline within the management bargaining team to insure that unexpected issues are not raised or unauthorized concessions are not made. The spokesperson decides whether, when, and how new ideas will be presented, agreement with a union position indicated, or concessions made. In order to maintain discipline, the spokesperson generally is the only person on the management team who speaks during a negotiating session. An exception might be made, for example, when the spokesperson is not sufficiently conversant with the topic being discussed, but usually such exceptions are by prior arrangement among the bargaining team. Management comments are rarely spontaneous and are discussed and agreed in advance among the bargaining team.

- Reporting back to executive management on the progress of negotiations.

- Renegotiating delegated authorities if it becomes necessary to make larger concessions that originally planned.

- Meeting privately with union spokesperson to address especially difficult issues.

- Managing communication of the company's version of the status of negotiations to managers, supervisors, employees, and external contacts as deemed appropriate.

Mutual Gains Bargaining. Collaborative bargaining requires different composition and roles for the bargaining team. The team should include all those who can reasonably make a contribution to solving the issues being addressed and should specifically include staff with expertise in problem solving and the substantive areas being discussed. A management bargaining team might include a team leader, the person or persons who worked on pre-negotiation research, the company's substantive specialist(s) in the areas being discussed, and someone with operational responsibility. Team members should be active participants in mutual problem solving and personally contribute all they can.

The duty of the spokesperson, as in position bargaining, is to manage the entire process from the company's perspective. But the actual role is different and may vary depending on what stage negotiations are in. The spokesperson cannot be a "talking head," as there are no pre-decided arguments, positions, or authorities. Rather, the spokesperson must understand broad company objectives, make decisions on the fly, and know when decisions must be deferred to executive management. Within this context, the principle role of the spokesperson should include:

- Coordinating with the union spokesperson on the process for mutual pre-negotiation planning and preparation.
- Understanding company interests, constraints, and objectives to the extent necessary to insure problem-solving dialogue and discussion are within acceptable parameters.
- Working with executive management to develop processes for their continuing involvement and quick turnaround of needed management decisions during the bargaining process.
- Working with union spokesperson to develop problem-solving approaches and processes.
- Facilitating dialogue during bargaining by inviting comments and asking questions of members of both the company and union bargaining teams.
- Insuring that the union bargaining team understands the company's interests and the company bargaining team understands the interests of employees and the union.
- Functioning as company spokesperson when position type trading is necessary to resolve an issue.
- Speaking definitively and clearly for management where appropriate to communicate its bottom line.

Using Power

Both unions and management have three basic types of power: coercive, utility, and collaborative. In position bargaining coercive power is frequently emphasized and used in ways that are self-defeating. In mutual gains bargaining, management takes an integrated approach, giving priority to collaborative power and using coercive power only when necessary as a last resort.

Position Bargaining. Use of the various types of power in position bargaining varies from case to case, but management frequently uses them generally along the following lines, particularly where the relationship is of an adversarial nature:

- Coercive power—Management uses its legal rights and bargaining power to limit topics for meaningful negotiation and do as it pleases to the extent possible. It refuses to discuss or provide information on permissive subjects of bargaining. During the contract term it refers questions of contract interpretation to the grievance procedure and gets its way on matters not covered by contract by proposing changes, negotiating to impasse, and implementing its last offer. If the union proposes changes, it bargains hard and refuses to concede. In both cases, the union's power to prevent or force action while the contract is in force is limited by a no-strike clause. When the contract expires, the parties are on more equal footing, but if a company has significant bargaining power relative to the union, it is likely to make proposals, bargain hard, and make as few concessions as possible. If the union has the power, it takes advantage of the open contract to force what it could not get management to consider during the contract term.

- Utility power—After management does what it can through use of coercive power, it addresses remaining issues by using its utility power. It pulls together staff resources to argue its case and convince union representatives of its merit. Failing that, it uses financial power to buy what it wants with money or other concessions of value. Utility power may be combined with coercive power, as management might try to force its will by actions such as imposing deadlines for acceptance, communicating its last offer directly to represented employees in hopes they will pressure the union to accept, unilaterally implementing its final offer, or locking employees out.

- Collaborative power—All matters are likely to be resolved by utility and coercion if one party has more bargaining power than the other. If their power is approximately equal, however, a stalemate is likely to result. When this happens, management turns to collaboration to try to resolve the outstanding issues. Collaboration begins with off-the-record discussions where the "real" needs of the parties are discussed, involves a mediator to facilitate problem solving, includes experts who really understand the problem, and considers creative options for meeting the needs of both parties and resolving the stalemate.

Such use of power in position bargaining gets settlements. But it also carries negative baggage. Use of management rights to foreclose discussion or force management's will allows concerns to grow into festering problems, creating hard feelings and mistrust, and it fails to take advantage of the synergy that can arise from the constructive consideration of countervailing views. Use of coercion early in the bargaining process destroys the opportunity for effective dialogue and problem solving and can cause a hardening of positions that makes later resolution much more difficult. When settlement is reached, one or both parties frequently do not like it and continue to resist, making implementation difficult if not impossible.

Mutual Gains Bargaining. Difficult power issues cannot be eliminated from bargaining. Their impact can be greatly reduced, however, by a collaborative approach that reverses the priority of various types of power and uses them generally along the following lines:

- Collaborative power—Almost nothing the union sincerely wants to discuss is off limits. The line between mandatory and permissive subjects is essentially meaningless because management wants employees and their union representatives to understand more about the business, and it wants to understand more about union institutional and security issues. Whether or not a matter is covered by contract does not affect the willingness to negotiate because both parties try to resolve problems during the term of the contract rather than allow them to fester until the contract expires. When matters are negotiated, the parties start with dialogue that explores respective needs and interests in a sincere effort to find mutually advantageous solutions.

- Utility power—When collaboration alone does not resolve a problem, management uses its financial power to buy a solution through trading money or other things of value.

This works much as in position bargaining but is more likely to succeed because it is done in a climate of understanding and trust resulting from the preceding dialogue.

- Coercive power—Ideally, use of coercive power is not necessary in collaborative bargaining. Unfortunately, however, this is not always the case. Some issues simply cannot be resolved so that everyone gains, people frequently cannot agree on the appropriate division of gains, and when buying a deal is necessary, disagreements as to price are predictable. Where the parties do not have the ability to walk away from a negotiation, an understanding that the other party can potentially impose a cost for failure to agree may be necessary to drive the parties to agreement. Therefore, use of coercive power will be necessary in some cases and should be considered as a legitimate tool in the bargaining process. Each party must understand that the other is free to impose whatever power it has, provided it does so as a last resort after other efforts have failed. Use of coercive power is not the primary tool but is the lubricant that allows the parties to move to agreement. An additional round of dialogue, discussion, and problem solving will in the end probably be necessary to resolve final outstanding issues.

IMPLEMENTATION

Moving from a history of position bargaining to effective mutual gains bargaining is not easy, free, or without risks, and it cannot be done in one step. Rather, the parties must start from where they are and build a foundation with accomplishments such as:

- Building trust among core leaders.
- Finding mutual success stories that can be built on.
- Expanding the union's role in the day-to-day business setting.
- Learning by using collaborative practices in a low-risk environment where all are likely to win.

In addition to creating a foundation, management should seriously consider a number of issues and concerns before attempting to make such a change.

Systems Thinking

The mutual gains bargaining process has been presented as a discrete model with elements emphasizing interests, effective problem solving, and respect for the paradoxes of power; contrasted with a discrete position bargaining model based on positions, compromise, and use of coercive power. In fact, however, bargaining is not that clear-cut and will inevitably include aspects of both. Movement from a history of position bargaining to mutual gains bargaining takes time, and the parties frequently must decide on a case-by-case basis where changes should be made and how far they should go. They must view the collaborative process as their goal but concentrate on existing processes and changes in them that are necessary to attain that goal. After they are well into a collaborative mode, the parties will find it necessary to move back and forth between types of practices, go further in some areas than in others, and learn from their mistakes.

One must think of the process as a system composed of continuums of practices, where collaboration is favored but where each practice must stand on its own in the context of the overall process. Figure 12.1 is a summary comparison of various elements of position and collaborative bargaining that establishes the continuums. It is not intended to suggest old and new or wrong and right; nor should one view either model as all or nothing. Rather, it describes ranges of bargaining practices from which the parties should select those that best fit their situation, recognizing that to move from position to collaborative bargaining one must tend toward the collaborative model whenever feasible.

Systems thinking should dominate the parties consideration of when and how to implement more collaborative practices. Such thinking must apply both within the bargaining process and external to it. Internally, when moving from position toward collaborative bargaining, various elements should be synchronized and brought along together. For example, fully collaborative pre-negotiation work would be made useless by power-based position processes in actual negotiation. Or setting up the room to encourage dialogue would have no value if the company spokesman adopts a position-based bargaining demeanor.

Systems thinking should also apply outside the bargaining process. For long-term success the attitudes and general approaches used in bargaining should fit with other aspects of the union/company relationship and other related management systems. For example, processes of employee involvement, dialogue, and problem solving similar to those used in bargaining should also be used in making work assignments, addressing day-to-day issues and problems, handling disagreements under the grievance procedure, and in addressing issues involving non-represented employees. This will create reinforcing feedback cycles that solidify use of collaborative processes and encourage use of additional ones. Failure to do so will create inconsistencies, thwarted expectations, and mistrust, casting doubt on the credibility and sincerity of the company. When this happens, the likelihood of a successful bargaining effort is greatly minimized.

Buying the Process

A collaborative bargaining relationship can present several disadvantages for union leaders, causing them to view it as a no-win situation. Employees expect union leaders to counter management: to protect them from management whims and abuses of authority or help them elicit concessions. If collaboration works and accomplishing such things is not necessary or appears too easy, the role of union leaders may be seen as diminished or not needed. Even worse, cooperation with management can be perceived as union leaders being too close or having been co-opted by management. If collaboration doesn't work from the employee perspective, union leaders may be perceived as having failed or having been

Figure 12.1
Bargaining Continuums

	POSITION	COLLABORATIVE
Pre-negotiation assessment	Each party does its own assessment.	Parties jointly assess the environment.
Negotiation objectives	Each party sets its own objectives.	Parties jointly set mutual objectives and standards for assessing results.
Timing	30-90 days before contract termination.	On an evergreen basis when issues develop.
Initial demands	Each party develops its own initial demands.	There are no initial demands as such. Parties jointly determine the issues to be bargained.
Subjects covered	Mandatory subjects only.	Any relevant subject.
Compiling bargaining data	Each party compiles its own. Company provides only "relevant" information.	Data is compiled by joint committee. Company provides whatever is available.
Spokesperson	Does all the talking; maintains discipline among committee.	Functions primarily as a facilitator; encourages exchange among all participants. Experts available to address appropriate topics.
Authority	Management has pre-approved authority for proposals. Union proposals subject to member ratification.	Pre-approved authority is limited to major strategic issues.
Offers/Proposals	Parties exchange and discuss series of unilaterally developed proposals.	Bargaining agenda addresses issues and needs. Proposals limited to final agreed proposal for execution.
Bargaining exchanges	Discussion and persuasion.	Dialogue, discussion, and persuasion.
Horse trading	Primary method of reducing areas of disagreement.	Used when problems cannot otherwise be solved.
Room set-up	Rectangular table. Parties on their respective sides with spokesperson in the middle.	Round workshop tables with participants interspersed.
Bargaining demeanor	Close to the vest; poker-faced. Conceal the bottom line.	Open and honest. No bottom line in attempts to find a solution.
Recesses/ caucuses	Frequent, particularly in later stages. Used to develop solutions to problems. No contact between parties.	Less frequent, as problems are addressed mutually. Informal exchanges continue during recesses. Dine together.
Record	Most exchanges on the record.	Most exchanges off the record; final agreement recorded.
Power	Coercive, utility, and collaborative power, in that order.	Collaborative power, then utility power. Coercive power used only as a last resort.
Agreement	One party accepts other's final proposal.	Jointly developed solution is executed.
Communication	Each party communicates its version of status and final results.	Joint mutually agreed communication.

duped by management. Either situation can present union leaders with political difficulties and the risk of not being reelected.

From a substantive point of view, the bargaining relationship is frequently viewed as a zero-sum game. When this is the case, union leaders and employees assume that a bargaining process management wants is intended to get it more, which necessarily means employees get less. Union leaders naturally are reluctant to engage in such an endeavor.

Union leaders need to see clear opportunities for gain for the union and/or represented employees if they are to engage in collaborative bargaining. Such a process must provide sufficient incentive to overcome the negatives associated with it. Management should not, however, attempt to provide such incentives by trading matters of substance to get participation in the process. The gain to both parties must be inherent from the synergy of the relationship in which the size of the whole increases and is divided equitably.

Many labor/management relationships have as a basic tenet "never give something for nothing" and the corollary "always get something if you give something." If a management in such a relationship seeks a more collaborative bargaining process, the union is likely to expect a quid quo pro in return for its willingness to cooperate. Such expectation may seem quite reasonable if what the union is asking for could be seen as related to the management's drive for more collaboration. Examples of such union requests are:

- Organizing neutrality, where the union asks management to maintain a hands-off, neutral stance in organizing activities at the company's non-union locations.
- Union security, where the union asks, for example, for an agency shop where it is legal.
- Increased compensation for increased employee involvement.
- Job security, which may include guarantees associated with seniority rights and layoff protection.

This discussion does not address whether such union proposals are appropriate for a particular situation. No doubt some, or perhaps all, are appropriate under the right circumstances. Rather, the point is that management should not grant these types of substantive concessions as a quid quo pro for a more collaborative bargaining process. The process should stand on its own and provide an improved vehicle for addressing issues such as those mentioned above on their substantive merit. Trying to buy a process with substantive concessions is a string with no end that will destroy management's credibility and ultimately fail. As the authors note in *Getting Together*, "Trying to buy a relationship is like paying blackmail. The more blackmail I pay, the more I will be asked to pay. And neither paying blackmail nor extorting it is likely to prepare the way for fair outcomes in the future."[15]

A union that has implicitly or explicitly entered into a more cooperative relationship may also attempt to use continuation of such relationship as a hostage for attaining substantive concessions. For example, in a mutual gains negotiating process a company may take a hard line and perhaps exert its power to a greater extent than the union believes appropriate. In response, the union may threaten to discontinue participation in union/management committees or withhold other types of cooperative activities unless the company accedes to its position on the substantive issue in question.

Buying a process relationship with substantive concessions is intellectually inconsistent with the basic principles of collaborative bargaining: that properly managed disagreement and conflict can be used in a synergy that works to the mutual benefit of all parties. Reciprocity in how the relationship is conducted is essential, but maintaining such a relationship by trading substantive concessions for an improved process will not work over the long term. It is giving in to a "get all you can get" approach and simply results in a different division of the same whole, when the real purpose is to increase the size of the whole and provide an improved process for dividing it. In addition, such trading fosters a relationship seen as requiring agreement, when the essence of what is being sought is a relationship that exploits the value of disagreement. These are internal inconsistencies that can only lead to failure.

Although the company should not try to buy a relationship, the process must provide the union and employees an opportunity for gain just as it does the company. Collaborative bargaining requires all parties to devote resources and take risks to continuously overcome the structural inertia tending toward position bargaining. Therefore, for collaborative bargaining to function over time, all parties must feel they benefit more from it than from position bargaining. There must be net gain from the process and this gain must be shared on an equitable basis. The gain may be more than economic, however. For example, providing union leaders enhanced status and influence in the workplace through involvement in a broader range of business issues is a gain to them that is just as important in many senses as an economic one.

All this means that management attempts to improve a bargaining process solely for management's own benefit will not work. Changing the process to get more bargaining leverage, win more in negotiations, or get the union to give greater concessions will be counterproductive. Rather, management's advantage from a process change must come from actions that get away from the zero-sum game and expand the size of the whole by considering more options, reaching better decisions, and enhancing the contribution of all employees in ways they feel good about.

Managing Expectations

All parties must be realistic about the promise of collaboration for it to succeed. In particular, they must understand that the size of the whole cannot always be expanded, and all parties do not benefit in every case. Collaboration does not mean that either the company or the union will be any more willing to give up matters of principle than with position bargaining. It doesn't mean that the parties will always be successful in expanding the size of the whole. And it doesn't mean that either party will be unwilling to take a hard line and ultimately use whatever bargaining power it has. It means only that the parties are in good faith using a process that has an increased probability of maximizing the benefit for all involved.

If executive management, union representatives, or employees are expecting more from the process than the participants are able or willing to deliver, and if their expectations are thwarted, the attempt may do more harm than good. Trust will be destroyed, animosities created, and positions hardened, making meaningful agreements more difficult to attain than in the past. Therefore, it is the responsibility of any person advocating mutual gains bargaining to provide the education and involvement necessary to insure that management, union representatives, and the employees they represent have an accurate, realistic understanding of the process, the associated risks, and the likely results. The parties should not proceed unless such understanding exists.

Process Risks

Collaborative bargaining, with its openness and willingness to explore the unknown, exposes both parties to substantive risks associated with discussing previously forbidden areas, having to consider surprising options, and needing to defend one's interest with logic rather than power. Such situations are part of the process and are the tradeoff for the increased creativity and ability to solve problems that collaboration can bring. The process also raises certain process risks that have little to do with substantive matters. These risks can be prevented with thoughtful planning, trust, and communication among the parties.

Spokesperson Authority. Collaboration is enhanced if the company spokesperson does not have set authorities in advance that limit problem-solving options. On the other hand, the management spokesperson not having the authority to make proposals or counterproposals, agree to union demands, or conclude an agreement can be evidence of an unfair labor practice for failure to bargain in good faith. Concerns about this issue are best addressed by insuring an understanding up front as to the reason for the spokesperson's lack of specified authority, obtaining the union's concurrence with the process, and assuring the union spokesman that if this becomes a problem, the management spokesperson will be granted authorities sufficient to meet traditional legal tests.

Limiting Proposals. Mutual gains bargaining envisions collaborative identification of the issues to be addressed and a problem-solving approach with few if any formal, on-the-record proposals, offers, counteroffers, or explicit concessions. The NLRB, however, has judged whether bargaining is acceptable by looking at the totality of conduct and considering whether the company has made proposals, offers, counteroffers, and concessions. Thus, there may be a concern that if collaborative bargaining goes sour and the union charges the company with failure to bargain, the company will not have the evidence traditionally available to refute the charges. In this case, however, the same test that may create a concern solves it. The totality of conduct in good-faith mutual gains bargaining overwhelmingly meets the test for good-faith bargaining. The additional information sharing, union leader and employee involvement, active dialogue between the parties, and ultimately the company's willingness to make a formal proposal all tend to support the case for lawful bargaining.

Bargaining on Permissive Subjects. A company's willingness to discuss essentially any subject with the union, regardless of whether bargaining is mandatory, may raise a concern that once such practice is started, it can't be stopped. Discussing a permissive subject creates expectations that it and similar issues are always open for discussion, and if a dispute goes to the NLRB, a prior practice of discussing similar topics could hurt company arguments that bargaining is not required. For a company interested in increased involvement and employee participation over the long run, this is an issue without substance. Management should be more concerned with getting employees and the union involved in many permissive areas than preventing involvement. If, however, a management is concerned about the precedent effect of discussing a permissive subject, this can be addressed by agreeing to a waiver under which the union agrees that discussing a particular permissive subject will have no effect on that or similar issues in the future.

KEY POINTS

1. Mutual gains bargaining is based on the concepts of interest-based negotiations, discussion and dialogue, and constructive management of conflict. Its goals are to use diversity and conflict in the organization to increase the size of the whole and to divide it equitably.

2. Mutual gains bargaining is a more collaborative model than position bargaining. Key elements of mutual gains bargaining are:

   • Developing collegial relationships.

   • Working jointly with the union on pre-negotiation planning and preparation.

   • Moving seamlessly into a collaborative negotiation process.

   • Rethinking the role of the spokesperson and bargaining team.

   • Using coercive power only as a last resort.

3. To move from position to collaborative bargaining management should:

   • Concentrate on changing the existing process while viewing collaboration as a goal.

   • Refuse to buy the process with substantive concessions.

- Manage expectations.
- Minimize process risks where possible.

NOTES

1. Roger Fisher, William Ury, and Bruce Patton, *Getting to Yes*, 2nd ed. (New York: Penguin Books, 1991), p. 4.

2. Ibid., pp. 17–21.

3. Ibid., pp. 40–41.

4. Ibid., pp. 56–57.

5. Ibid., pp. 81–88.

6. Peter M. Senge, *The Fifth Discipline* (New York: Doubleday, 1990), p. 240.

7. Peter M. Senge, Charlotte Roberts, Richard B. Ross, Bryan J. Smith, and Art Kleiner, *The Fifth Discipline Fieldbook* (New York: Doubleday, 1994), p. 358.

8. Senge, *The Fifth Discipline*, p. 241.

9. Ibid., p. 243.

10. Carsten De Dreu and Evert Van De Vliert, eds., *Using Conflict in Organizations* (London: Sage, 1997), pp. 9, 24, 88.

11. Ibid., p. 88.

12. Ibid., p. 92.

13. Ibid., p. 39.

14. Samuel B. Bacharach and Edward J. Lawler, *Bargaining: Power, Tactics, and Outcomes* (San Francisco: Jossey-Bass, 1981), p. 104.

15. Roger Fisher and Scott Brown, *Getting Together* (Boston: Houghton Mifflin, 1988), p. 22.

Chapter 13

Supplemental Teams

Mutual gains bargaining uses dialogue and discussion in bargaining to take advantage of constructive disagreement and address the interests of the parties. It is a collaborative effort that uses union leaders' information and expertise along with that of management to improve organizational performance and meet the needs of employees.

Mutual gains bargaining offers a great deal, but its value is limited by the number and expertise of the people involved and the scope of the issues they are allowed to address. No matter how good the process, the full value of collaboration will not be realized if few people of limited knowledge, expertise, and vision are able to participate in it or if the participants are limited to addressing narrow bargaining issues. On the other hand, the value of collaboration will be greatly expanded if a large and diverse group of union leaders, employees, and management staff are allowed to share their broader perspective and understanding.

Use of supplemental teams is a vehicle for expanding participation in the collaborative process. Such teams are additions to existing formal organizations and structures and should be distinguished from work teams, which are groups assigned to a designated area in a functional hierarchy using team principles to do their regular, frequently repetitive work on an ongoing basis. There is much to be said for—and much has been said about—work teams, but they are not the subject of this chapter. The ability of work teams to grow and become self-reliant is largely a function of the management/union relationship, and how their work gets done and the implication for employees may raise difficult bargainable issues. Work teams, however, are different from and addressed by the existing labor relations structures, while supplemental teams are part of and add to those structures.

Supplemental teams involve processes that generally support, change, or compete with existing management or labor relations structures. Use of such teams can be a daunting challenge in a unionized workplace, where the presence of a union leads to political issues and legal requirements that are quite complex. This chapter presents ideas for meeting that challenge. It starts with a brief overview of teams and team management in general as a context for a later discussion of their use to supplement existing organizations and processes.

PRINCIPLES

The definition of "team" is in the eye of the beholder. It is "*a group of people who are necessary to accomplish a task that requires the continuous integration of the expertise distributed among them.*"[1] Or it is "*people doing something together.*"[2] Katzenbach and Smith define a team as "*a small number of people with complementary skills who are committed to a common purpose, performance goals, and approach for which they hold themselves mutually accountable.*"[3] The authors of *The New American Workplace* note that the concept of team covers a wide spectrum of behavior, and "the meaning of teams varies considerably as defined by their involvement in different domains of decision making . . . and their degree of autonomy or control over substantive decision making."[4]

Supplemental teams can vary greatly in characteristics such as size, composition, longevity, and purpose. For our purpose, however, two types are defined as follows:

- Committees—Individuals brought together to accomplish a common purpose on a continuing basis. For example, a health and safety committee might be formed to provide continuing advice and counsel to the safety department or address specified issues over the long term.

- Task forces—Individuals brought together to address a particular issue or problem on a one-time, ad hoc basis. For example, a task force might be named to solve a problem, develop a plan, create a product, or support a common cause.

Teams also can be characterized on the basis of their decision-making authority. Appelbaum and Batt note three types: "consultative, giving workers a voice or input into management decisions; substantive, allowing workers the power to make decisions over certain production issues; and representative, providing workers with a role in decision making through their unions."[5]

"Team" is to be distinguished from "teamwork," which is the actual cooperative effort made by a group of persons acting together as a team or in the interest of a common cause. How the people on teams actually work together and whether they engage in teamwork can, of course, vary greatly. The authors of *Creating the High-Performance Team* describe three stages of team development that define a continuum.[6] These stages are:

- "Collection of Individuals"—Members are individual centered, have individual goals, and do not share responsibility.
- "Groups"—Members develop a group identity, clarify their roles, and establish norms for working together.
- "Team"—Members understand a common purpose, are committed to it, and use it to guide their actions and decisions.

In most cases only the last stage involves true teamwork. While teamwork is the goal of most teams, whether or not it exists has little impact on how a team is managed or how its results are implemented in a unionized setting. Therefore, this chapter defines supplemental teams to include any formally designated group of individuals who are expected to follow the same rules and contribute to the same end regardless of the extent to which they actually engage in teamwork.

The objective, of course, is for members of a team to demonstrate teamwork and effectively accomplish their purpose. There is no magic formula for causing this to happen, but most effective teams have certain predictable characteristics, such as the following:

- The purpose of the team is directly related to business success or another common cause, and it is accomplished better with a team than with an individual or an existing structure.
- The team is comprised of the right people with adequate, complementary skills and experience to accomplish its purpose.
- The team, its expectations, and its processes fit within the culture of the organization of which it is a part.
- Team members know who the customers are and what their expectations are.
- The purpose of the team has been clearly articulated and is understood by team members, sponsors, and customers.
- Team members and sponsors agree on to whom the team is accountable, what goals it is expected to accomplish, and how it will demonstrate its accountability.
- Participants and the broader organization understand the authority of the team and the extent to which it is consultative, substantive, or representative.
- The structure, practices, policies, and systems that govern the team are effective and well understood by team members.
- Team members work well together and communicate effectively within the team and with external stakeholders.
- Team members trust each other, their sponsor, and others with whom they must deal.

This list of characteristics provides a framework for management of supplemental teams in a unionized setting and for the discussion to follow.

SUPPLEMENTAL TEAMS IN A UNIONIZED WORKPLACE

Teams have been used in unionized operations for many years. Some have been broad in scope, while others were limited to narrow areas such as safety and health, drug and alcohol abuse, or employee counseling, where the mutuality of interests between employees, union, and management increased the possibility of success. Many were part of a "two-track" system, in which joint structures were established outside the collective bargaining process to address issues that were not part of the bargaining agreement or a required subject of negotiation. Unfortunately, many have ended in failure, leading to decreased trust and increased skepticism between labor and management. The sections that follow use the characteristics listed above as a general framework for discussing ideas for structuring and managing supplemental teams to improve their chances of success.

Establish Business Need

Supplemental teams may be formed for many different reasons: to solve a problem, perform specified work, manage a project, support a customer, design a process, plan a strategy, advise management, and on and on. Most of the work involved, however, can be done by individuals, or a collection of individuals, doing their assigned job within existing organization structures. So what can a supplemental team contribute that individuals and existing structures cannot? Under what circumstances should a supplemental team be used? When should they not be used?

Supplemental teams should not be used because they are a program of the day or a fad with management consultants. In *Why Teams Don't Work* Harvey Robbins and Michael Finley discuss the myth that teams are always better. They note, "Teams are great. Cuisinarts are also great. But you wouldn't mow your lawn with one."[7] Teams should not be used if the need can be met through individual actions or collaborative management of existing structures, nor should they be used in lieu of attempts to improve individual performance or fix organizations that are not performing up to their capability. Underperformance should be addressed head on. Nor should supplemental teams be established when teamwork within the existing structure can be just as or more effective. Establishing a team to do someone else's work reduces incentives, interferes with the ability to learn, destroys morale, and leads to a cycle of declining performance in the primary organization.

Circumstances do exist, however, where supplemental teams can contribute something that doesn't already exist and enhance overall organizational performance. Teams should be used only in such situations: where there is a business need. To understand when there is a business need, one must peel back the layers and look below the surface. The first layer, the obvious reason for teams, is a reasonable expectation that their use will improve organizational performance or employee work life over what it would be without teams. Improvement in organizational performance in a for-profit business usually means improving the bottom-line financial result, which frequently goes hand in hand with improvement in employee work life.

Beneath this obvious objective is the expectation that using a team will foster improvement in those key financial or other factors that contribute to profitability and organizational purpose: those factors that are usually measured and tracked over time, continuously improved, and used to dominate the competition. For example, a supplemental team could lead to more effective bargaining, better conflict resolution, improved productivity, lower cost, enhanced problem solving, or better quality. Such changes lead to the ultimate objective of improved organizational performance or work life.

But what causes improvement in these key factors? How can a supplemental team contribute? It can contribute by enhancing the performance of the people of the organization, both individually and in the aggregate. This can happen in four ways, which are the core reasons for using supplemental teams. Teams can:

- Exploit diversity by bringing together individuals from various parts of the organization with different knowledge, experience, ideas, and points of view.
- Improve organizational learning by exposing more employees to cooperative behavior, broader information, and new ways of working.
- Strengthen employee commitment and support through representative involvement in decision making or implementation processes.
- Enhance collaborative processes by encouraging synergy and teamwork that for political reasons may be limited in the normal structure.

Upon reflection, these reasons for using a supplemental team closely mirror what a union can bring. Unions bring diverse individuals together to represent all employees. They foster a form of cooperative behavior among a cross section of employees and are based on the concept of representative involvement. Collaboration within labor/management structures is encouraged and possible. Therefore, when considering the need for a committee or task force, management should ask not only whether there is a need that cannot be accomplished by individuals or an existing management structure. It also should ask whether working with and through the union, perhaps by using existing structures in a more collaborative way, is not a better way to accomplish the need. Supplemental teams should not be used to try to fix the management/union relationship, but rather to enhance it by involving more people.

Bargain Establishment and Parameters with the Union

There are both legal and practical reasons for bargaining with the union about establishing a supplemental team. The requirement that bargaining must be with appropriate union representatives rather than directly with employees applies if mandatory subjects are to be discussed by a supplemental team. A team's discussion of such subjects probably would be "bargaining" even though the stated purpose might not include bargaining in the normal sense of the word. Therefore, since the union has the legal right to bargain through representatives it designates, it also has the right to determine who its participants on such a supplemental team will be.

The labor contract may also indirectly require bargaining. Most contracts cover matters such as work assignments, seniority, and the appropriate compensation for specified work, which limit management's flexibility to change work assignments, as would be the case in assigning an employee to a supplemental team. In such cases, management would be prevented from unilaterally assigning a represented employee to a cross-functional team and could make such assignment only after negotiating an exception to the contract.

The real need for bargaining, however, goes beyond the legal requirements, as the union support necessary for a team to succeed can only be obtained if the union is involved from the beginning and agrees with the approach being taken. This involvement, which must be through the bargaining process, must address the controversial nature of supplemental teams and allow union leaders to become comfortable with their use. Those who are against teams argue that they equal co-optation, or cooperation only where workers give away their knowledge to the disproportionate benefit of management. Supplemental teams that address bargainable issues also may be seen as a subversion of the collective bargaining process. Such concerns may be offset by the view that teams make work more satisfying, ease worker/supervisor tensions, and give workers recognition. Properly managed, supplemental teams also may be seen as improving the collective bargaining process and enhancing the ability of the union to influence the decision process.

Regardless of which view is more accurate, management must recognize that from a union perspective there are advantages and disadvantages to teams and legitimate reasons for union leaders to consider opposing them. In deciding whether to support use of teams a union must consider the pros and cons and decide whether participation is in the best interests of employees and the organizational integrity of the union. When advocating use of teams, management must empathize with potential union concerns and recognize that the union has a legitimate say in whether they are established and how they will function. The bargaining process must accommodate such considerations and capture a common vision of what the team is to accomplish, develop a joint commitment, and agree on how success will be measured. It may also address issues of an operational nature dealing with how the team will function. Bargaining should lead to a binding social contract, or a formal agreement if necessary, that provides the best chance for obtaining union support of the ultimate results.

The parties should also reach an understanding on procedures for ending teams. Teams may be on a trial basis, with continuation to be jointly evaluated against agreed standards at a specified point in time. They may be for a certain time or until a specific task is accomplished. Or they may be subject to termination at any time by either party for any reason. Whatever the conclusion, the parties should concur in advance on the life of teams and how they will be ended, if at all.

Integrate with Existing Organization Structures

Joint teams or "partnerships" that are separate from and parallel to the collective bargaining process, and limited to non-bargaining subjects, are of limited value because they exclude important matters and fail to address the systems aspects of change. These deficiencies can be largely overcome if joint teams are integrated with and supplement existing management or labor relations structures and include bargaining as well as non-bargaining subjects. They must be available for use on all types of workplace issues and operate in sync with existing organizations and processes.

The need for integration and operating concurrently with existing structures raises several issues. How those issues are managed depends in part on the type of subjects the team will consider, which could be either of the following:

- Bargaining subjects, which are mandatory subjects of bargaining or those covered by existing contracts. For example, a team might be assigned to address a clearly mandatory subject like high turnover among jobs across the organization that is thought to be caused by seniority and pay concerns among employees.

- Non-bargaining subjects, which are permissive subjects of bargaining or those where the final decision is considered within management's unilateral prerogative. For example, management might want a cross-functional team of represented employees to pursue ways to better understand customer needs and improve customer satisfaction or to pursue areas of mutual interest such as public service or charitable endeavors.

- Mixed subjects, which involve both bargaining and non-bargaining elements. For example, management might have a team explore opportunities for improved communication across the organization. This could involve changing technology, which typically would be within management's discretion, or changes in conflict resolution procedures that are bargained.

The type of results expected of the supplemental team also affects how integration takes place. The following descriptions of potential types of results draw from, but slightly alter, those listed by Appelbaum and Batt:

- Substantive results, where the team is expected to adopt its own processes, make decisions, and implement them. Such teams require a process for making decisions and proceeding with implementation.

- Consultative results, where the team is expected to gather and consider data, agree on the optimum decision, and recommend it to another entity for consideration and final

Figure 13.1
Characteristics of Supplemental Teams

Subjects ⟶ Expectations ↓	BARGAINING	NON-BARGAINING	MIXED
SUBSTANTIVE	Decentralized Bargaining	Decentralized Management	Combination
CONSULTATIVE	Decentralized Bargaining Centralized Authority	Decentralized Management Centralized Authority	Combination
TASK	Centralized Authority Decentralized Support	Centralized Authority Decentralized Support	Combination

decision. These teams require a process for internal decision making, even though their decision may not be accepted.

- Task results, where a team is expected to do assigned tasks that do not require decisions. This could include gathering data, analyzing it, and preparing options for referral without recommendation to another entity for consideration and final decision. Such teams have no need for a decision process.

Thus, nine different combinations of subjects and expected results are possible, as demonstrated in Figure 13.1. Each combination results in a team with different characteristics. For example, a team addressing bargaining subjects with a substantive expectation where members can decide and implement mandatory subjects is really a delegated or decentralized bargaining team. At the other extreme, a team with task expectations addressing a non-bargaining subject where the team can only do work on non-mandatory subjects is decentralized support to the management, which retains decision-making authority. Or a team with substantive expectations addressing mixed subjects has elements of both bargaining and management.

Each combination raises different integration issues. The key issues, however, always revolve around responsibility, accountability, and governance, raising questions such as: What is the team accountable for? Who are its customers and to whom is it accountable? Who has decision-making authority? How do the answers to these questions relate to existing management or labor/management structures? Reference to Figure 13.1 suggests an approach based on two fundamental types of teams: bargaining teams and management teams.

Bargaining Teams. When a team is dealing on bargaining subjects—either

Figure 13.2
Supplemental Bargaining Team

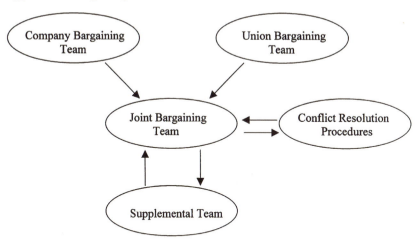

exclusively or in combination with non-bargaining subjects, and regardless of whether it is expected to decide, recommend, or provide input—it is involved in bargaining covered by the NLRA. Under these circumstances, it is an extension of the designated bargaining team and must be accountable to it, as demonstrated in Figure 13.2.

In this situation, the joint bargaining team composed of management and union representatives authorizes the supplemental team and receives its feedback, whether it is a report of results accomplished, a recommendation, or information to be used for bargaining a final decision within the joint bargaining team. In this situation, the joint bargaining team is the ultimate decision maker, following the rules of collective bargaining established by law. The supplemental team follows rules established by the joint bargaining team. If irreconcilable conflicts develop within the supplemental team, they are deferred to the joint bargaining team and ultimately may be decided through use of normal bargaining practices or existing legal or contractual conflict resolution procedures.

Management Teams. Matters can be more complex where non-bargaining subjects are involved. Management may wish to turn an issue over to a team for complete handling, or it may want employee or union input and involvement, with management retaining the final decision for itself. In either case, however, it may wish to protect its right to manage the business in the non-bargaining area concerned. Formation of an intervening steering committee between the joint bargaining team and the supplemental team, to which the supplemental team is accountable, as indicated in Figure 13.3, can provide a way to manage this dilemma. The steering committee could have the same membership as the joint bargaining team but preferably would be composed of representatives from management and union whose expertise relates to the subjects assigned to the

Figure 13.3
Supplemental Management Team

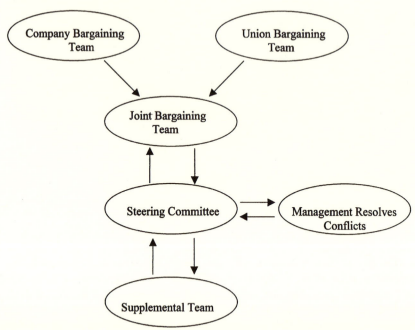

supplemental team. The steering committee's role would be to oversee and direct the supplemental team and receive the team's recommendations where appropriate. Its primary purpose is to provide a vehicle for involving senior union leaders in oversight of the team, while avoiding bargaining as such, co-management, or limitations on management's right to make the final decision where necessary. Accordingly, how final decisions will be made in the steering committee must be clearly understood from the beginning. The following approach is recommended:

- Do not vote. The prospect of voting tends to polarize the parties and impede the discussion and dialogue necessary for effectiveness. More importantly, decision by voting is an abrogation of management's responsibility to its stakeholders.

- Attempt to decide by consensus. Consensus implies general agreement or harmony where all parties consent to the decision. The decision may not be their preferred solution, but they can live with and support it. A process for obtaining consensus requires thorough dialogue and discussion of the type that can lead to effective synergy, problem solving, and commitment to the result. It is the best approach to attaining agreement without abrogating management's ultimate responsibility.

- Be willing to agree to disagree. Some issues simply cannot be resolved to the satisfaction of all parties. Hopefully these can be limited with good-faith dialogue and discussion. But when the situation does occur regarding non-bargaining issues, both parties must understand that management has the right and responsibility to make unpopular and even painful decisions. This right to make the decision at the end makes it safe to involve the union from the beginning. This continuing involvement places union representatives on the steering committee in the room where the decision is made and provides them every opportunity to influence decisions and make every effort to insure that actions of the supplemental team are appropriate and acceptable. Such involvement can at the least minimize resistance to a management decision and at most garner support for it.

Select Appropriate Participants

Many considerations are relevant when selecting members of a supplemental team. Early consideration should be given to broad issues, such as whether the team is to be composed entirely of represented employees or both represented and non-represented individuals; and whether union leaders who are not employees should be team members. Once such decisions have been made, individual participants must be selected.

Additional factors should be considered when selecting individual participants. For example, pertinent expertise, ability to work in teams, likelihood of active participation, organizational balance, racial or gender diversity, internal politics, and the extent of involvement/commitment necessary for implementation are all relevant. Where a union is involved, however, the primary consideration should be the position of its leaders.

Law and contract are likely to require union agreement on selection of participants. Even if they do not, however, it is nearly always in management's best interest to get it. Union representatives frequently have a good knowledge of which employees will make the best contribution, and their perspective on who has the needed knowledge and expertise is different and in some situations may be better than management's. Because of this different perspective, they are likely to add helpful diversity to a team. More importantly, union leaders are likely to have a better understanding than most managers of personality issues, political considerations, attitudes toward management, and other similar considerations that can materially affect the contribution of a team member. Although union leaders may be affected by seniority or other considerations management has little sympathy with, jointly establishing objective standards for team member selection can minimize the potential negative from this concern.

Having union leaders agree on the participants helps minimize potential concerns about the team being established in the first instance. Their being comfortable with who is on the team also increases the likelihood union leaders will monitor the behavior of team members, coach them, and otherwise support the actions and recommendations of the team. Union leader support can be critical to accomplishing the ultimate objectives, because they are a major factor in whether the team's results actually have broad employee buy-in and are effectively implemented.

The best course is for management to collaborate with union leaders to select participants who are in the parties' mutual best interest. Working together through the joint bargaining or steering teams, the parties can select participants who provide the best chance of getting all relevant information on the table, developing a synergy of ideas, and addressing the differing interests of both parties. In working together to select team members, the parties should address issues such as the following:

- Clearly understanding the need for a team and why normal structures are not sufficient.
- Agreeing on what type of talent is needed for the team.
- Understanding concerns of both parties that relate to team participation, such as internal politics or personal attitudes.
- Clarifying the role and expectations of the participants and selecting participants most likely to meet those expectations.

When the company and union collaborate on such issues, their joint decision is likely to lead to selection of the most appropriate team members.

Provide Team Leadership

Leadership has two faces in supplemental teams: external leadership from the chartering group and leadership within the team. Both are critical for success.

External Leadership. The chartering group must provide strong leadership. It must, for example, be clear about purpose, select the right participants, provide resources, and take other actions the team itself cannot handle. Its most difficult task, however, may be to exhibit the confidence and integrity to let the supplemental team do its work in the face of the risk that bargaining positions will be compromised. Both management and union must understand that the team will not always behave exactly as they think best but still be willing to allow it to accomplish its purpose. They must avoid imposing requirements or constraints that defeat the team's purpose and instead deal openly with whatever it does. This may require both management and union leaders to think differently about various issues and deal with information or recommendations that are contrary to their stated positions. Such concerns can be minimized if the chartering team is clear about the supplemental team's purpose, objectives, and operating parameters, but both parties must be aware of the risks involved.

Internal Leadership. The specific role of leadership within a supplemental team will depend on its purpose and its relationship with the negotiating team or steering committee that chartered it. Is the supplemental team a substantive, consultative, or task team? What obligation does it have to the chartering team?

As a general rule, however, the leader of any supplemental team will be expected to perform duties such as:

• Keep the team on track with its purpose and goals.
• Manage the relationship with the chartering team and externally if appropriate.
• Facilitate internal team processes and decision making as appropriate.
• Support and reinforce the contribution of each individual.
• Insure administrative trivia is handled.
• Do real work.

Several of these duties convey power on the selected leader. Therefore, a leadership position is apt to be highly desired, as neither the company nor union wants the other to have additional power to influence the outcome. This issue must be decided within the chartering team, which has three realistic options: a single leader who is a representative of either labor or management, co-leaders, or co-leaders working with an external facilitator selected by the parties. Each approach has advantages and disadvantages. A single leader has clear responsibility and accountability but may not be accepted or supported by one of the parties because of a perception of bias. Single leaders work well where management has clear responsibility for the issues to be addressed and the purpose of the team is to provide input or support to management. Co-management avoids the appearance (and perhaps fact) of bias but diffuses accountability and may make decision making difficult. Co-leaders with an external facilitator, while less than perfect, frequently is the best option. A facilitator who is carefully selected and whose duties are carefully defined can perform many of the ministerial duties of the leaders, chair meetings, and mediate decisions if necessary. This can avoid bias and free co-leaders to coach individual members or do other work.

Clarify Roles and Responsibilities

Individuals are likely to have little or no knowledge of their roles and responsibilities when they are assigned to teams. This lost feeling may be exacerbated by concerns about working in a world of arcane laws and rules seen to govern labor relations and by questions as to whether participants were selected to represent a constituency or to provide their own individual input. Clarity as to roles and responsibilities is necessary to prevent polarization along company and union lines. Without clear roles and responsibilities, a team can easily degenerate to an adversarial, quasi-bargaining group.

To minimize such polarization, all participants must understand the specific tasks or areas for which they are accountable. If they do not, work assignments can become redundant and overlapping, or gaps can exist. Unhelpful competition can develop in which participants gravitate to their respective management and union sides rather than work collaboratively.

Participants must also understand how the team will function and how they should relate to other members. They should understand how decisions will be made, how communication to the chartering committee and employees will be handled, how information will be gathered, and other procedural matters. More specifically, participants must understand and respect where the team, and they as individuals, fit relative to the bargaining process. Is the team a substantive, consultative, or task team? Are individuals to represent a constituency, or are they to function only as an individual? Failure of the chartering group to be clear on such issues can lead to a team that is ineffective or counterproductive.

In summary, team participants are likely to be selected specifically for their differences, their individuality, and their conflicting needs. If these characteristics are not properly channeled, unhealthy competition or destructive conflict can develop. If they are channeled through clearly understood roles and responsibilities, however, positive synergy can result.

Improve on the Bargaining Processes

Many bargaining teams are not structured for optimum collaboration. They are comprised of individuals selected on the basis of their political or bargaining skills rather than their substantive knowledge of the issues being addressed or their ability to work collaboratively. Bargainers are accustomed to representing their side and are likely to be averse to risk. Concerns about the impact of proposals or discussions on future grievances or arbitration cases, or the possibility of compromising a tactical bargaining advantage, may limit their willingness to explore an issue. The effect of such structural disadvantages can be reduced with mutual gains bargaining, but even that process cannot avoid all the legal and political realities that make collaboration difficult. There is always room for improvement, and supplemental teams can be a source for it. Teams that address bargainable subjects can improve the bargaining process and foster more effective problem solving by using internal team processes that are unlikely to occur in normal bargaining.

A supplemental team should refrain from the use of coercive power in order to encourage risk taking, sharing, and collaboration. This requires labor and management membership on joint teams to be balanced. Membership should be comprised of an equal or approximately equal number of management staff and represented employees or union leaders. Members of the team should be of roughly equivalent stature within the organization, and supervisor/supervised relationships should be avoided. Where possible, experts in the area being addressed should be included. This equivalency of numbers, stature, and expertise can lead to an equality of power within the team that will foster effective teamwork. If use of coercive power is necessary for certain decisions, those decisions are made by the chartering team or committee.

To further encourage open exchange of ideas, the team should be assigned responsibilities that are narrow enough to discourage trading. If several different issues are handled by one team, as is necessarily the case with a joint bargaining team, there is a tendency to trade issues rather than develop the optimum solution for each. If, on the other hand, a team is asked to address only one issue, or one issue at a time, it must concentrate its efforts and seek the best possible solution.

Team members should agree on what is to be communicated to the chartering team, management, union, and employees, and issue such information jointly. Beyond this, discussion and dialogue within the team should not be considered part of the bargaining history of the issue being addressed. Reference to or use of comments made or proposals advanced in a supplemental team should not be allowed in a subsequent joint bargaining team discussion of the same issue and should be prohibited from being used in future legal or arbitration cases. This explicit exclusion allows team members to speak and act freely in an attempt to solve problems without concern for the future impact of discussions or proposals that failed.

Facilitate Joint Training

People brought together from various parts of an organization do not necessarily know how to work together, even if they are accustomed to teamwork in a different environment. In a supplemental team, they are likely to face new people, new processes, and new challenges. They will need to be trained to adjust to these changes and become effective in their new role.

Supplemental teams should receive training that is jointly administered by the company and union, particularly where bargainable subjects are to be addressed and the union's interest in performance of the team is similar to the company's. Union involvement can improve the relevance and quality of the training and also is a demonstration of support that can foster commitment of employees the union represents.

Joint training should cover a wide array of subjects. Katzenbach and Smith suggest that teams must have or develop complementary skills in the following categories:

* Technical or functional expertise.
* Problem-solving and decision-making skills.
* Interpersonal skills.[8]

Presence of such skills and expertise is likely to be a criteria for team member selection, but this will not be enough. Even the best in these areas may need additional training, and other selection criteria, such as seniority, need for diversity, or need to insure a particular political situation is addressed, may lead to selection of less qualified members. Thus, some training and development of team members is essential in nearly all cases. Such training should give special attention to the following:

- The team should be free to learn and develop for itself. In a unionized setting, management is likely to have a tendency to over-engineer and impose training to compensate for a perceived lack of control. Doing this, however, may impose constraints and rules that defeat the purpose of the team. If objectives and parameters are clear, team members can identify deficiencies and learn for themselves. They are motivated to learn by their common purpose and goals.

- Where training is required, involve the union in diagnosing the need and developing training programs. Involving union leaders can lead to better decisions as to both the substance and process of training. More importantly, their involvement will be obvious to team members and help increase their commitment to the training objectives. And finally, where bargaining subjects are concerned and ultimate decisions are made by the bargaining team, union involvement in all aspects of managing the supplemental team provides the perspective that improves the final decision process.

- Create a productive team culture. One reason for forming a supplemental team is to enhance collaborative processes beyond what is likely with existing structures. In a unionized workplace team members are likely to have mental models and habits developed in an adversarial relationship. Therefore, training must concentrate on teaching participants new ways of viewing the relationship and new, more collaborative ways of addressing issues. This can be the basis for developing a team culture that is a microcosm of the collaborative culture desired in the larger organization. It serves not only to foster a more productive team but also as one small step toward broader organizational learning.

KEY POINTS

1. Supplemental teams should be used only if they will improve on individual or organizational performance by utilizing more diversity, improving organizational learning, strengthening commitment, or enhancing collaboration.

2. Supplemental teams and their parameters must be bargained with the union.

3. Role, accountability, and authority of the team must be clearly established, and the team must be integrated with existing structures.

4. The union should concur with selection of participants.

5. Management and union must be willing to let the team do its work. Internal leadership is frequently best provided by co-leaders with the assistance of a facilitator.

6. Roles and responsibilities of team members must be clearly understood by all.

7. Teams must respect and improve on bargaining requirements.

8. Management and union must provide joint training.

NOTES

1. Anne Donnellon, *Team Talk: The Power of Language in Team Dynamics* (Boston: Harvard Business School Press, 1996), p. 10.

2. Harvey Robbins and Michael Finley, *Why Teams Don't Work* (Princeton, N.J.: Peterson's/Pacesetter Books, 1995), p. 10.

3. Jon R. Katzenbach and Douglas K. Smith, *The Wisdom of Teams* (Boston: Harvard Business School Press, 1993), p. 45.

4. Eileen Appelbaum and Rosemary Batt, *The New American Workplace* (Ithaca, N.Y.: ILR Press, 1994), p. 86.

5. Ibid., p. 249.

6. Steve Buchholz and Thomas Roth, *Creating the High-Performance Team* (New York: Wiley, 1987), p. 15.

7. Robbins and Finley, *Why Teams Don't Work*, p. 181.

8. Katzenbach and Smith, *The Wisdom of Teams*, pp. 47–48.

Chapter 14

Moving Forward

This book does not purport to tell management what to do to improve its management of change and its labor/management relationship. Rather, it is intended to stimulate thinking, assist managers in understanding their problems and opportunities, and provide a framework for collaborating with the union that represents the company's employees. Part II suggested a labor/management philosophy emphasizing collaborative change management among countervailing interests, and the preceding chapters of Part III presented practical ideas for implementing day-to-day operational change and for transforming the labor relations environment. This final chapter shares observations about integrating the philosophy and practice and presents ideas for starting an initiative to transform a labor/management relationship.

INTEGRATING PHILOSOPHY AND PRACTICE

A system of interrelated parts such as a labor/management relationship is not linear. There is no beginning or end, each part affects and is affected by other parts, and each is subject to external influences. The system is not static but instead is continually changing and evolving. Things don't happen sequentially like a book is organized but in fact are circular, messy, and always changing. Therefore, it is helpful to briefly revisit the theoretical change model developed in Part II and reflect on how the practice ideas discussed in Part III are integrated with it to foster the countervailing collaboration philosophy.

The change model for a unionized workplace presented in Part II is as follows:

Change happens if:
Management Drive $\times$ Management $\times$ Quality of the $>$ Individual $+$ Union
to Change $\quad\quad$ Rights $\quad\quad$ Decision $\quad\quad$ Resistance $\quad$ Resistance

Figure 14.1
Change Model System Relationships

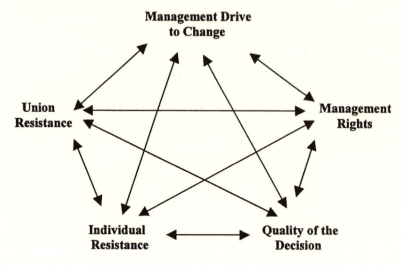

The model was presented in a linear fashion for ease of presentation, perhaps implying orderly or even sequential cause/effect relationships from one part to another. In actuality, it is not linear at all, but rather is a circular system in which each part affects, and is affected by, the other parts. Figure 14.1 is a more accurate depiction.

This model demonstrates the many relationships and shows how change really happens in a unionized workplace. For example, management drive to change, which is a function of vision and power, can overcome individual and union resistance but paradoxically can also increase the level of that resistance. Management rights can be used to overcome union resistance, but injudicious use can increase both union and individual resistance and reduce the quality of the decision. Improved quality of the decision can reduce both individual and union resistance and thereby minimize the need for use of management rights—and so on. These are the cogs in the machine of change. Turn one and others turn. They are not independent, and each reacts in predictable ways to changes in others.

But even this is an oversimplification. Each element of the change model is influenced by the environment within which they all operate. Many influences combine to fashion this environment, and the most important one is management. It exerts its influence through how it behaves and the practices it uses. Management's behavior and practices are the levers for turning the cogs of the change machine, and they work by creating the environment within which change takes place. In this context the change model looks more like Figure 14.2, which shows various management practices creating an environment within which the change model functions. For example, change in business need

Figure 14.2
Integrated Change Environment

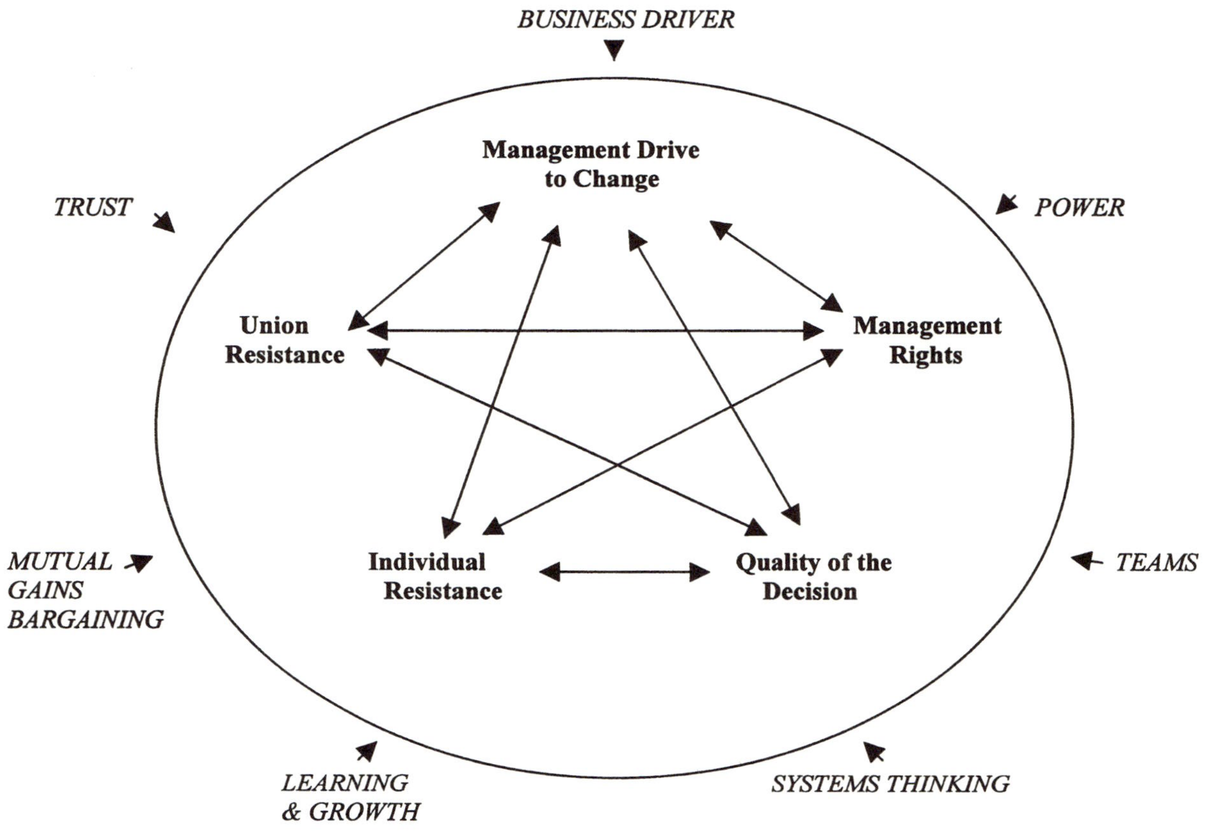

contributes to an environment that increases management's drive to change. But depending on how the need is presented, it may either reduce or increase union and individual resistance. Supplemental teams may improve the quality of decisions and increase the likelihood of a primary change attaining desired secondary results. Use of coercive power may cause an environment that increases employee and union resistance or use of collaborative power may reduce resistance. Mutual gains bargaining creates a synergy that leads to better decisions and reduces resistance. Trust reduces the need to rely on management rights and coercive power. Organizational learning helps the entire system learn from its experiences and evolve in the right direction.

In summary, the management practices that fashion the labor/management environment determine how each element of the model works and how each element reacts to change in other elements. If the change model is functioning badly—if the company's change management is ineffective—this can only be addressed through improving the environment within which it operates. Management practices are the best lever for transforming this environment. Deciding which levers to pull, how to pull them, and in what direction is at the heart of the management challenge. The answer cannot be form fit but must be figured out for each particular circumstance and approached as a never-ending journey. The purpose of the preceding chapters has been to stimulate thinking about these levers and how they can affect the change process. But as is always the case, a journey must start with its first steps.

GETTING STARTED

One of the beauties of the countervailing collaboration philosophy is its flexibility. Building collaboration into existing human resource processes and systems does not require a program or an identified initiative. Its essence is a fundamental change in how managers and other representatives of the company behave. Therefore, if there is a need for improvement, each individual manager, human resource specialist, or other company representative can begin to act differently and improve the relationship within his or her area of influence. As more of them behave differently, and union leaders reciprocate, a new and better labor/management relationship evolves.

But bottom-up, evolutionary change in the relationship may miss opportunities or be insufficient to meet competitive challenges. A more revolutionary approach may be needed: one that is intended to more quickly attain a critical mass of support and use the leverage of changing systems and processes to change the behavior of more individuals, more quickly. But where does one start such broad change in this messy, circular world? Management actions can have broad repercussions and must be considered from a systems perspective. All available levers must be used, but an established sequence for using them does not exist. What to do and when to do it will vary from location to location, and various practices must be used time and again as part of a never-ending journey. The first steps of the journey, however, are most important and perhaps more common for all situations. While there is no magic formula, the ideas presented in the following sections should be considered when starting an identified initiative to change the labor/management environment. These actions should be addressed early in the process, but not necessarily in the order presented. Instead, several should often be addressed simultaneously, and in all cases they should be addressed when they make sense in the particular case.

Assess Business Need for Change

Transforming the labor relations environment can be difficult, expensive, and risky. The effort and cost associated with such change are too great for it to succeed unless there is an obvious payback. Before initiating a change initiative, therefore, management must be comfortable that opportunities for improvement are available, and that pursuing those opportunities will further the business purpose. A critical mass of managers, supervisors, and employees ultimately must understand the business driver for change and be willing to commit their energy to insuring that it happens. Attaining this critical mass is difficult at best, and management must not try to build it by creating a need for change. Creating a felt need for change where it is not supported by the circumstances is not possible. Instead, management must find the need for change, if it is present, and effectively communicate it to others. Whether it is based on an immediate crisis or a longer-term necessity for maintaining competitiveness, the need must be obvious to most people, or the change effort will wither and die.

To find this need for change, management must accurately and honestly assess the current state of its labor environment and determine whether there is opportunity for positive transformational change that will improve how business gets done. The assessment must not be a general view of how the parties feel or seem to get along. Rather, it must assess the impact of the relationship on business performance in concrete terms.

It is easy for management to blame poor performance on employees or the union when in fact other causes are more significant. Therefore, assessment of need must start with a consensus that employee effectiveness or efficiency are performance factors contributing to a crisis, performance deficiency, or need for improvement. How to handle such an assessment involves basic management practices that are outside the scope of this book. But unless management is convinced that employee productivity is an area for improvement, it should not proceed with efforts to transform the labor/management relationship.

If employee productivity needs improving, management must next identify a causal link between the state of labor relations and the identified performance gap. Since how change is managed is at the core of the labor/management relationship, an effective way to concretely assess the relationship, and the need to change it, is to assess the effectiveness of operational change efforts. Management can do this by honestly answering a number of questions, such as the following:

- Are needed changes deferred because of perceived inability to make them?
- Are most needed changes deferred until the contract is open?
- Is change typically imposed by coercion rather than through collaboration?
- Do employees and union resist first and ask questions later?
- Do they resist for reasons that aren't understandable to management?
- Does conflict tend to be personal and about process rather than substantive disagreement on the issues?
- Does direct change frequently fail to deliver intended secondary results because it is not effectively implemented?
- Are employees and union leaders excluded from most significant business decisions?
- Do changes frequently have unintended results?
- Does one party lose when the other wins?
- Do union leaders condone or encourage behavior that makes implementation more difficult or that detracts from productivity?

If the answer to many or most questions such as these is "yes," one may reasonably conclude that the relationship with the union (the relationship, not the union) is a source of business problems. And since the relationship is a function of both management and union, one can also conclude that there are many opportunities available to improve it.

Insure Management Support

Identification of clear business need is critical to insuring management support for changing the labor environment. Management also must understand the other side of the equation: the potential costs and risks of a change initiative. Implementing broad and frequently controversial change is a long, time-consuming effort that will affect everyone in the organization, and all levels of management must be involved and supportive for it to succeed. All must be concerned about whether resources are available for the initiative and whether it is the highest priority use of those resources. And all must be concerned about the potential impact on their part of the organization if the initiative fails.

In addition to such broadly applicable concerns, each level of management has its own unique interests. For example, head office managers must understand the potential political and management problems associated with one location going in a different direction than others, the process working well in one location and less well in another, or response from the field being slower or different on some issues because new, collaborative processes are involved. Senior location management must be prepared to deal with troublesome corporate decisions, explain delays or setbacks, and accept the risk of devolving authority lower into the organization or to union leaders. First-line supervisors must accept that their jobs will change as represented employees and union leaders become more involved in the business. Managers at all levels of the organization, in their own unique ways, must assume risks that frequently are personal. All must understand the change effort and visibly commit to supporting it because without such support the initiative will be relegated to a secondary effort when more immediate but not necessarily more important issues arise.

Change Yourself

Management sets the tone for the labor/management relationship, and it must lead change if desired results are to be achieved. Since people tend to follow what they see rather than what they hear, those leading change must change themselves before they can reasonably expect the union and employees to follow. This means that both managers and management must change.

Managers Changing. Each manager and supervisor in the organization must engage in an individual, personal transformation if she or he is to lead a broader change process. While ultimate results are attained through mutuality, teamwork, organizational learning, and other collective actions, all are based on individual behavior. Only individuals can have values, think, act, or decide. Working together with others can enhance and leverage these individual capabilities, but they must exist in individuals in the first instance. Stephen Covey notes in *Principle Centered Leadership* that "Profound, sustainable cultural change can take place within an organization (such as commitment to Total Quality) only when the individuals within the organization first change themselves from the inside out. Not only must personal change precede organizational change, but personal quality must precede organizational quality."[1]

Identifying the need to change is one thing. Actually doing it is another. Each individual must see a need to change sufficient to disconnect him from his current personal state, overcome all those internal and external pressures to remain the same, and connect to a new way of being, thinking, and doing. To accomplish this, each individual must assess and understand herself and measure what she sees against her vision of what needs to be. This gap is an individual matter that will vary from person to person, but when transformation of the labor relations environment is being considered, the following opportunities for personal change should be given highest priority:

• Changing mental models. Mental models are at the root of all we do and usually are particularly relevant in a unionized setting where most managers carry baggage from the past. We cannot expect to change ourselves or lead change unless we first change the mental models that are driving our actions. To cite Covey again: "if you want to improve in major ways—I mean dramatic, revolutionary, transforming ways—if you want to make quantum improvements, either as an individual or as an organization, change your frame of reference. Change how you see the world, how you think about people, how you view management and leadership."[2]

• Changing knowledge and competence. Transforming a labor relations environment requires new knowledge, ideas, and skills, many of which can only be attained efficiently through focused education and training. Most such learning should be done jointly in connection with employees and union leaders. To lead this effort, however, managers must understand the opportunities available and what lies ahead. Developing this knowledge and understanding may require extensive reading, benchmarking leading companies, attending seminars, or other familiarization activities. It is also important for managers and supervisors to demonstrate leadership by being personally involved in educational activities. For example, they should serve on joint training design teams, faithfully attend and participate in joint training, deliver training where appropriate, and participate in other activities that will increase their own and others' knowledge and competence.

• Changing role of the leader. Managers and other organizational leaders must use both "managership" and "leadership" in order to be effective. Managership, which deals with matters such as procedures and structure governing how or how fast things get done, is probably the predominant role of management in most companies with poor labor/management relationships. Managership also is necessary in a collaborative environment. But leadership, which deals with matters such as vision, values, and what is to be done, is even more important in a collaborative relationship, where many typical managerial duties are delegated to or shared with employees and union leaders. Individual management styles that emphasize structure and control do not fit with collaborative labor relations. The predominant style must be to lead, and changing mental models and new learning should cause managers to move from emphasizing managership to emphasizing leadership.

• Changing personal objectives. Similarly, changing mental models and new learning should lead to new personal objectives. Objectives such as beating the union, winning all you can, or prevailing in power games must be set aside. These must be replaced with objectives such as personal growth, fairness, or improved business results that will drive the relationship with the union in ways that benefit all.

Management Changing. The collective effect of personal change in a critical mass of managers and supervisors results in a change in management. When this happens, managers and supervisors as a group talk and behave differently, and they make the systemic changes that are necessary to foster a more collaborative labor environment. These may include fundamental transformational changes in the values of management, the corporate vision of what can be, or the longer-term organizational objectives. They may also ultimately include operational changes in areas such as management authorities and reporting relationships, supervisory roles and expectations, communication procedures, and decision processes.

In particular, the role of the labor relations professionals and operating management must change from a rights-based, coercive orientation to a more collaborative one. Labor relations staff must move away from being a contract administrator, negotiator, policeman, and disciplinarian toward becoming a consultant, mediator, facilitator, and coach. Operating management must become less of a boss, planner, and decision maker and more of a visionary, participator, and collaborator. While such matters may or may not be a direct part of the labor relations system, changing them is necessary to support changes in the labor relations system. Doing so will help drive labor relations changes and create an environment in which they have the best chance of succeeding.

Build Islands of Trust

Employees usually elect unions because they don't trust management, and poor labor/management relationships usually exist because the parties don't trust each other. The origin of distrust may often be traced to the organizing campaign, or in older relationships to particularly difficult times when either or both parties used power inappropriately or took other actions that destroyed trust. Such events were perhaps exacerbated over the years by poor communication, indifference, or continuing events of bad behavior. Whatever the cause, lack of trust leads to personal antagonism, game playing, and reliance on rights and coercive power that will prevent transformation of the labor/management relationship.

Building trust in such an environment can be especially difficult. Many managers don't like the union, and employees are primarily loyal to the union, or at best have split loyalties between company and union. Union leaders may try to enhance their power by continually challenging the credibility or trustworthiness of management. Convincing a critical mass of employees and union leaders to trust the company and a critical mass of managers to trust employees and union leaders are difficult challenges.

Building this critical mass is a long-term journey that must begin with a few small steps by an individual manager or managers who are willing to expose their vulnerabilities and risk failure and embarrassment. They may be from executive management, senior location management, the Human Resources organization, or from operating units. They should be individuals who have an honest, sincere desire to change the relationship, the personal characteristics to succeed, and a scope of influence that will foster expansion from an initial success.

Such individuals should make specific, concerted efforts to develop personal relationships of trust with identified union leaders who are similarly situated. They should get to know them personally, go further and take more risks than the existing relationship justifies, and take other actions along the lines discussed in the chapter on trust. As reciprocal trust begins to build, the parties can work together to expand their success through creation of what John Kotter refers to as a "guiding coalition" of managers and union leaders who trust each other and share the objective of improving the relationship.[3] This coalition can then consider ways to expand the sense of trust to the broader organization through joint training, team building exercises, mutual gains bargaining, or other broader based initiatives.

External Assistance

We cannot change what we cannot see! This is the primary reason external assistance is important in a labor/management change effort. An external consultant cannot tell the parties what to do or how to do it. They must figure these things out for themselves by solving problems together, making mistakes together, and learning together. But someone from outside the system can remove blinders by questioning, observing, and providing feedback, which helps the parties to see themselves as they are and see opportunities for change. An external party can challenge mental models, help understand others' reactions, facilitate communication, and bring specialized expertise or broader knowledge to the table in two different situations.

Management Assistance. Depending on its level of expertise in labor relations, organization effectiveness, change management, and related disciplines, management staff and the company's labor relations team may need advice and counsel. A consultant might assist with management's assessment of need and opportunities for improvement and represent management as part of its labor relations team. Because of the need for systems thinking, all members of this team should be involved in or aware of a broad spectrum of the company's business (e.g., labor relations activities such as grievance handling or negotiations, management initiatives in the non-represented sector, etc.) as well as the labor relations change effort. Therefore, if consultants are used, they should become knowledgeable in a broad area of the company's labor relations business, well beyond those activities specifically identified as part of a change effort.

Joint Assistance. Where a union has agreed to a mutual effort to transform the relationship the parties should consider a neutral third party to facilitate the process. Some key duties of this person would include the following:

- Holding private discussions with each party to confirm that each is committed to change.
- Helping the parties develop a joint vision of what can be.
- Working with the parties, either independently or in joint executive session, to develop agendas or other plans for meetings or interventions.
- Developing consensus as to what joint training is needed and providing or arranging it.
- Serving as a process facilitator for joint meetings or work sessions.
- Teaching the parties new processes for solving problems.
- Serving as a mediator to assist the parties in solving difficult problems.
- Working with co-leaders of supplemental teams.

Selection of a facilitator should be by mutual agreement of the parties, as he or she must have personal and professional credibility with both. However, where differing views arise, credibility with the union must be given first priority. If the union's choice of facilitators is acceptable, management should accede to it even though another choice might be preferred. Doing this can be an early step in building trust and in many cases can also help management develop a better understanding of and empathy with the union leaders.

Arrangements for compensating the facilitator should be agreed in advance. Ideally, charges should be split to avoid any possible incentive for or appearance of favoritism. In certain cases, however, it may be appropriate for the company to pay the entire bill. In these cases, the union should be fully informed of how much and when the facilitator is paid, and the facilitator should clearly understand that continued employment is contingent on approval of both parties.

Don't Talk about It—Do It

Union leaders and employees have many reasons to resist change to a more collaborative working relationship, such as concern for politics, fear of co-optation, risk of embarrassment, and fear of the unknown. Their concern about such issues, and therefore their level of resistance, will vary with the circumstances but typically will grow larger as they perceive the magnitude of the change to be larger. As Conner notes, "A person's perception of a change situation determines whether resistance occurs."[4] Expansion of the perceived magnitude of the change can give resisters a bigger target and make it easier for them to solidify their support.

Employee and union leader perceptions about change are based on words and actions of management staff, who can easily make changes seem bigger and more ominous than they really are. To minimize the chances of this happening and resistance escalating, management should emphasize actions rather than words. This is not a suggestion to be less than forthcoming and candid about plans and actions. To the contrary, management should be open with its intentions, involve the union and employees whenever possible, and communicate more rather than less. But it should do so without causing the changes to be seen as bigger than they are. How it conducts its business in three areas will affect the results.

Communication. How management communicates with employees and the union will go a long way in determining how they perceive the changes. Approaches such as the following should be considered to help keep change in perspective:

- Communicate in the commonly accepted mode. The change effort should be, and should be seen as, a part of everyone's job. Where not inconsistent with common practice, matters should generally be handled informally.
- Avoid use of grandiose, programmatic titles for a change effort. References like "La-

bor/Management Partnership," "Labor/Management Relations Improvement Program," or other such titles arguably can be helpful. They can create an identity with the effort and communicate in real terms that the parties are working together. But they can create a big target and provide focus to individuals or factions that oppose the effort. They also tend to cause all improvement efforts to be viewed as one, so that a failure in one small area can bring down or hurt the entire "program."

- Avoid buzzwords and "consultantese." Thoughtfully using new words or a language of change may be helpful in communicating accurately and rallying participants around a change effort they can identify with. But new language should be clearly defined, broadly understood, and limited to specific uses, or it will become a rallying point for resistance. Buzzwords frequently are associated with "flavor of the month" programs. And just as judicious use of new words can bring focus to a change effort, injudicious use of buzzwords can become an object of ridicule and provide focus to a resistance effort.

Planning. In addition to the way it communicates, management must recognize the limits of long-term planning and utilize "logical incrementalism" for most efforts. There are too many uncertainties, complexities, and conflicting views to develop and publish a plan that communicates one right approach. A different approach to planning is required. Kees van der Heijden notes in *Scenarios: The Art of Strategic Conversation* that a rationalistic approach to strategy "starts with the concept that there is one answer and the task is to find it."[5] One right answer does not exist where a key objective is to develop a synergy that will lead to better answers, so the rational approach will not be effective.

Van der Heijden also describes a processual paradigm for strategic planning, which is much more appropriate for labor/management change, as follows:

The processual view starts from the premise that business success cannot be codified, but requires an original invention from the people involved. This implies that the resource the company needs to mobilise is the brain power of its people and their networking and observational skills. The organisation needs to engage in a process to make room for ideas. Any inventive idea directed towards improving the match between the organisational competencies and the business environment needs to be surfaced and considered, wherever these may originate in the organisation.[6]

This approach, which leads to organizational growth and mutual learning, is the one that fits in the labor relations environment. It avoids publication of a "plan" that probably won't work and can easily be shot down and ridiculed, and adopts a process that provides its own strategy and direction. Further, even if a rationalistic approach to planning would work in a narrow sense, having the company unilaterally develop a plan would be self-defeating. The primary objective is to involve the union and take advantage of what it has to offer. To start this process with a company-initiated plan would send the wrong message from the start. Rather than overplanning, management must take the first right step.

Informality. The parties must decide whether the change effort should be pursued on an informal basis or pursuant to a specific, "formal" agreement. The union's acknowledged willingness to work with management to foster collaboration is desirable, although it is not necessary for significant improvement if management is willing to take the initiative. Mutual commitment to work together, however, can increase the speed of change and lead to more far-reaching results than a unilateral effort.

Whether the parties execute a formal agreement should be a mutual decision. They should recognize that the answer depends on the circumstances and weigh the potential advantages of a formal agreement against possible disadvantages. A formal agreement has several advantages. It clarifies the "rules," hopefully narrows the area for misunderstandings and disagreements, and provides a visible concept around which people can rally. It also may have disadvantages. A formal agreement may create need for additional risky and time-consuming union membership votes, possibly limit flexibility on the part of all parties to change direction when needed, and create an even bigger target for resisters. Therefore, both parties should thoughtfully consider the advantages and disadvantages and decide how to go forward. In the final analysis, however, the union's need should be the deciding factor, for its leaders are most affected by the decision and best positioned to predict the likely impact.

Generate Substantive Successes

When moving to a more collaborative relationship, the parties should from the beginning work on real issues that have a business purpose or respond to employee needs. Changing the labor/management relationship is changing a process, not substance, and process cannot stand alone. It must be in association with substance. Holding conferences, conducting training, or other such interventions to address process issues, whether for management alone or jointly with union leadership, will have minimum impact unless they are in the context of the current, substantive issues the parties need to deal with. The substantive issues provide the incentive and immediacy for commitment to change, the laboratory conditions for learning from doing, and the clear and immediate feedback necessary for continual learning and development.

This raises the question of which substantive need or issue should be addressed first in the improvement process. The answer is that issues should be addressed in order of business priority, so the next change needed to further a business purpose should be the starting point to an improved, more collaborative relationship. It may be small or large. It may involve handling an employee's minor complaint, processing a union grievance, changing a work assignment, responding to a union initiative, or negotiating revisions in substantial portions of a benefit package or labor agreement. Regardless of the size or difficulty of the issue, however, the highest priority business change is the place to start.

A more difficult question is how to start: what to do differently this time to improve results. To answer this question management should think in terms of a learning organization and a journey into the future, rather than of immediately jumping to the desired state. It should start from where things are at the time and decide what to do next by balancing the magnitude of the possible process changes against their likely difficulty and the risk of doing nothing. For example, if the existing relationship is adversarial, and the next needed change is urgent and could have a major impact on the business, the risks of moving too quickly might outweigh the likelihood of success and dictate proceeding with a comfortable, predictable process. In such case, management might make only a minor process change: perhaps providing unsolicited information to the union or making a greater effort to understand their needs and interests. On the other hand, if a reasonable, accommodating relationship already exists and/or the impact of the substantive change is not large, the risk is minimized and the parties may go substantially further and experiment with new and untested ways of doing things.

A key consideration in balancing the magnitude of the initial process changes against the risk of failure is the need for short-term success. A journey to a better relationship must build on a succession of gains for both parties. Trying to improve a labor/management relationship generates skeptics on both sides, and even those who are committed to improvement need continuing reinforcement. Therefore, while some initial steps may be small and relatively obscure, it is also important for the parties to generate some recognizable wins. Kotter notes that a good short-term win has at least three characteristics:

1. It's visible; large numbers of people can see for themselves whether the result is real or just hype.
2. It's unambiguous; there can be little argument over the call.
3. It's clearly related to the change effort.[7]

These are the types of wins that help maintain the support of both company and union leaders, and a critical mass of employees. Without such support significant change initiatives cannot succeed.

FOLLOW-THROUGH

Follow-through is probably the most neglected yet critical aspect of any change effort. The energy and mutuality that exists at the start frequently decline as reality hits and people begin to appreciate the extent of the effort required and the number of opportunities for conflict. Unfortunately, getting started and then dropping the ball wastes resources at best and most probably exacerbates the problems that led to the effort in the first place. Paradoxically, however, at this point I must bring this book to a close and suggest that managers and others fostering change in a unionized workplace proceed on their own. This book has been about managing institutionalized conflict between parties with different roles, who are accountable to different constituencies, and who operate in very different circumstances. I have argued against quick fixes, how-to formulas, or programmatic approaches for developing a more collaborative labor/management relationship. Managing such complex organizations is too difficult for cookie cutter, predetermined solutions, and to avoid trying to do what I say cannot be done, I will refrain from trying to prescribe a solution. However, as managers and others work to figure out their own answers in a thoughtful and collaborative way, I hope they will:

- Recognize the differing legal context and increased opportunities for resistance to change that exist in a unionized workplace.
- Develop a labor relations philosophy that emphasizes collaboration among countervailing interests.
- Work from an integrated change model that includes elements unique to a unionized workplace.
- Avoid change not driven by business need, and clearly articulate the business need for change that is initiated.
- Take a systems view of everything that is done.
- Recognize that mistakes and setbacks will occur, and learn and grow from them as well as from other learning opportunities.
- Build trust among individuals and throughout the organization.
- Recognize the paradoxes of power.
- Approach change with the view that synergy among management, employees, and union leaders can lead to increasing the size of the whole with gain for all.
- Use teams as appropriate to supplement existing processes.

Only the parties involved—management, employees, and their union—can decide what to do. The ideas presented in this book must be filtered through the lens of their own experience and fit to the circumstances of their particular case. The parties must work together to make the choices necessary to build an ever-improving labor/management relationship: a relationship leading to improved organizational performance and mutual gain for the company, employees, and union alike. But on the fundamental proposition, the parties have no choice. Once they have gone to the brink and seen that there is a better way, they must begin the journey. I hope the ideas presented in this book will prove valuable in traveling it.

KEY POINTS

1. Integration of philosophy and practice must recognize the need for management to create an environment in which the changing, circular, messy labor and management systems can best function.

2. Although transformational change of a labor/management relationship must be addressed on an individual, case-by-case basis, several important issues must be considered at the beginning of all change efforts.

3. Transformational change of the labor/management relationship requires tenacity, continuity, and follow-through.

NOTES

1. Stephen R. Covey, *Principle Centered Leadership* (New York: Summit Books, 1990), p. 265.

2. Ibid., p. 173.

3. John P. Kotter, *Leading Change* (Boston: Harvard Business School Press, 1996), p. 51.

4. Daryl R. Conner, *Managing at the Speed of Change* (New York: Villard, 1993), p. 127.

5. Kees van der Heijden, *Scenarios: The Art of Strategic Conversation* (West Sussex, England: John Wiley & Sons, Ltd., 1996), p. 25.

6. Ibid., p. 36.

7. Kotter, *Leading Change*, p.121.

Selected Bibliography

Ahl, Valerie, and T.F.H. Allen. 1996. *Hierarchy Theory*. New York: Columbia University Press.

Argyris, Chris. 1992. *On Organizational Learning*. Cambridge, Mass.: Blackwell.

Argyris, Chris, and Donald A. Schön. 1996. *Organizational Learning II*. Reading, Mass.: Addison-Wesley.

Cohen-Rosenthal, Edward, and Cynthia E. Burton. 1993. *Mutual Gains*, 2nd ed. Ithaca, N.Y.: ILR Press.

Collins, James C., and Jerry I. Porras. 1994. *Built to Last*. New York: HarperCollins.

Conner, Daryl R. 1993. *Managing at the Speed of Change*. New York: Villard.

Covey, Stephen R. 1990. *Principle Centered Leadership*. New York: Summit Books.

De Dreu, Carsten, and Evert Van De Vliert, eds. 1997. *Using Conflict in Organizations*. London: Sage.

De Geus, Arie. 1997. *The Living Company*. London: Nicholas Brealey.

Dilenschneider, Robert L. 1994. *On Power*. New York: HarperCollins.

Drucker, Peter F. 1982. *The Changing World of the Executive*. New York: Truman Talley.

Ferguson, Marilyn. 1980. *The Aquarian Conspiracy*. Boston: Houghton Mifflin.

Fisher, Roger, and Scott Brown. 1988. *Getting Together*. Boston: Houghton Mifflin.

Fisher, Roger, William Ury, and Bruce Patton. 1991. *Getting to Yes*, 2nd ed. New York: Penguin.

Fukuyama, Francis. 1995. *Trust*. New York: Simon and Schuster.

Galbraith, John Kenneth. 1983. *The Anatomy of Power*. Boston: Houghton Mifflin.

Handy, Charles. 1994. *The Age of Paradox*. Boston: Harvard Business School Press.

Kanter, Rosabeth Moss, Barry Stein, and Todd Jick. 1992. *The Challenge of Organizational Change*. New York: Free Press.

Katzenbach, Jon R., and Douglas K. Smith. 1993. *The Wisdom of Teams*. Boston: Harvard Business School Press

Kotter, John P. 1996. *Leading Change*. Boston: Harvard Business School Press.

Loughran, Charles S. 1992. *Negotiating a Labor Contract*, 2nd ed. Washington, D.C.: BNA.

Price Waterhouse Change Integration Team. 1996. *The Paradox Principles*. Chicago: Irwin.

Ryan, Kathleen D., and Daniel K. Oestreich. 1998. *Driving Fear Out of the Workplace*, 2nd ed. San Francisco: Jossey-Bass.

Senge, Peter M. 1990. *The Fifth Discipline*. New York: Doubleday.

Senge, Peter M., Charlotte Roberts, Richard B. Ross, Bryan J. Smith, and Art Kleiner. 1994. *The Fifth Discipline Fieldbook*. New York: Doubleday.

Shaw, Robert Bruce. 1997. *Trust in the Balance*. San Francisco: Jossey-Bass.

Sullivan, Gordon R., and Michael V. Harper. 1996. *Hope Is Not a Method*. New York: Random House.

Ury, William. 1991. *Getting Past No*. New York: Bantam.

Walton, Richard E., Joel E. Cutcher-Gershenfeld, and Robert B. McKersie. 1994. *Strategic Negotiations*. Boston: Harvard Business School Press.

Woodworth, Warner P., and Christopher B. Meek. 1995. *Creating Labor-Management Partnerships*, ed. Edgar H. Schein and Richard Beckhard. Reading, Mass.: Addison-Wesley.

Index

About the Author

KIRK BLACKARD, a mediator and consultant based in Houston, Texas, worked for Shell Oil Company, a recognized leader in developing labor/management collaboration, for nearly 30 years. His assignments included service as president of several operating subsidiaries and as head of Shell's industrial relations function.

ISBN 1-56720-348-5

9 781567 203486

HARDCOVER BAR CODE